# The Last Dynasty
# of the Angels

# The Last Dynasty of the Angels

George Papadopoulos

Translated from the Greek by
Charles Moore

OCEANTIDES PUBLISHING
Chicago

An OceanTides Book
Published by OceanTides Publishing

Copyright © 1998 by George Papadopoulos

Library of Congress Catalog Card Number: 98-68080

ISBN 0-9668015-0-4

Designed and composed by Sans Serif, Inc.
Printed by Bang Printing

Manufactured in the United States of America

Composed in Cochin 12/14, display font is Gaelic

First Edition: September 1998

*This book is dedicated*
*to the first human clone*
*Who, I hope, will be you, Walt Disney!*

# Contents

# About the Author

"Using earth and water man produces mud while God creates life," remarks author George Papadopoulos, even as he challenges our views about creation in "The Last Dynasty of the Angels," his latest work. He describes his own work as a constantly renewed vision of what is probable.

"The writer of Science Fiction," he says, "is like the great lover who reaches the zenith of flirting but never completes the act of love. He creates and describes a million potential discoveries but he never has the fortune to implement them. He is a warehouse of ideas where everyone can find something valuable and useful."

George Papadopoulos was born on September 22, at midnight, 100 years to the day from the death of Jules Verne. A famous general and vascular surgeon in his native Greece, he graduated with High Honors from the Univercite Catholic de Louvain (Belgium) and completed his specialization at the Univercite de Strasbourg (France). George Papadopoulos' writing has drawn significantly from his academic and professional experiences.

He is a pioneer in the writing of science fiction in Greece where he previously wrote, under the pseudonym Graham Still, "Attack of the Brains," "The Borders of the Impossible" and the "Fourth Dimension," a work of travel in time.

Under his real name, George Papadopoulos has written "Idols of Reality," a philosophical discourse, "Silly Hippocrates," a play, and "Theocide." He next work, "Breaking the Barriers of Time" is going to press now and he is working on the "Fury of Archimede's Clones."

An avid traveler, George Papadopoulos lives and writes in Thessaloniki, Northern Greece, not far from where Aristotle tutored Alexander the Great. His own work intertwines strains of philosophical concern, scientific challenges and flights of the imagination. In "The Last Dynasty of the Angels," the heroes glance at creation the way it may have happened (why not?) even as they are unwillingly swept up into a world of intrigue and blackmail that leads from Africa to Europe and the Americas.

# A Strange Discovery

Several decades had passed since David Mason, then a university student, had attempted to receive his doctorate in Paleontology and Biotechnology. To achieve his goal, he had to write a doctoral thesis on an original subject approved by the university committee. Until that moment, his university life had been smooth, and prospects for a brilliant career path excellent.

David's unusual abilities as a scientist were well known in scholarly circles. That's why they saddled him with a most difficult task for a thesis. According to information emanating from the African Congo, unusual phenomena were recorded in an area northeast of Stanleyville, during excavations for construction materials.

At first, authorities had assumed that the nature of the reports, which originated with the local community leaders, was tainted by the superstitions of the area's pagan tribes. Specifically, unexplainable sounds and kinetic phenomena were recorded near the town of Beni. They were thought to be em-

1

anating deep in the guts of a cave inhabited by more than an estimated million bats. Thus, "research into the Beni cave and determination of the origins of the phenomena," was the mission handed to David Mason.

David's arrival fired up a titanic effort on the part of all local authorities to assist in the accomplishment of his goal. On his part, David possessed a characteristic dynamism. That, combined with a passion for hard work, made it possible for him to complete the search of the haunted cave in the northeastern province of this vast country. The natives spoke with reverence and terror when referring to this region. It was a taboo subject for them.

David Mason toiled non-stop for many months, dealing simultaneously and successfully with the excavation problems and the superstitions of the natives. In addition, he had run out of money but his stepfather, Harold Sheridan, had come to his rescue. Neither the heavy tropical climate nor the sluggishness of the workers was able to hinder the researcher's progress.

He finalized his conclusions and put the finishing strokes on his writing and, as far as he could tell, the time had come to deliver his thesis to the committee. He was full of hope and expectation.

Not giving a second thought to the potential for collegial envy in the university community for the extent of his findings, David made some bold assertions on what he discovered at the Beni Cave. His thesis asserted that he found buried, "a substance of unknown origins," in other words, an extraterrestrial being. Naturally, the committee, always biased against such discoveries, was taken aback by the young researcher's chutzpah.

The university community's conservative position and the professorial presumption of "higher knowledge" rendered it impossible for David to defend his thesis successfully. The committee's forceful rejection made him the butt of jokes in the scientific community.

David's professional disaster spilled over into his family life.

His life story was a drama in many parts. He was the only child of a Norwegian immigrant. David's mother died when he was three years old. His father, Eric, was killed in action a couple of years later, during an ill-fated, clandestine search-and-rescue operation in Iran. Sergeant Eric Mason's helicopter crashed in the desert and so did the mission to rescue the American diplomats held by the Iranian fanatics. But a survivor of the hellish mission, Colonel Harold Sheridan, a close army buddy of David's father, stood by David's side not only as a step-father but as if he were his real father.

The Colonel had noticed early on that David was not an average person but had the mind of a genius. So he made it his life's mission to help David climb as high as he could at the university and as a scientist. David was not the ungrateful type. His stepfather's sacrifices had a serious impact on his own thinking and feelings. He responded similarly with respect and love.

David's failure to defend his thesis struck the Colonel like a bolt of lightning. Harold Sheridan's already weak heart literally gave up. And this meant a double strike for David.

Still, David Mason would not break. Despite his loneliness and his tattered career, he persisted. He often recalled his stepfather's advice, "You must be like a steel rod that bends but does not break. You may lose a battle or two, but that does not mean you cannot win the war."

David knew that he had no more room for failure. He had indeed lost two battles. Before too long, his fate took a turn for the better. David's drive to regain his prestige and job led him to a position on the team of paleontologist Tom Rich and the "gulf of the dinosaurs" in Australia. The success he shared in that expedition proved decisive in burying his own past. The "extraterrestrial affair" was all but forgotten.

But David Mason could not forget. A compelling voice inside him gave him the courage to remember. "Something, indeed, exists down there. It is not the product of my imagination, and I must not let it go. I need to know for sure!" The feeling had become a recurring thought.

David kept a close watch on developments in the African region and began creating a systematic plan that would lead to fulfilling his goal to uncover the truth. He knew that his own resources were too meager to handle the entire cost of a new safari and excavation, so for many years now, a sizable part of his annual income was set aside in an account labeled "Beni Cave."

He would not trust his plans to anyone, but he had silently decided that this year, during his vacation time, he would return to the location in Africa where his professional dreams had been buried, where he would resolve the issue in a dynamic way.

This time, as an experienced scientist, he wanted to revisit the same problem and resolve this issue once and for all. David wanted to be "cured" from the nagging thoughts, hoping that if he could justify his original conclusions of an important finding, he could finally put the entire matter behind him.

This time he was armed to the teeth. He had already assured the presence of earth-moving machinery at Beni, in addition to the most important electronic equipment. This way he was certain to identify with precision any important discoveries and to interpret their importance to science.

The morning David arrived at the cave with the bats, everything was exactly the way he had left it. "I am the only one who got older," he thought, although he also knew that, in his forties, he was vigorous and a tireless fighter.

He was well prepared, bringing with him a dozen laborers and two excavator operators. For a few dollars he had secured the permit from the local government in Bounia, a beautiful town that was the administrative center of UELE, the eastern province of Congo. David wanted to identify the region first and then make his final, all-out effort.

Driven by uncertainty about the outcome of his new research, and wishing to avoid another disaster, he avoided any publicity about his trip. Even people in his immediate circle were unaware of his new attempt.

The very first afternoon of his arrival at Beni, the excavating equipment went to work. The ear-shattering noise of the machinery forced the countless bats to flee the cave in terror. Excavations lasted three days and three nights, on a schedule of three shifts daily.

On the first day of excavations, the laborers had dug to the top of the huge metallic object that David had described in his original thesis as a spaceship. His instructions were very clear this time. They had to dig deeper to completely unveil all the sides, including the underbelly that was to be exposed for the first time ever. The man in charge of the work, Manuel Calango, reported at the end of the excavation that he had found something interesting.

David Mason's excitement was great, as one can understand. He felt a lump in his throat even as he tried to thank Manuel, but he was unable to muster any words. "They found something! My God, I would like to finally feel justified," he thought. "Even at this late date, I would like to claim back my reputation." Too bad that Harold Sheridan was no longer around to witness that his own sacrifices were not in vain.

With Manuel's assistance, David carefully entered the huge opening and began to climb down the rope ladder. He was holding a stormlamp in one hand and had a camera around his neck. He continued his descent. The well was more than 35 feet deep and was dug following the sides of the object. These sides were stronger than steel.

At the top of the well, Manuel realized that his boss had reached bottom and shouted: "Buana, there is an opening; you can go inside."

David could feel his heart pounding so heavily that it felt as if it would explode in his chest. His veins were throbbing on the sides of his head. He could hear Manuel's words reverberating in his mind, "You can go inside." The words created their own unending echo. The far-away dream was now a reality. It was a step forward, a step that would bring him closer to the raw truth. He would be proven right—that was a fact.

The first time around, the wells into the earth had been dug facing the wrong sides, or at least at the sides that had no egress."

"Whoever does not believe in the goddess of fate has never met her," David shouted with enthusiasm.

The loyal Manuel heard him speak and thought something was wrong. "Did you say something, Buana? Do you need something?" he asked anxiously.

"No, Manuel . . . I am just talking to myself because this time we got it!" He had progressed hardly two meters when his stormlamp lit a long corridor on the side that was dominated at the far end by a round massive sphere, an opaque ball that looked as if it were made of opal.

At first, David thought there was light coming from the surface of the ball, but soon concluded that it was the reflection from his own lamp that played all those games on the sphere's surface.

He continued as if sleepwalking, with his eyes open wide. He took six steps. He could now see an octagonal opening in the middle of the corridor, and a round hall. In the center was a huge chair, raised like a throne, overlooking the space so that the chair's occupant might have easy access to the endless line of levers and screens. He walked a bit further. Now facing him was the mysterious sphere.

Silence was king, but it was a threatening silence. "The calm before the storm," David thought. He laid down his lamp so that it continued to light the opal sphere, unhooked his camera, and shot.

Lightning filled the room, not the flash from his camera! It was so strong that it blinded him. As if that were not enough, the thunder that followed burst like a scream into his ears and deafened him. David collapsed lifeless. It felt like thousands of bites pierced his body—hundreds of thousands of bites. "It is the End," he shouted just before he lost consciousness. He was carried by a whirlwind, falling into a bottomless pit. It was painful, but his mind refused to recognize his body.

As if in a film, his life's important moments flashed in front of his eyes. He saw himself playing chess with his father. He saw the Colonel bidding him adieu as if he was embarking on a journey, perhaps his final journey.

It took superhuman work for the laborers to retrieve David from his spaceship grave, the grave he had chosen for himself. He was barely breathing, and that gave them some hope. The explosion caused the opening to cave in, but a little air was still escaping to the interior of the mysterious object. There was also the oxygen that was pumped in with a pipe, and the two sources of air saved him from certain asphyxiation.

Manuel Calango insisted that David be speedily transported to Kisangani, the old Stanleyville, and from there, by airplane, through Brussels, to the United States. The faithful Manuel accompanied David like a guardian angel. Manuel was the son of one of the natives who had toiled in the first expedition and was later killed in a car accident.

The sudden explosion of the mysterious, massive sphere caused David's trauma. Naturally, the news spread immediately throughout the country. The press, thirsty for sensational science stories, reported every scrap of information, embellished by innuendo. News reports talked about extraterrestrial phenomena, but nobody could find out exactly what occurred.

Fortunately for David, the specialists at Memorial Hospital were ready and waiting for him when he arrived. Saving David became their top priority. The fight to save him was touch and go for awhile, but they finally succeeded. Once more, science defeated death, but there was every indication that the adventure would leave its indelible marks on David, if not on his body, at least on his psyche. It was not at all certain that science would succeed in restoring him to his former self.

On the sixty-first day after his accident, David was able to walk about on his own and to be fed without the help of a gastro-intestinal tube. To the great relief of his friends, he had finally gained the full use of all his senses.

But the peculiar conditions that led to his injuries had also led him to the edge of a breakdown. It was impossible for anyone to discern the storm that raged in the depths of his soul. "It's as if I am not the same person," he thought, but did not tell anyone while trying to overcome this feeling. "It's as if I have a partner under my skin, and in my brain!"

The attending physicians, dealing with his physical problems, determined that he was finally healthy, but kept him under observation. The media was relentless in its requests to the doctors for interviews, claiming the public's right to know the exact circumstances of David's accident. They also wanted to know what the reasons were for his visit to the "Cave of the Bats." Eventually, after a medical committee meeting on the media requests, the hospital agreed to allow a press briefing by a specialized physician as it was expected that some unusual circumstances would have to be explained. They deduced the latter because of David's condition at the time that he came out of his coma. In his dreamlike state, David mentioned strange happenings that possibly took place in the distant past. It could be that in addition to the ordinary medical information, they would hear about "a life he had lived before this life!"

The doctors were neither romantics nor driven by curiosity, but they sought to determine to what extent the accident had influenced David's ability to reason. They sought to determine if their patient would be balanced in his presentation and if, in his drivel, he was coherent and if he was saying anything worth studying or researching.

In David's case, the injuries were multiple, with tens of wounds caused by the impact of broken objects. His entire body and his skull were riddled with openings. In fact, patients with severe skull injuries often suffer from a loss of coherent thought. But in David Mason's case, it was everything but incoherent. His speech had all the elements of a scientific narration or lecture.

That's exactly what drew the attention of parapsychologists and anthropologists, and their colleagues, the biotechnologists.

The first two months after the trauma, David was completely comatose, fed through the G-tube. With the use of lasers they were able to manage the problem of the pieces found in his brain, except for one pyramid-like piece. Only time could tell the long-term results of this heroic battle for life.

The post-operative observation was on a constant 24-hour basis. Days and nights passed routinely but were stressful. The sixty-first night was the exception!

That night an intern spent eight hours near the comatose David. To pass the time, the intern was studying with the assistance of a tape recorder. It was the intern's assigned task that night to observe the patient closely because the latest tests had shown increased encephalic cell activity. Physicians expected that the body would respond to the brain's activity and the immediate outcome would be particularly critical. The night passed, however, without any apparent change in the patient's condition.

At the end of his shift, when the time came for the intern to leave, he forgot to turn off the tape recorder. It was a voice activated recorder with a 90-minute tape, and it was easy to forget about it if the room was silent.

The head nurse that was scheduled to follow the absent-minded intern at David's side was more than an hour late. When she finally entered the recovery room, she witnessed a strange sight. The critically injured David Mason was seated at the edge of the bed with his eyes wide open, talking calmly. He spoke in a mercurial manner, as if dictating, but seemingly unaware of what he was saying.

His dialogue was not the usual chat of a patient. It was a kind of monologue, a confession, centered on topics suspended between the imaginary and the real. The casual listener would have considered it nonsense.

For a moment, the head nurse became alarmed that her tardiness would be noticed. Then she saw the red light of the recorder indicating "On" and relaxed in the thought that David's "strange tales" had been saved. "Everything is on tape," she told herself. Without any hesitation she buzzed emergency.

In less than ten minutes renowned professor Larry Keith

was at David's bedside. Dr. Keith had been the coordinator working to save David's life from the very beginning and knew exactly what to do. Dr. Keith checked the electronic monitors, which did not suggest any cause for alarm. He helped David lie back in bed, and congratulated the head nurse for demonstrating the presence of mind, as she reported, to use the tape recorder left by the intern. Now they had David Mason's first unsolicited confession in his own words. Soon David ended his "broadcasting" and fell into a deep, restful sleep that was nothing like his coma.

As he walked out of the room, Professor Keith took the valuable cassette and went straight to his office to listen to its contents.

Larry Keith had learned from David's cousin, Natalie Mason, the only person who visited him at the hospital, that David's years as a child and a teenager had been rough. For his own reasons, Dr. Keith was deeply touched.

Larry was the grandson of an Irish immigrant. His grandfather joined the thousands that had been forced to leave the old country during the potato famine. Larry was the only son and the oldest of four children. His mother abandoned them for a life with an Argentinean musician and Larry's father, Jonathan, moved the family from their home in Milwaukee to Brooklyn, New York.

Jonathan Keith was penniless and without any acquaintances in New York, but he was determined to do whatever was necessary to survive. He joined the army and fought valiantly in Korea where he was awarded three times for bravery under fire. In the meantime, Larry worked to support his younger sisters and to go to medical school. Despite his sacrifices, his sisters did not keep in touch once they grew up and had their own families.

Larry felt a certain sympathy and compassion towards David. Before Larry fell asleep that night he murmured to himself, "So, there are others who had it even worse. Let's hope that David Mason will be able to overcome this new trial."

# Survival and Side Effects

The professor bounced from one surprise to another as he studied the contents of the cassette. It became increasingly apparent that the case of David Mason, the man with the multiple traumas, commanded tremendous interest beyond the immediate medical circles. Of course, it was proper to begin the briefing with his own associates.

Larry Keith was in no hurry to call a medical conference. When the time came, he would prepare a list of invitees that included all the distinguished colleagues, and anyone who would be concerned with this subject. Before issuing invitations he listened one more time, ever so carefully, to the mysterious text and he made sure that references to religious matters had been erased. He acted instinctively, thinking that such matters would be best heard by an audience with direct interest in them. Of course, the text for the associates would be on another "clean" tape.

Scientists from many related fields rushed in record time, in response to his invitation, to hear the professor's cassette. The meeting was held at Memorial Hospital, in the conference hall near the Recovery Room.

The head of Memorial's public relations department announced Larry Keith's arrival to the meeting. The latter, without any guilt feelings for bringing a "clean" tape, something he considered necessary, was ready to begin the briefing. The conference participants welcomed the professor with a warm applause and he took his seat at the speaker's chair. The applause was followed by a silence, pregnant with anticipation and respect.

Larry Keith squinted, uttered a nervous cough, forcefully landed his open palms on the table and said, emphasizing his every word, "Friends and colleagues, all my life, during my entire career, I have been a cool-headed realist. I always categorized visions only where science allocated a place for them, in other words shelved them as metaphysics or stashed away where they were soon forgotten. Today, after you hear this text and participate in the discussion that we have placed on the agenda, it is possible that some of our basic theories will be destroyed or will be placed under serious doubt. That, of course, is something you will decide and I will respect your opinion. Today, without the benefit of satellites, telescopes and other such complicated equipment, we will touch the unknown past of another world, a different form of life. It is all implemented through the brain of a wounded man who is playing the role of a mouthpiece, a transmitter. Be careful! We must be skeptical. Today we may be enthusiastic about it, but it may consequently be proven that it is all a sick farce, one being perpetrated on us by a satanic, sick brain used as a go-between."

As soon as the public relations representative of the hospital heard the Professor's last words, especially the phrase "sick farce," he got up in protest. He cut off the Professor as discreetly as he could, and he stated unequivocally, "I would request all of you not to discuss this matter with anyone outside this room, or make any premature personal comments, at least not until after the committee has come up with its final conclusion on the subject. Gentlemen, anything different could tarnish, now and in the future, the image of this hospital, this unique financial and medical colossus!"

With a distinct murmur, the audience indicated its solid agreement and intention of complying with this statement.

Care had been taken for taping the entire speech and for producing a separate tape for each individual person attending the conference, in order to enable each person to review the proceedings at his or her own pace and provide an analysis. Speaking on behalf of the group, researcher Renato Lunetta addressed Larry Keith, "If luck would have it and David Mason remains in this limbo, this psychological condition for a long time, I believe that a dialogue would give us a great deal of material valuable to our research. It would be like a mild interrogation . . . provided that we do not affect his health adversely. In fact, I think that, as you said, that is one of the conditions."

Professor Larry Keith hurriedly agreed and repeated that it was, indeed, his intention. He was also thinking that after they listened to the taped monologue, they would vote to appoint the most appropriate person to carry on this sensitive dialogue. However, since the issue came up now, he was not opposed to holding the selection of the appropriate person immediately.

The overwhelming majority voted for Larry Keith. He would now be the man to decide how to handle things. The professor thanked them for the great honor, but he declared that another man, Oliver Sachs, the philosopher-doctor, would be better than he for the task before them. The great philosopher had stated in a recent interview: "Questions inundate us like waves that produce many answers, and these answers become the bridge that leads us to a new series of questions."

It was agreed that after listening to the cassette tape, and after they had the opportunity to discuss it with David Mason, they would meet in the same place again, if and when that was deemed necessary.

Everything was ready. An explosive silence hovered over the entire hall. The scientific interest in this peculiar case kept everyone at the edge of his or her seats. The professor pushed the button. At first, they heard sounds as if a man was trying to clear his throat. Slowly, the coughing subsided. Then, a voice, "It is in the inner depths of all existence . . . there, where the most sophisticated technology has been unable to penetrate or search . . . worlds are born and worlds die . . . worlds that meet their extinction sooner or later . . . willingly or not. Yet, despite the nature of these relentless rules of nature, one planet, one strange heavenly body, refused to succumb to its fate. It reacted and was successful at the end to survive." The audience began shuffling in their seats during the full minute of silence that followed until Keith motioned them to remain calm.

David continued his monologue, "Attention. I will attempt to describe the geology, so to speak, of this strange planet because I consider it very important to the understanding of what follows. A planetary system with two suns and the unbreakable hold of their magnetic fields kept everything in place among the 32 planets. Of the latter, the 17 closest to the suns were almost complete balls of fire. The 12 furthest away were completely frozen, their frigid masses spinning forever, without hope, like lifeless bodies. Of the three remaining planets, only one was able to resist the inevitable, to raise its head and to create a miracle. It cooked on its soil all the necessary conditions to see the rise of Life!"

Several scientists in the audience began to express their discomfort with what they termed romantic nonsense dished out by David Mason. Larry Keith looked at them pleadingly, giving them to understand that the main course was still coming.

"Let me give you a good idea of the shape of planet

KEROPS. If you apply a solid, irregular ring on a sphere so that it divides it into two hemispheres, the dividing mountain range is called KOX. Fortunately, the seven dormant volcanoes—each on its own mountaintop—rarely became active. When they did, however, their explosion had nothing to do with that of volcanoes as we know them today. They did not spew lava; they were dry. Instead, the gases burst from the depths of the volcano, under a tremendous pressure, and found their way out through the cracks near the peak of the mountain.

"The explosion around the ring made a sound that seemed as if it said "KEROPS," and it christened the entire planet with that name. This planet had no nucleus, just two oceans of about the same size. The two were completely separated by KOX, the ring that I mentioned earlier.

"KEROPS was ten times larger than the earth, and all seven mountaintops greatly surpassed earth's Himalayas in height. For all the similarities, one mountain peak was quite distinctive because of its height and shape—almost a perfect sphere.

"The shorelines rose almost vertically from the oceans, in an inhospitable environment that was not conducive to the cultivation of crops. Lakes that absorbed the color of the rock filled the spaces among the range's peaks. Without exception, their water was salty. On the other hand, the oceans contained fresh water, just like our rivers. But there were no rivers. There were very few arable prairies that could provide enough food for only one in every twenty creatures that lived there. One ocean was shining bright, the other dark.

"This peculiarity resulted in a decisive level difference, where the bright ocean was much higher than its opposite dark ocean. The drop was more than 750 earth feet! The inhabitants took advantage of this idiosyncrasy and were successful, after a titanic effort over 276 earth years, to create a unique tunnel that cut through the KOX range and connected the two oceans. This created an artificial waterfall, which, however primitive, became their first source of energy!

"Endless water reserves channeled through a dam were used to provide abundant energy for all their needs, as long as population remained low. For thousands of years, limited arable land, affected by the salt of nearby lakes, forced severe limits on population growth because of the danger of starvation.

"During one of the famines on planet KEROPS, the victims numbered more than one million souls in the earth equivalent of two months. In order to survive, entire tribes offered themselves as slaves. One would have to consider both the scientific miracles and the peculiarities in the living conditions of these creatures. In this strange world, unusual and innovative concepts developed about justice, liberty and individual rights. It was natural that a flexible, moving dynasty would come to dominate the planet. It was the Dynasty of the MANTA.

"Strange!! I feel as if we are in a theater and someone is feeding me my lines. I am a human loudspeaker! That's it! I am a transmitter that broadcasts the contents of a text. It is possible that my limited knowledge of what I am transmitting creates some gaps . . . sorry, not my fault. And if there is repetition, it won't be my doing, either."

David paused. When he spoke again, he sounded exhausted.

"I am very tired . . . I feel nauseous . . . as if I worked all day. I need some sleep."

He fell asleep immediately, but the audience in the conference room remained in their seats. Their amazement was reflected on their faces as they waited for the next round, the discussion between David and Professor Keith.

# Contact with a Strange World

The Professor entered the Intensive Care Unit. David Mason was waiting for him, wearing an electronic helmet, the communications system that connected them with the audience in the hall next door. To prepare himself further, David also drank a cocktail of several medications that included scopolamine.

As had been previously decided by the committee of experts in the hall next door, Larry Keith was given the difficult role of questioning David Mason so that he may skillfully receive as much information as possible. The hour had come.

"I am Larry Keith. David, how are you feeling today?" the Professor asked with hesitation but calmly.

David answered without moving, "I feel like a pregnant woman just before delivering . . . I feel that I have been given this role by fate and that I will be revealing a chain of incredible events from the time of creation. I am not the Messiah and certainly not crazy . . . !"

Larry answered readily. "David, let's not delay any longer

since birth pains have already started . . . and I am the midwife
. . . and I am present!"

David offered a bitter-sweet smile and said as if to himself,
"Humor—here is something that is exclusively ours, human.
Humor is like the aroma of the flowers and foreplay in love,
something that does not exist on another planet."

"I see you are a romantic."

"You must be aware of two things, Mr. Keith. The world
whose history you are about to hear was filled neither with ro-
mance nor humor. Fortunately, neither is essential for life to
progress. Too bad that life loses its beauty without them."

"We have heard what that world had not had. Can you tell
us what was in their place?"

Without hesitation David pronounced, "Hate and Love.
Eternal light and eternal darkness. That's what gave birth to
the life I am about to describe."

The Professor interrupted. "David how is it possible for
eternal light to co-exist with darkness. Isn't this a conflict?
They are two opposing states; one neutralizes the other."

David smiled as if he understood. "Even so, this superfi-
cially strange condition was absolutely true on KEROPS. Let
me explain. One side of this planet was permanently turned
facing a twin sun. On the other hand, the other side was protected by the KOX ring, which acted like a curtain and cast
eternal darkness. This darkness was not pitch black."

"Didn't the planet revolve around an axis?" Larry asked.

"Of course the planet revolved around itself. One of its
poles had as an epicenter the multiple bright solar system. It
never experienced night! All that was generally correct. Undoubtedly, in the deepest recesses of the salty lakes, waters
from the two sides met and bright reflections blended with
darkness."

"And how do you explain that the oceans had fresh water
and the lakes salty water? Is there a reason?" Larry asked.

David, irritated by the assortment of wiring and the tight
helmet, suddenly tried to rid himself of the entire system. Fortunately, the monitor did not malfunction as the system was

made to withstand such an attack. In any case, technicians were waiting outside his door to correct any problems.

David did not forget the question. "The lakes with salty water are the products of torrential rain that filled the valleys, just like filling a cup."

"If understood correctly, the rock at the lake's bottom contained salt deposits. So the presence of water continuously diluted the rock and created these peculiar, hanging dead seas. My dear David, allow me to return to the issue of the complete darkness that prevailed at one of the two seas.

"The lakes with salty water are the products of torrential rain that filled the valleys."

David grimaced with discomfort. "To begin with, do not confuse me with the word sea. They were oceans."

"I will be careful!"

"I am not saying this out of stubbornness, I have the feeling that I act as the transmitter of a vast electronic memory that has scripted everything in detail. It is exacting in what it states as it dictates it to me."

"You are very clear in describing the events that took place."

"What events are you talking about? Up to now we have been talking about geology, so to speak . . . the geology of planet KEROPS. It's impossible to imagine what . . . what you can expect when it comes to events. You are in line to hear such earth shattering occurrences that it will radically change your beliefs and principles. Serious matters will eventually be turned into children's bedtime stories."

"What would you say if we continued," Larry interrupted in order to cut short any philosophical discourse that would border on drivel and get them into unrelated topics. "We should not waste any valuable time."

Before the session, the parapsychologists had arranged for David to travel to the past through hypnosis so that they may get precise answers. But it was uncertain how long David could last and endure the questioning under the stressful conditions of the machinery selecting and decoding David's manner of speech.

"So, we talked about the light . . . dear David."

"The dark ocean never got a glimpse of light except on the rare occasion when a deep crevice in the mountains would allow a stream of light to caress the ocean's fresh water, like the single spotlight that flashes in the darkness of a prison camp.

"Slowly but steadily the dark ocean began to receive light and to reflect light through the phosphorus of the tiny plankton. It formed solid masses composed of trillions of plankton floating in the vastness of the dark ocean. They were the first floating 'natural batteries' of light-reflecting protein. They were readied by nature to eventually nurture the chain of living creatures that were to follow. Thus, dynamic, self-sufficient, intelligent creatures found themselves under new conditions and in an environment that was rich in food containing phosphorus.

"At first the environment in the inhospitable, dark ocean, though rich in food, was a tremendous obstacle. However, the light creatures were endowed with superior adoptive powers that produced changes in the DNA. Evolution is the award of the eternal struggle for survival!

"Finally, the harmonic symbiosis of the higher forms of life of the lighted plant with the abundant living masses of food led to the evolution of life forms with a lightning speed.

"Undoubtedly, they would have all remained in a state of co-existence and inter-dependence. Their digestive system was such that, in order to survive, they had to consume large quantities of food. They searched for food ceaselessly, day and night. Of course they were also driven by the propagation instinct, but that did not claim any of their valuable time since they were hermaphrodites!

The professor interrupted the speaker, saying "I wish to submit a question."

"I am listening!" David said dryly, taking the opportunity to down a glass of water.

"You, Mr. Mason, please allow me to address you this way . . ."

"Of course."

" . . . you lived in what evolutionary stage on that planet?"

David appeared to have been taken by surprise and showed his anger. His eyes were almost bulging. He thought for a moment that his colleague had underestimated his intelligence.

" . . . I did not live on that planet, Mr. Larry Keith. Anyway, had I lived during that period of the evolution I would have been plankton or some brainless creature. What is your opinion? I think that we are not here for you to examine my scientific knowledge. We are here to learn the translation of the transmission that they are sending and which you are pressing me to find out. Let's take an example.

"Did you, Mr. Larry Keith, learn about the ice and the water underneath Europe, Zeus' satellite, because you lived there? Of course not. But you know about it. Did you find out about the deluge on Mars because you lived there? No, but it is part of your education." The professor moved around in his chair, feeling bothered by the possibility that his subject of inquiry might get mad and discontinue the transmission.

"I humbly ask your forgiveness, David," he said sincerely.

"Let's continue . . . my remarks were also out of place," David agreed.

"David, you explained the biological evolution; I would also like to hear something about energy. Was this planet active? Did it have a nucleus? Were there volcanic explosions?"

"I think that I have already talked about that. Let me repeat and also provide some additional details. Inorganic substances created complex reactions in the gut of ring KOX. Under that tremendous pressure, gases were first liquefied and then solidified. This natural chamber of explosives often found its own way of release. Fortunately, only in some rare cases, did the underground explosions shoot rock formations into the heavens. In those instances, the speed of the rock defied gravity and turned them into meteorites or even satellite bodies. All this was but a rehearsal performance by the gases for the forthcoming cosmic explosion."

"Please be more specific about the phrase 'cosmic explosion?' Why?"

"Allow me to explain something else first, before I speak on the issue at hand. I promise you it is not unrelated and it will be of interest. It will compensate for your time."

"I cannot wait."

"The ring of mountains consists of many parallel ranges that are only rarely interrupted by vertical cracks or valleys. The ranges finally converged at a huge, pointed rock formation that looked like a navel. In earth terms, the size of the peak of the range was slightly larger than the continent of Australia. The peak was created by lava excreted at the time when the volcanoes of the planet were still active. The surface was dotted by holes and gave the appearance of Swiss cheese. In fact, the maze that followed these entrances became the home of the more advanced form of life, those that had left behind the waters, their 'stepmother.' These creatures came from the bright side of the planet. Their dark skin color protected them from the intense rays of the sun. Their underwater origins resulted in an ability to fly."

"Incredible! Were they birds? Bugs? I beg you, David, please describe these flying creatures for me." Larry could hardly hide his enthusiasm.

"In earth terms, again, the evolution of these creatures took several hundred billions of years. I will try, anyway. They were neither birds nor bugs. Basically, their bodies had four feet that evolved into bodies with two feet and a set of very strong muscles in their shoulders. These muscles powered two wings that were able to help them move among the mountaintops. This trait gave them the power to overcome all other creatures and to lord over the food resources. Their brain capacity, however, would never improve, because of their peptic system. They were carnivorous creatures with a very high metabolism rate that compelled them to permanently make food hunting their main concern."

"Fantastic! David, you have more or less described to me winged, carnivorous creatures that patrolled the bright side of KEROPS constantly eating whatever they came across."

"Exactly, everything that was alive or has just died, even if it were a winged body. At the end they were forced to eat even decomposed corpses."

"You are talking about cannibalism . . . "

"Yes! When it was the rule during periods of starvation— which occurred quite frequently."

"What did they look like in comparison to the various animals on earth?" Larry Keith asked with obvious eagerness.

David grimaced. He sighed a couple of times before he dared utter the answer. "Well, Professor, my answer might displease you or even create serious doubts regarding what I have described. It might even become the basis, somewhat understandably so, to interrupt our scientific collaboration.

"We will risk it, David. However, I can assure you that my tolerance has no limits."

David continued though he did not appear totally convinced.

"In their faces, they were truly beautiful, Apollo-like with baby looks; their bodies were like Hercules, but their brains were a disappointment. In fact, besides the pretty face, they had very a tiny cranium and a tiny brain."

"You want to say that . . . "

"Yes, and I repeat! They had small heads, even though their body resembled that of a body builder."

"Really, I am uncertain whether to accept the veracity of your description," Larry stated with an obvious disappointment despite his previous statement about being tolerant.

David expected such a reaction.

"You see what man's arrogance does? Unconsciously you identified with the winged creature for no good reason. It is normal for us to react when we are being compared to a sorry-looking, ugly-faced chimpanzee or to a humanoid bat. Besides, this has got to be the reason that we rejected the evolution theories of Darwin the Terrible. On the other hand, when it was explained to us that we are created according to God's image, we became religious! The same holds true now. You were disappointed by what I told you; but I did not exaggerate at all in my description. They were humanoid, winged destroyers who terrorized everyone else."

"Everyone else?" Larry asked with renewed interest.

"Of course. The creatures I described were only the inhabitants of the sunny section of the planet. Parallel to this evolution, on the dark side, evolution had a different result and so did the form of the species. The 'others,' Professor, those who dwelled in the dark side of the planet were colorless and their faces were just like the face of a four-month old embryo."

"In other words . . . ? Real freaks!"

David was absorbed in his narration and did not pay much attention to the offensive characterization. He continued, "They were albinos, they lacked melanin; it is obvious that the absence of light had created its own set of conditions. Otherwise, the outward appearance and the ability to fly were their only common characteristics with the black Apollo-like creatures on the other side. The albinos had an ugly face, but could see in the dark. Their hair was long, platinum blond, almost white. They had a large cranium and they weighed hardly one-third of their dark counterparts. The albinos looked like huge, winged, human embryos."

"Were they strong? I mean of equal muscle appearance?" the Professor asked.

"No comparison! But whatever they lacked in muscle-power they had gained in their superior intellectual development. They had a different digestive system. They could eat anything, a trait that made them independent from food sources, and their metabolism was normal."

"Therefore, they had plenty of free time to think, to develop intellectually. Is that what you mean, David?"

"That's right. Even the problems they faced in darkness were difficult, and so they were forced to search for solutions. Finding solutions were a matter of life and death for them. They discovered foods with special nutrients and the stress of searching for food became secondary. Their metabolism, regulated by a special body organ, adjusted according to conditions and the energy they consumed."

"So, it resembled our own thyroid gland? After all, they did resemble us."

" . . . but, not their faces. Their looks were freakish, I could almost describe them as 'winged devils.' Expressionless, with bulging eyes." "Even though the dark-skinned, handsome ones were superior in doing evil and in their destructive mania," Larry Keith added. "You will be the judge of that, later on," David Mason said, pointing his finger meaningfully. "Don't hasten to come to conclusions." David made his point succinctly and then continued in his enigmatic style.

"The white wings of the albinos, with their rosy tint, often became the target of their strong, mountainous, dark, hungry competitors. The final supremacy of the latter on the entire mountainous ring, KOX, naturally made the albinos vulnerable. They lived under the shadow of constant danger. They were forced to live defensively. It was not a struggle between equals. It was fortunate that their adversaries could not see in the dark and would lose their sense of direction in the hunting fields. But they had superior sense of smell and hearing. An albino would save his hide only if he could find a hole whose opening was so narrow that it would not allow the hunter to push his way into the hole. For that reason, the Albinos dug deep hiding places along the rocky coast and used them as their permanent living places. This one-sided, cruel war finally tipped the survival scale for the benefit of the black ones, and would have meant the total annihilation of the Albinos, if something totally unexpected had not decisively influenced the fortunes of the two fighting camps—something that would decisively influence this clash to the death." Larry Keith, of course, was literally riveted to his seat! He listened to the incredible story, uttering not a single word. And David continued.

"In one of the few bright crevasses of the KOX mountain range that allowed a large region to become slightly bright, the

Albinos had created an inhabited place, a labyrinth of underground tunnels and shelters. They lived in peace in their cav-
ernous capital for quite some time. As was expected, their
carefree existence made them careless. The guards slowly
began to disappear and enjoyment of abundant food increased
their body weight to a dangerous point."

"Your description, David, is so lively and detailed that one
would think you actually lived those moments."

"Thank you for the compliment. Let's not get into that
again."

Larry bit his lip; he had totally forgotten their earlier conversation.

"Nevertheless, the lack of physical exercise had weakened
those muscles that helped them fly. The feeling of contentment
also led to a population burst."

"But, they were hermaphrodites."

"No! Those were the black ones. The Albinos had separate
sexual features and sexual organs. You might say that their
method of reproduction was ritualistic. This was a handicap
when they were compared to their foes with the Herculean
strength."

"I am really eager to listen to the rest of the story. What did
finally happen?"

"The light beam, during this period, revealed the endless
tunnel exits and, at the same time, brought unusual heat to the
network of tunnels. This might be the reason why tens of
thousands of Albinos dispersed and were occupying all of the
partially lighted mountainsides. They could only remain in the
tunnels brief periods of time, every once in a while. Their enemies, hungry as ever, kept a vigil wandering about in gangs on
the mountain range. For hundreds of years they had not
crossed the Bright Valley because it was inaccessible and hostile. Now that food became rare, they would go anywhere to
survive. They were like mad dogs in search of anything edible.
Suddenly, their scouts could not believe their eyes. There in
front of them, on the rocks, was a banquet. This potential feast

had dimensions they never had seen before. Let alone quantities of food. . . ”

“I can imagine what happened! Catastrophe,” Larry said to himself.

“Starving, they fell upon their victims without pity. The attackers were more than 800,000 and the victims exceeded 50,000,000. About 1,200,000 of them were eaten or imprisoned, while the rest died in the tunnels they had built—what an irony!—for their protection. The hunters sealed the openings of the tunnels so that they would have meat for a long time to come, even though the bodies of the Albinos would rot. It was a terrible genocide.”

“What was the population of the Albinos?”

“Before the bloodshed, they were approximately 100,000,000. Half of them paid with their lives for the lack of organized defense and security. Thoughtlessness is always paid for the hard way. Loosely translated, the devastation has historically been called ‘demons’ assault against the bright valley.’ But they learned a lesson. After they reassembled their forces, they organized themselves on a sound basis. They installed life-size models of the enemy all over the place so that every Albino, from early childhood, knew to watch out for the enemy. Drastic measures were taken. Gaining excessive body-weight meant a sentence to death; that is, exile to the bright side. There were only two sports: flight speed and javelin throw during flight.

“It was accidental that the Albinos’ heads were larger than those of the swarthy creatures. The brain substance was triple in weight and performed much better. In other words, they were incomparable when they needed to think and make decisions. They were the first to use everyday items as weapons and to lay traps. They had a lot of free time that allowed them the luxury of thinking, as I have already mentioned.”

“You mean, David, they finally managed to deal with danger and to neutralize it?”

“No, my dear Larry, despite their progress and desperate attempts, the Albinos diminished in number, not only due to losses in the undeclared war for survival, but also due to lack of fields to grow crops for food. They could not get enough food. They lacked vital space."

"You hinted at something unexpected but we digressed. The digression was very informative and interesting but we should get back to the main subject."

David Mason smiled. "It was not really a digression, but now we have arrived at the crucial moment so that I can explain to you the salutary event that had multiple consequences. Perhaps you remember that I talked to you about a huge formation, a sphere almost the size of Australia. This formation caused a geological asymmetry on KOX's stone ring. The tremendous pressure from this mass created one more side effect, a lake made of condensed liquid, a lake of plasma."

The professor interrupted him. "I remember. You've made me understand that most of the swarthy creatures inhabited this gigantic rock."

"Yes, they had nested in labyrinthine, deep, dark tunnels. It was like a colossal ant nest that sheltered almost 70% of the swarthy creatures. They lived in groups, just like bats do in caverns."

"So?" Larry asked, obviously impatient.

David swallowed hard—indicating he was thirsty—slowly emptied a glass of juice that was on the table close to him and continued.

"Nobody could predict what would come up during that apparently ordinary day."

# The Satellite God

The first time Larry Keith listened to the tape, his secretary, who was working in the office next door, pricked up her ears. Through the intercom system, she managed to record the part where David was speaking about the religion of KEROPS' inhabitants. In fact, she managed to record David's revelations in their entirety. The secretary, who was present at the meeting where her boss was presiding, noticed the omission of this part and suspected it was done on purpose.

At the same time, she fumed with rage because of Barbara Haim's appearance and her visits to the professor. Yes, Dorothy was madly in love with her boss and, as long as he lived alone, she didn't mind. The hope that, perhaps, some day, he would pay attention to her as a woman kept her going.

For his part, like the civilized person he was, the professor often offered her presents. Although they were everyday items, they acquired a particular importance in her lovesick mind.

Everything was fine until Larry went on a vacation to

29

Greece. Then, suddenly, a six-foot doll with a tempting body and an alluring personality invaded their lives. Almost every day she came to visit the professor and the two usually left together, holding hands.

Dorothy even entertained some very well founded suspicions they, once or twice, had made love in the office, right under her nose.

Barbara Haim was a zoologist with top credentials from the University of California. She frequently participated in missions to save the wild kingdom in the Amazon region and in Central America.

She had met Larry in Mykonos, the charming island that makes you forget all your troubles and awakens old feelings and sensations. If they had had time, they would have been married there. And now they lived the most intense phase of their affair. Love-stricken Dorothy could sense it.

What a cataclysm! All her dreams were wiped out! Her hopes that they would, some day, live together, gone with the wind. "Vinegar made from very good wine tastes more sour. . . Hatred runs deeper when it springs from a scorned love."

She had lost Larry and she was determined to destroy him. Her revenge passed over Larry Keith's corpse. There was no greater transgression, for a university professor, than to hide information of the highest scientific interest!

She felt mighty having this weapon in her hands.

"You shouldn't have come out of the blue, dear Barbara, to seduce my Larry! If I cannot have him, no one else will! Justice shall be done!"

Dorothy repeated these thoughts out loud as she stood naked in front of her mirror at home, admiring her sensuous body. On such occasions, she could imagine Larry's hand caressing the curves of her body and embracing her in his arms.

Without much thought, Dorothy took a copy of the tape and went to the Cardinal's office. She was a Protestant but believed that the Catholic dogma offered a greater potential for reaction to Larry Keith's tapes. What a scandal!

"You asked for an audience, my child?" the Cardinal asked.

"Yes, Your Eminence," the hypocritical Dorothy answered, bowing her head.

"What can I do for you, my dear child?"

Dorothy, with an arrogant smile, opened her bag and took the tape out.

"I would like to trust you with its content," she said with false respect. "It constitutes a serious evidence that might undermine our religion, our institutions, World Peace, our Church. . . "

The cunning Cardinal, before granting an audience to Dorothy, had been informed that his visitor was a Protestant. He also knew her parents lived in Belfast. Before the meeting, his counsel had said it might be an attempt to trap or discredit the Catholic Church. He had to be careful.

The Jesuit, pretending to be interested in her offer, said, "Oh, my child, I thank you! Your interest in our Holy Church will certainly be rewarded."

He took the tape in his hands and escorted the foxy Protestant to the door. Everybody was satisfied.

The Cardinal gave the tape to the senior counselor. "Listen to this tape. Make a copy of it and send it to the Holy See, to Father Patrick."

Some time later, the Bishop reacted. "But this tape offers nothing interesting, Father!"

"The Devil himself offers nothing interesting, yet we do study him. All information, even distorted, may be worth something. Knowledge is power."

Dorothy now felt fully satisfied. "I will teach him to flirt right in front of me with that slut! The mighty Church will come crashing down on his head like thunder. Fortunately, the Cardinal didn't ask the name of my parish. . . in fact, that is strange . . . he must have been in a hurry."

With these optimistic predictions about her boss's destruction, she entered the hospital. She went up to the second floor and silently entered the booth where Larry was listening to David Mason's confession. Taking care not to draw anybody's attention to her presence, she sat in a corner pretending indifference.

David knew she was Larry's secretary and paid no attention.

"So what happened that day, finally?" Larry asked David with obvious impatience.

"A cosmogony! It's the only word I can think of that describes what happened! Suddenly even the dark ocean flashed with light. Something like a thunder from deep space fell upon the planet and uprooted it from its eternal orbit. The explosion this phenomenon produced could only be compared with those taking place on the surface of the sun. The energy it released can only be compared to that of all the atomic bomb reserves on planet Earth. And this explosion happened exactly under the phalloid top of KOX's mountain range. The explosion grabbed this spherical, mountainous mass and launched it into space, just like a gun shooting its speeding bullet. In two minutes' time, the spherical mass had already become a satellite."

"So, it was transformed into a satellite," the Professor repeated stupidly, hiding his face in his hands. "But this is terrible! Inconceivable! Wonderful!"

"The amazing thing was that the final position of this satellite and its speed turned it into a permanent celestial inhabitant. It had the ideal orbit that gave life and light. Light, for the first time!"

"If I understand it correctly, this is tantamount to having a satellite the size of Australia. . . "

"Don't hurry. Allow me to complete the description of the effects of this incredible event. First of all, the explosion's thrust caused a slight shift to KEROPS itself. It changed that planet's orbit. Fortunately, it was a minor shift whose effects weren't crucial to the living life, to plants and animals. The most important consequence was, of course, the increase of atmospheric pressure that led to a doubling in the force of gravity. This, in turn, made it very problematic for the swarthy creatures to move, because their bodyweight increased dramatically."

"Didn't the same thing happen to the Albinos?"

"No, because they were much lighter and agile. The effect on them was equivalent to one-third. Minor. Their wings became slightly weaker but were still usable. On the other hand, the swarthy creatures could now only move on foot. Their wings were useless. This gave a terrific advantage to the Albinos. Yet, there was something much more important."

"I think you are exaggerating, dear David. Is it possible to have an event more important than the sudden disappearance of 70% of one's enemies who certainly were vaporized the moment the explosion went off? As you already mentioned, 30% of those who survived had nevertheless lost their wings. In other words, they were disarmed, they were deprived of this great advantage, the ability to fly from mountaintop to mountaintop. I cannot see what could be worse than that."

"Indeed, it was the worst that could happen to the swarthy creatures. Yet it was the greatest and most unexpected gift for the Albinos."

"And since they are the only ones able to fly from then on, let's call them Angels," Larry Keith added. "Don't you think it's both reasonable and practical?"

The familiar enigmatic smile appeared again on David's face. "Although I disagree with the term you proposed, for now and until you change your own opinion, I shall call them Angels."

"You have this unique way of surprising me, my dear David."

"It's not me, Keith, but the facts, the crude and tough reality. The future shall prove it. I am just asking that you be a little patient."

"So, what was the happy event that pleased these newly baptized Angels so much more than the annihilation of their enemies?"

"In fact, there were many events! Let's take things one by

one. First, the explosion, let's call it the mini 'Big Bang,' caused 132 crevasses from one end of KOX's ring to the other. This brought in direct contact the two oceans, which were at levels 900 feet apart. So the explosion created 132 natural waterfalls, with no effort at all!"

"If you consider", Larry said, "the heroic struggle of the Angels to create the first one, I can understand the relief they felt to receive such an unexpected gift. You are right, my friend!"

David appeared to be paying no attention to Larry and continued his train of thought. "Suddenly, nature awarded them 132 waterfalls, 'white coal,' that were eventually utilized to produce energy."

"What do you mean? Wasn't this a major development?"

Again, David gave no direct answer. He kept his trump card for last.

"I forgot to mention, too, that the satellite-rock was named ANOL. The cataclysmic events that led to ANOL's creation had literally immobilized everybody—the Albinos, the swarthy ones and all the other living things on planet KEROPS. All the living creatures that had time disappeared deep in their hiding places. The Angels, as you prefer calling the Albinos, moved by their curiosity and hunger, were the first who ventured out after the initial shock."

"Curiosity is the father of intelligence and, therefore, the father of research," Larry said in a monotone. "What's next?"

David appeared to be toying with Larry's impatience. "The Angels reappeared from their shelters, in large groups, many holding each other's hand as if to draw courage. Their surprise was justified. This was the first time they had seen the dark ocean reflecting light, as if myriad tons of silver was sprinkled in abundance on its surface. Yet, this time, the light had nothing to do with the plankton. They looked at each other, filled with amazement and unanswered questions, confused. They were like prisoners who have been pardoned and, after many years, again face freedom's light. They tried to explain the unexplainable.

"Of course, you couldn't compare this with the hemisphere

of light they had known. However, the new situation constituted an unexpected progress that would measurably improve
their future living conditions. They now enjoyed 'silver light'
instead of the other side's 'golden' shine."

David stopped talking, his lips dry and sticky. With obvious
delight he downed a big glass of fruit-juice.

"And now, dear Professor Keith, get ready to listen to something astounding! When terror was replaced by an awareness
of their enemies' misfortune, messages arrived asking everybody to gather in the precise part of the Bright Valley where
the genocide had occurred. Taking with them food for only
four earth days, they gathered in that historical place. The
gathering had been organized by MANTAS."

"Who's that? I think this is the first time you mentioned his
name."

"Yes. I forgot to. . . introduce him to you. For several centuries, there was one tribe that had as their patriarch a creature, MANTA, who was the most intelligent and, therefore,
most powerful. It was the tribe of MANTA that had discovered weaponry and traps, and had established the laws governing them.

"You see, the Angels also had their Archangels. At the beginning, the brightest among their children was called
MANTA and, in fact, after the extermination of all the enemies, he was accepted as 'chief of the planet.'

"In order to distinguish themselves from the others, the
MANTA and his court in the same tribe cut off their wings,
thus demonstrating they didn't need them. In the face of danger, the brave do not flee but stay and overcome with their
wits."

"This, David, reminds us a bit of the Pharaohs' dynasty in
Egypt."

"Exactly. But let's return to our main subject. The MANTA
in this particular case had asked for this huge gathering because he thought the time had come for something big, something historic. Standing before the pink sea of his winged subjects, he no longer had any need for auxiliary techniques to

help transmit his message. The Bright Valley, shaped as an amphitheater, had the perfect acoustics of Epidaurus' ancient theatre.

"MANTA raised his hands, as if to bless the crowd. In fact, he was instructing them to be silent. He began, 'You all observe the sea; you all observe our silver ocean; you are all pleased with the light you see for the first time, yet no one has lifted his eyes to the sky.' His was a thunderous voice, a voice extraordinarily appropriate to the melodrama of the occasion.

"Like an echo came the answer from the Angels, 'No one!' He raised his hands high, and the sea of Angels imitated him instinctively. He looked at the sky, staring at the huge, bright meteor—as if seeing it for the first time—and howled with a voice from another world that brought shivers to everyone."

"ANOL," "NOO," "ANOL," "ANOL-GOD," "ANOL-LIFE."

The countless crowds repeated echoed the words, "ANOL-GOD-LIFE."

"MANTA, in a ritual manner, bent his body the way religious Muslims do to indicate repentance. His subjects did the same. They lowered their ugly faces, still unable to realize that today their God was born! They hadn't yet comprehended that this gesture of theirs signified submission to something supernatural. Until then, the word God—NOO in their language—did not exist because, until then, they were animals. It is the privilege of rational beings to admit submission to a superior power. NOO was the name for what was stronger than the strongest. Yet they didn't define some god. They now had the privilege to know the godly substance. At least, that's what they thought."

"But they were still in an infantile intellectual stage, immature."

David was startled by Professor Keith's reaction. He tightened his eyebrows and the pursing of his lips meant to show displeasure if not disappointment. Suddenly he realized that his companion was attempting to ridicule the seriousness of his narrative. Apparently he was unable to understand that this journey into the affairs of another world could have held tremendous interest historically and scientifically. David himself lived the agony and the problems of those beings who were able to master a logical explanation to what was happening only through the revelation of a deity expressed in the incident of the satellite.

"Their faith in something supernatural united them for the first time. They finally belonged to something. They felt stronger."

"With all due respect, Professor, allow me to disagree with you. You clearly missed the point this time."

The professor had already got up, so embarrassed that he didn't know what to do with his hands. He finally murmured, "I sincerely apologize. I am very sorry for the crisis I caused. For God's sake it was not my intention to bring the discussion to such a low point."

David allowed fifteen seconds of total silence to prolong the Professor's agony, then he began talking again.

"The rays of the suns fell on the new-born satellite, like on a mirror, and for the first time spread light to the hemisphere of the Angels."

"Just like our moon."

David smiled. "Certainly not, Larry. That moon, or rather that natural satellite, lived its one-and-only sunrise, and perhaps, its one-and-only sunset would have meant its disappearance. There had been no sunrise and there would never be any sunset. From the moment it became a satellite, by simple coincidence, the combination of the forces pulling it and its speed—had it nailed exactly in the middle of the distance between the dark pole and the rocky equatorial ring. Our telecommunications satellites are a good example of what had happened.

"With the speed of lightning, MANTA made sure that his message, including the upgrading of the satellite to a god, reached even those who were unable to attend the meeting. For the first time, something common would unite them all, their faith in the one and only divine superpower - the light-giving ANOL, God, NOO.

MANTA was the first to understand that if the power of faith were correctly directed, that is, in a constructive way, his Angels would do miracles. Because 'faith is what creates the miracles'. Yet, for this to happen, it was, of course, necessary to establish disciplining methods for those who violated the course set by MANTA. In his wise speech he had added that, 'ANOL, God, has destroyed most of our enemies, paralyzed the rest of them and, at the same time, he gave us the light. As much light as we need.'

"Of course, there were also the super-pessimists, though believers, who continued talking about possible dangers. 'Our ocean will flood us! We counted 132 crevasses through which tremendous water falls into our sea at great speed.' Others cried, 'Water levels will rise and our coasts will be inundated, our fields will be destroyed and we'll die from hunger!'

"A sort of Council, more appropriately called a Parliament, that always followed MANTA during his tours, said, 'MANTA, our Leader, you should ask God what we are to do.'

The supreme and indisputable leader, MANTA, who expected the question, answered with great pleasure. 'I will consult God and I shall decide. Last time, he told me that if we did not obey his will, he would return ANOL to our planet, thus bringing back our enemies who are imprisoned but alive. It shall no longer provide light and protection.'

"The threat of such a disaster filled the hearts of both believers and non-believers with terror. Their Leader's ominous words convinced even the most reluctant that it would be useless to challenge God and, by extension . . . "

"Or God's representative, MANTA! Isn't it?" Larry added.

"You're being rather literal in your interpretation, although MANTA presented as the God of Vengeance nothing but a common satellite which, however, occupied a large part of the firmament because it was close to their planet."

"A God who was born to serve selfish aims."

David showed his disagreement, shaking his head. It was obvious his opinion was, again, different from Keith's.

"No, their Leader's aims weren't really selfish. He wanted to convince them to agree so that they would implement an ambitious development plan. This plan would upgrade them from the animal state to a sphere where thinking and rationality would precede action . . . although what is considered rational sometimes requires serious discussion."

David sighed.

"Larry, I'm tired!" David said, closing his eyes.

Dorothy, in a conspiratorial mood but obviously disappointed by the strange things she had heard, left the room drawing as little attention as when she had entered. She returned home and was disappointed again to discover that there was no message from the Church.

# Doubts

Before Professor Keith even had the time to respond, a snore-that sounded more like a death rattle-echoed in the interrogation lab. The emergency plan was immediately activated. All hell broke loose in seconds, as doctors, nurses and technicians rushed in with life support equipment. David was wearing a hospital garment, with a zipper but no buttons that made it look like a modern straitjacket.

In a few seconds, the computer that was connected to David's electronic helmet reached the diagnosis-"Intellectual polarization due to exhaustion and precipitated hypoglycemia." In other words, stress induced exhaustion. They all breathed easier. The storm had passed.

Fortunately, the situation was reversible, as far as David's life was concerned. Yet, no one, either man or computer could assure that this man-who had literally returned from the grave bearing the odd mythology of the unknown god ANOL-could ever fully recover his senses and continue with his monumental narration. In any case, one wondered if the narrative might be the product of a delirious mind.

Was it true that what he described was a novel myth or prehistoric tale? It's certain that if David had been a mythomaniac before the accident or, at best, a gifted spinner of fantastic stories, then no one would have paid any attention to him. Yet, the detailed description of another world that perhaps never was, but could exist in the future, sounded awesome. Who could ever exclude the possibility David Mason was a prophet, just like Nostradamus?

During David's narration, in a room next door specially outfitted with teleconferencing equipment, a group of highly interested scientists were following the discussion between David Mason and Professor Larry Keith. The narration enthralled them to the point of forgetting their thirst and hunger. To those among them who began belatedly the study of "Subject David" or more correctly, the "David File," Professor Keith obliged them with a complete briefing.

At the advisors' demand, the professor offered to recount the history of the entire incident. He explained how David Mason had his first contact in the region and where the tragic explosion occurred. The briefing took place while the doctors took care of David, who had passed out.

"Gentlemen, David Mason's recent visit to the BENI cave was the second one after many years. The first visit occurred when he was still a student at M.I.T. and was writing his doctoral thesis. His thesis was finally rejected because it was considered inaccurate, containing para-psychological beliefs, and was of no substantive scientific interest!

"So, during his last descent into the cave, although everything seemed to be progressing as predicted, David was injured from the fragments of an exploding opaque mass. As most of you know, at first he thought it was opal rock, although its bright reflection made it appear rather peculiar.

"According to Mr. Mason's opinion, it was part of a self-destructing material, whose function and use is unknown to us. To be more accurate, we are just beginning to have some notions about it. Several laboratories undertook experiments with samples of this material almost immediately. And some neuro-physiologists have made important progress in their research but have not reached any conclusions. I kindly ask our colleague, Professor Maier, to replace me at the podium and continue this briefing."

Speleologist and paleontologist Arthur Maier began to speak. "There were literally hundreds of points where the fragments from the explosion entered Mr. Mason's body and caused a multitude of injuries."

"I think that surgical intervention removed all the alien parts," one of the participating scientists said. "I mean, all mineral fragments."

"Yes and no. . . because some of them were of very small dimensions and penetrated, in some cases, deep into the brain area. Their presence theoretically poses no danger."

The neurosurgeon who had been involved in the removal of the fragments interrupted without waiting for an invitation. "Gentlemen, at the risk of appearing careless, or even that mythomania is contagious, I wish to add something. After several days of studying this phenomenon, I dare suggest a truly revolutionary and, therefore, original explanation."

The tone of his voice allowed no objection! Professor Vangehuhten's scientific credentials, his bright mind and his up-to-now outstanding career, were in danger of being irrevocably tarnished before this group of distinguished personalities, if the theory he supported did not prove to be the correct one. Would he jeopardize his reputation?

The professor continued. "All the fragments but one have been removed or destroyed by laser, by my team. By coincidence, the triangular object that we left there and which looks like a miniature pyramid has lodged itself exactly at the center of a region where most recent research places the memory file."

Larry Keith interrupted, "I do apologize, but an injury there should result in loss of memory, yet. . . "

The neurosurgeon interrupted in the arrogant style he was known for when he was angry. "It may have caused a loss of memory, Professor Keith, yet, at the same time, it created an explosion of 'fertile' imagination. Memory and imagination seem unrelated in this case. In fact, this is the essence of the problem we're facing. The product of an active imagination cloaked with the pretense of memory. That's what we have heard and will, probably, go on hearing for, I hope, a brief period of time.

"Undoubtedly, Mr. Mason's utterances show some coherence and logic, yet, as far as I am concerned, they are nothing but a horrible fairy tale that, I predict, will have no ending. It is impossible for him to claim that what he narrates is factual, because in that case it would mean he has lived three billion years or that he simply has read about them. From what I have heard, Mr. Mason never had anything to do with science fiction literature, either as a writer or as a reader. As far as I am concerned, he is delirious."

"Or, perhaps, thought transference," another member of the audience threw out the idea.

Professor Vangehuhten struck him mercilessly with his answer. "You must certainly be joking, dear colleague! He who would be able to do this, I think, would prefer to write a book of his own. He could gain glory and make money. I see an incentive. The Von Danickens await us, although they are out of fashion. I protest and claim that the opal mass is not a part of any technological product. Gentlemen, sometimes nature likes to play games with human intelligence and credulity. It is possible that concentrations of gases inside this mass caused the explosion as soon as human presence altered conditions of temperature in the cavern.

"Without underestimating anyone of you, and although I accept anyone's right to believe in anything he wants, nevertheless, I propose we should be dealing with matters that are important and extremely urgent; specific problems that demand solutions. We should not continue listening to this imaginary description about the purported past of a completely fictitious planet. I am completely unmoved by this melodrama. I consider the case closed."

He concluded his statement with that sarcastic comment and waited for his colleagues' reaction.

But no one in the audience even thought of applauding the famous scientist. Strange! Vangehuhten himself was surprised not to find one single ally among the participants. "And what if it is true?" he asked himself, as he was leaving the meeting with the excuse that he had to respond to an urgent call.

Professor Keith spoke again. "I personally do not risk expressing a pessimistic opinion as our colleague Professor Vangehuhten just did. Anyway, I absolutely reject his suggestion to shelve the David File. If the narration goes on, as I hope it will, with the same harmony and coherence, and with the reporting of increasingly more interesting facts, I dare to predict we may find ourselves in front of something very big, very. . . powerful. It may overshadow even the most amazing achievements of our century.

I instinctively believe this man really lives the story he tells. One might even say that the facts he mentions are really part of his personal experience."

"This is, of course, exaggerated because how would it be possible for him to have lived. . . thousands of years?" someone in the room asserted.

The professor pretended he did not notice the sarcasm and went on. "One might say this man is a kind of a historian, the Cosmographer-Astronomer of this strange planet KEROPS.

A knock on the door interrupted the discussion. The doors opened. This time, optimism filled everyone as soon as they heard the good news. The medical report announced that David Mason had completely recovered. He had even been telling jokes, which was a clear evidence of the recovery of his intellectual capacity. Specifically, David declared, "The only way for somebody to get any rest, when he is dealing with so many scientists-interrogators, is to pretend he's dead. I warn you, if you make things difficult for me again, I might stop. . . pretending!"

The stimulant David had been given brought a sparkle to his eyes and expression to his face. . . and the mood for chatting. The scientists went back to their seats in the room next door. Larry Keith sat right in front of David.

# The
# Hermaphrodites

"David, progress is not compatible with the consumption of abundant and, if possible, cheap energy any more, is it?"

"Your point is well taken, my friend. For several hundred years, the 132 waterfalls were more than sufficient to supply electricity to the inhabitants. The energy needs of the Angels, industrial and many other, were met by this single source. Yet, one problem, that of storing energy in appropriate batteries, prevented them from building flying machines. The batteries were just too bulky."

"But they themselves could fly!"

"The muscles that powered their wings atrophied as time passed, and those who followed the trends, decided to eliminate them through surgery. Of course, the courtesans who, literally, constituted a 'state within a state,' not only did not cut off their wings, but, on the contrary, made them more splashy in order to increase their appeal to the opposite sex."

"So, the Angels frequented the ladies of the night?"

"No. These women reproduced their own partners through cloning. This means the sexual act aimed not at the fertilization of the partner's ovary. It simply aimed at her satisfaction. Yet, they were under the illusion that the opposite was true. The partner reproduced himself once, twice or even more, according to his financial ability. This was slowly abolished and cloning became, by law, a one-time activity for everybody."

"What about the women?"

"The same was true for the women. They made love for money and pleasure, but without bearing children as women do on earth. They worked until they had the financial possibility to reproduce themselves and hired a 'prostitute, who was beautiful like an Angel. . . "

"What about love?"

"What love? It had not been discovered. You mean sex."

"Whatever!"

"Free sex, without caprice and hypocritical shyness. The Angels, as far as this matter is concerned, were already in paradise if, of course, entry to paradise was prohibited to those who had feelings."

"You mean those prostitutes, let's call them the 'birth-givers,' those whose only work was to give birth."

"Ha, ha, ha! A new and very correct term, professor! Those birth-givers were, in reality, the economic giants of the planet. They control the future of the entire population."

"And what about MANTA?"

He was their leader, their procurer, in a general sense, as his power depended on a strong economy. Even in our own world, a man's power is directly related to the love women have for him. And the MANTAS who knew that acted accordingly. But this situation changed and birth-givers became almost useless when the geneticists discovered in-vitro fertilization, which in this case meant fetuses conceived in-vitro and also brought to term in incubators."

"In other words, just like farms where chickens are raised."

David answered calmly, "You are absolutely right."

The professor interrupted. "But, we got to talking about

women and we completely forgot all about the forms of energy I asked about."

"Yes. Besides white coal-the waterfalls-the turbines and the very heavy batteries, there was also the problem of the work force. There were jobs that were not done by machines or, if they were, cost too much."

"Yet, with the technology they had developed they certainly had made electronic computers and robots."

The enigmatic smile reappeared on David's face. "Computers, yes. . . robots. . . of course, the manufactured robots that were much more perfect than what we've achieved. Only. . . "

"Only. . . ?"

"Financially, it was totally counterproductive to use robots in tasks like agriculture and building construction. The Angels could not get themselves to go to work and their lack of physical strength made it even less likely."

The professor smiled. He had thought of something that pleased him.

"I see! They made copies of themselves by cloning, and sent them to work."

"Error! Huge error! Even though what you say was feasible."

"Then, how is it an error?" the professor wondered.

"When the reproduction law was finally implemented, as soon as the Angels were born, a clone was created. Yet, they didn't want to keep their successors, and that's why they put them to death."

"And ate them? Cannibalism also existed among them, right?"

"No, Larry. In fact, I meant they sacrificed it."

"If I understand things correctly, they sacrificed them to their god, NOO," Larry said.

"What god of theirs? When they advanced, intellectually and scientifically, there was no way to convince the bright, very intelligent student at school that a satellite was their God! The Gods are dependent on their believers, their followers. First you find followers and then you create a god according to preferences, to the model constructed by the imagination of the believers."

"So, even that depends on marketing?"

"Especially that."

Such were the subject and the thoughts expressed in the tape the medical student had forgotten and left running near David, and Larry had tried to hide. Yet, now, whether Professor Keith wanted it or not, it all came out. The professor could not censor the discussion. The only thing he could do was to try to guide it in another direction.

"Since they did not sacrifice them to gods or demons, what did they do to them?"

"They sacrificed their clone in order to harvest future spare parts of themselves. Each one then had secured parts and did not have to look for donors should the occasion arise."

"When they got sick, their cloned self came to the rescue," Larry said.

"You have stated it succinctly," David said with a smile. Of course, the Albino's swarthy opponents were once again destined to suffer. They were turned into slaves through cloning."

Suddenly, a small red light came on. This signified that the period allowed by David's doctors for questioning had run out.

"Time out, Larry! See you around!"

"Certainly!" Larry answered. "I am already warning you that I want all the details about the black creatures who became slaves and what was their final fate."

Of course, David Mason had secretly asked Larry for a tape-recorder to use if and when he felt like it. Larry gave him one. For Professor Larry Keith it was the end of the working day.

His colleagues left the hospital in deep thought and with mixed feelings. He took the stairs down to Memorial Hospital's parking area.

The professor drove home wondering in amazement about all the strange things he had heard that day. He felt as if he was standing at History's door peaking inside. He had the feeling that nature itself was narrating its life. Maybe the barrier to the most distant past had been shattered and he had been the chosen archaeologist to dig into David's memory and to discover something that could be precious, or simply strange. Only time could tell. The next appointment was to take place in ten days, in the same room.

# Theories on Creation

The missions to Mars, under the generic name New Millennium, used space vehicles called Microprobes. These probes gathered some amazing information about the probable origin of "Mars's stone face."

At the same time, the 'Athena' plan was advancing and global information channels kept people informed in detail about achievements in astronautics.

Suddenly, there was a long period of complete blackout on everything that concerned space. This blackout coincided with the opening of the David File.

During that time, the messages between the Pentagon and NASA were dispatched only with special couriers.

For a long time-in fact, many years-measures concerning security and top secret documents between those two super-services had been loose because the deadly Soviet threat no longer existed. In the absence of deadly enemies, security measures had relaxed.

Yet, recently, there seemed to be a revival of heightened security. As time passed, use of special couriers increased and even journalists began to notice that news sources in the two agencies had dried up. The use of couriers was anachronistic, but it presented the advantage that any messages delivered that way did not pass through intermediaries. The person who carried the bag with the messages also chose the travel route he was to take in order to reach the destination.

A special courier, riding fast on his Harley Davidson to Houston in order to deliver his message to the Space Centre, skidded off the slippery road. He was critically injured and died in the ditch where he fell.

The local police, not realizing the identity of the dying man, paid little attention to the partially open bag with the papers marked top secret.

A woman journalist managed to put her hands on the top secret documents and, unable to understand the coded content of one of the letters, published it in the local newspaper, just as it was, without any comments. It dealt with a program named "The B of the B."

It took a few days but the journalistic eagles managed to decode the message. The very beginning of the introduction was already puzzling. It could have been an action plan but did not sound very interesting and certainly would not be a hot selling item. Thus, the major TV networks gave little play to the story.

Larry Keith's father was a retired marine. Decorated by the President for heroism in battle, Jonathan Keith tried to remain occupied with a variety of interests, but there was nothing specific demanding his time. Since he lived in Texas, he went to meet the woman journalist in person. The old man gave almost all of his savings to recover some "secondary" documents that were joined to the main report and handed them to the police.

Of course, before doing so, he copied them and sent the copies to his son, Larry.

When Larry received them, he first laughed at his father's persistence and sense of patriotism. Yet when he carefully studied the text he found it particularly interesting.

". . . Launches will be pursued even after the end of program Athena. The U.S. Congress's Appropriations Committee had allocated $4 billion."

"A huge sum! But what was the mission?" He thought, "Just as in the Apollo series of flights, astronauts were launched to conquer a foreign land; maybe something similar was planned for Mars, after Pathfinder, or the satellite to Jupiter.

"At least, there was plenty of water there. Under the ice, there might be life, even at a very early stage. At least, that's what they say." Larry was almost sure that this was the meaning of the text. Still, he was unable to explain the reason for all the secrecy.

"Hello, Larry!"

"Is that you, Father? Sorry I forgot about your birthday."

It had been a long time since they had spoken to each other, and the documents were an excuse to renew their ties.

"Listen, Larry! Don't give it another thought, but as you know, we old men like to complain."

". . . You, the elderly, you mean, Father."

"Anyway. . . ! We gather at the Entertainment Center and the only things we talk about are our children's achievements."

"After you add a bit of spice, you mean, Father," the son added in laughter.

"That's also true, but the description of an astronaut's deeds that I heard the other day clearly exceeds the limits of imagination. It makes me jealous."

"What do you mean, Father?" Larry asked, pretending he was interested in order to give his father the opportunity to talk.

"I don't know if you remember Dean Thompson?"

"Of course I do. He's the one who was saved as if by a miracle."

"Well, he has a son, Patrick."

"Ah. . . that's his son? He's known because of his many trips to the Space Station."

"Precisely, that's who he is. His father recently revealed to me something extremely confidential. It seems Patrick and some companions are getting ready to stay permanently on the moon. Theirs will become a permanent base. Do you think the $4 billion. . . "

Larry interrupted. "Father, what you say is, of course, very interesting but I must be going now. I'm late. We can finish this conversation tomorrow. I will call you."

He thought his father was obviously jealous because of the legendary deeds of the other father's son. Who knows what he was telling about Larry to the other elderly friends?

The Professor was methodical in everything he did. Before filing away the documents his father had sent him, he examined them once more. One document had two signatures. One was difficult to read. The second signature was that of the Secretary of Defense, Michael W. Donovan.

The Professor stood there, confused. But, a short time ago, immediately after he first listened to the tape the student had forgotten he had something to do with this name. Oh, yes! Now he was certain.

"Things get a bit messy here," he said to himself. "I remember clearly that someone by that name called to ask for information."

Larry reached for the computer that recorded all of his telephone calls. He pressed the buttons, typed in the necessary information and, finally, the communication's text appeared on the screen.

"Mister Larry Keith?"

"Himself."

"This is Donovan! Michael, to my friends."

"Hello, Michael! What can I do for you?"

"I forget the name of the prophet you've discovered! Ha, ha . . . ."

"David Mason. Researcher, anthropologist and paleontologist," Larry informed 'Michael, an unknown.'

There was a pause on the other end.

"I can't hear you. Do you want anything else from me, Michael?"

"I was looking for him in the files, Larry. I can't find him. For routine, informational reasons, I would like to ask you to send me all possible information concerning the tapes."

"Michael, you speak as if you were. . . a member of the President's Cabinet."

"That's exactly who I am, Larry! Ha, ha, ha! OK? Bye now!"

Of course, Keith had made that remark jokingly.

That moment he felt he was in a cold sweat. Considering this entire adventure, and developments in David's case unfolding around the clock, he had completely forgotten to inform the Secretary of Defense.

Through e-mail, in a few minutes, he sent the following message: "My sincere apologies for the delay in communicating information on David Mason's file. Up-to-the-minute details will be sent immediately to your department."

Larry was extremely tired. So, he lay down.

" It's better to keep things friendly with military!".

He had just closed his eyes when, suddenly, an e-mail arrived. "That's really fast. . . ! That Donovan!"

He got up and approached the computer screen. His eyes bulged. His mouth froze wide open. He was reading a message from the least expected sender. The Holy See itself! The Vatican!

"The Holy Father shall be very pleased to receive you on Thursday, at 8.00 p.m., in the Vatican. The necessary documents have already been sent to your department, including reimbursement for several days' absence from your important duties. PS: Do not forget to bring the entire David File."

This was truly beyond reality. "Am I dreaming?" he wondered. He read the message again. The invitation was real and most urgent. In 48 hours he would be face-to-face with God's representative on Earth! He, a simple professor-researcher, one out of thousands in this world. . .

An ironic smile bloomed on Larry's face. He finally had the opportunity to teach a great lesson to somebody whose arrogance was legendary.

What would Professor Vangehuhten think if he knew that the Secretary of Defense and even the Pope himself were interested in David's fairy tale?

"I owe him that!" Larry thought. "He was so offensive and selfish when he withdrew from the committee of experts, that he must be punished."

"Hello!"

"With whom would you like to speak?" said a steely voice.

"Professor Vangehuhten!"

"Speaking! Who is it, please?"

"Larry Keith!"

"Oh! What can I do for you?" Vangehuhten asked in his most arrogant style.

"Well, in two days I am meeting with the Pope. . . "

"Who? The. . . Pope? In Rome? Are you crazy?"

"Why? Is it so terrible?"

"How long ago did you ask for an audience?"

"Just an hour ago the Pope himself asked me to meet him. This meeting was arranged at his request." There was a long pause.

"He wants to learn all about the 'story-teller' David. I'm calling you because I wanted to know if I have your permission to give to him, among others, the tape segment that contains your opinion in this matter."

The longer his victim took to answer, the more satisfied Larry felt.

"Hello? Are you there? Do I mention your opinion or not?"

" No! No! In God's name, don't do that!"

"Very well. Then you'll have to retract. . . "

"I will do so. I am retracting immediately. I'm doing it in writing and sending the department a memo about it. We all do foolish things in our lives. This was a serious mistake and I apologize!"

"Do you persist on withdrawing from the committee?"

"No! I'll be present at the next meeting. When is it?"

"In ten days, at the same place."

"I'll be there! Congratulations! And, again, I sincerely apologize!"

"Revenge is a dish you eat cold," says the proverb. Nevertheless, Larry noticed, in this case it did not lose any of its flavor.

The Pope would certainly be interested in the creatures, both the blacks and the Albinos, or Angels, and their religion.

Larry felt as if he were the Inquisitor who traveled to the New World with Christopher Columbus, and reported in detail about what he had seen and done.

A slight difference, of course. It was David Mason who had taken the journey, and he did so only in his imagination.

"Damn!" he thought. "Things are becoming dangerous! As time goes on, more and more highly placed individuals are getting interested in David's case. It's time to make sure he is absolutely safe! Because, when elephants quarrel in the swamp, it's the frogs that pay for the commotion with their lives!"

The first thing Larry did was to locate all the text relating to religion. It was puzzling. The minute David woke up from his coma, alone in the Intensive Care Unit, he began speaking precisely about that matter. Why was it so? The student's tape, as Larry referred to it, not censored, was already in place and Larry, with his eyes closed, was ready to listen to it again to refresh his memory.

"It was better when one could imagine god in the heavens, when one feared him as a father or a teacher and adored him. When satellite ANOL received its first visitors, religion was ruined because the granite god was immediately demystified.

Everyone was now aware of the crude truth. Poor is a god that doesn't have devoted ones.

"During the period when KEROPS was unreligious, the MANTAS of this intelligent dynasty understood that the void that had been created had to be filled as soon as possible. 'There is,' the MANTA declared and he was believed, 'a superior force that is the addition of matter, energy and psychic power. This Superior Force is our Creator and the creator of everything.'

"Of course, this news was not spread in the same ritual manner that MANTA's ancestor used when he claimed that NOO, God, the stone-satellite, would punish them if they did not do what they were told. There were scientific symposiums organized before the proclamation. This was the unanimous decision of the planet KEROPS' intellectual class.

"The fact that a part of energy was idealized as psychic is what finally gave our race Reason. Each one of us has his own that passes from one body to another, being indifferent about the temporary corpses it lets recycle. The soul's recycling does not demand its disintegration and re-creation. Soul consists of a permanent entity that is not influenced by Death, that simply relieves it from life's memories, purifies it."

"This will certainly please the Pope", Larry thought, ". . . soul's immortality." Yet, on the other hand, the text reinforced the reincarnation theory.

"Death is an eternal sleep, a sleep of the spirit, yet it presents features of the real one. As there is no body, no external disturbance influences dreams. If, during your life, you were right, just and compassionate, your dreams will be wonderful. It is as if you really lived in paradise. Yet, if during your life you were unfair or arrogant, or a murderer, your eternal sleep is constantly troubled by terrible nightmares. You are in hell itself."

"That's also good, this concept of dreamed nightmare hell and paradise with MANTA-David's lyrics and music.

"Schools for good behavior and penitentiaries are our own adoration spaces", the MANTA declared through David.

"This will certainly not satisfy the Pope," Larry thought. So many mouths are filled through rituals being performed. Wouldn't it be a pity to throw them into unemployment?"

"On KEROPS, there were scientists, psychologists, not priests, a kind of HOLY PHILOSOPHER. The ones that did not respect the laws were sent to the swarthy slaves' camps to be treated just like them."

"I won't speak about that," Larry thought, "it will undermine David's style."

It is true that David Mason had studied at the famous M.I.T. and, most certainly, this fact had its importance as far as the Pope's sensibility was concerned. He must have been informed about David's doctoral work that had been rejected after many months of research in Congo-Eastern Congo, to be more precise, 350 miles from old Stanleyville, today's Kishangani.

Larry Keith did not think, even for a moment, that the one who had betrayed him was his jealous secretary, the heartbroken Dorothy.

# Action
# on All Fronts

Larry searched his personal computer files and located the address and phone number of the man who accompanied David on his first trip to the Congo. He was the civil engineer, Theodore Papadopoulos, who now lived in Athens, Greece. He had previously made a name for himself as a pioneer in construction methods for high-rises in tropical climates. He had lived in Africa with his engineer father during the period called by white settlers the "Golden Age."

At the time David Mason arrived at Kishangani-Stanleyville, the THEO-PA Group had just completed plans for construction of a giant hotel, the Congo Palace.

Financing had been approved and the group was ready to begin construction. Yet, there was a problem that seemed impossible to solve. Where would they find the necessary sand and gravel? It might seem ridiculous at first, yet, that was a real problem since the tropical soil lacks both of those ordinary materials.

In Africa the soil, down to 6 feet deep, is like a layer of half-rotten vegetation. Deeper down follows a layer of clay, but there is no sand and no gravel.

The THEO-PA Group had dispatched teams of workers to do test borings at various sites in Congo's Eastern Province. They particularly worked close to Roentzore Mountain, the one also known as Kilimanjaro. It was located close to the new borders with Kenya.

Theodore's first encounter with David was accidental. When David arrived on a Sabena flight, Theodore's group offered to help David deal with customs formalities. Afterwards, they guided him to a building with rooms to let, in the town's square, run by a Cypriot woman.

As was the custom among whites in those days in Africa, Theodore invited David to dinner. He immediately accepted with enthusiasm, and that was the beginning of a friendship that would play an important role in David's life.

Larry thought he could get some valuable information from Theodore and called him in Greece.

"Hello. . . I would like to speak with Mr. Theodore Papadopoulos, please."

"He isn't in Athens, sir," the secretary answered. "He is with his son, Basil, in Belgium. I will give you the phone number, if you wish."

Larry called the new number:

"Mr. Theodore Papadopoulos, please?"

"Speaking! Who is it?"

Larry was very excited. He was finally speaking with David's main collaborator in the first, unsuccessful search.

"Larry Keith on the phone! My name may certainly not mean anything to you, but. . . "

"Oh. . . but, yes! You are the one conversing with my old friend, David Mason. I read about it in the papers, but lately I haven't heard anything new, even though I've been looking.

Exactly what is going on with David? I'm worried about him!"

"It's difficult for me to explain over the phone. But I would like to ask you, if it's possible for you, to send me a written report on what happened during that first search effort which took place on. . . "

"I don't retain dates either; they age us faster. Nevertheless, I'll be happy to do what you are asking of me. After the rejection of David's doctoral work, I had made a personal report, under oath. I have a copy and it would be easy for me to send it. You'll find a detailed analysis of the facts as well as the narration by the region's medicine men about strange events that took place."

"Whom did you report to?"

"To the Ministry of Education and Sciences in Greece and to the Education Department in the USA."

"What was their answer?"

"If you can find one, we will let you win an empty Coke bottle!"

"You mean they never answered?"

"Congratulations! You've won! Where can I send you the bottle? Ha, ha, ha!"

And to think that this guy, even then over eighty years old, had sensed the seriousness of the findings, Larry thought. Yet it had been impossible to interest the government officials. They certainly had received the report and certainly had not read it.

First thing in the morning, Larry Keith would call the hospital's security department to arrange without failure that David Mason would be guarded discreetly by three men, day and night.

Later that day, Larry sat in front of his computer to compose his report to the Pope. In a sense, this was tantamount to taking exams on good behavior as much as it was an exercise of writing a careful, informative report. Larry buried himself in the report for more than four hours. He was so absorbed that he answered the telephone after several rings.

"Larry. . . hello!" The voice sounded official, but Larry recognized it immediately.

"Michael! I mean, Mr. Secretary. . . "

"Forget about that 'Secretary' stuff and listen to me carefully!"

Larry noticed that the last phrase was an imperative that would take no objection.

"I'm waiting for your orders, sir!"

"We've been informed about the Pope's message and I already have read the report you've sent by e-mail. By the way, it's a mistake to use the Internet for such things. I also took the necessary measures so that there will be no trace of your report on the computer's hard disk."

"I am sorry! I thought. . . "

"At the beginning, we also considered this whole story a rather funny affair. Yet, David Mason's case is now being considered top secret. No information may be given to anyone."

"The Pope. . . "

"A nice person, a holy man. But, at least for the time being, he also has no right to the information."

"What about the audience with him?"

"Put if off claiming illness until we tell you exactly what you shall tell him, if you're allowed to meet with him."

"Mister Secretary, I believe we live in a free country. What I hear and the manner in which you speak to me remind me of a Banana Republic."

"Concerning information on David Mason's File, the same procedure is to be followed as for the 'B of the B'."

"But, how are they related?"

"There might be no relation at all, my friend, but, if there is any, as we seriously suspect, then you must know that not even a World War would shake up this planet as much as this whole story!"

This statement filled Larry's soul with awe. He could not imagine how this rather romantic story for imaginative minds could undermine our society's peace and social order. In fact, he could find no logical reason to support Michael Donovan's statements.

"That's the reason I called you, Larry. Written instructions will follow and I would advise that you follow them to the letter."

"I don't know if I can oblige. . . "

"You are considered deputized, Professor Larry Keith," the Secretary interrupted. "Your mission is confidential. As a hero's son you have to undertake your responsibilities seriously."

The phone conversation was ended abruptly. The Secretary of Defense hung up without as much as saying a simple goodbye! Everything is cancelled, Larry thought. Why all this mystery, this conspiratorial atmosphere? Imagine. . . they don't even trust the Pope!

Waiting for instructions, Larry halted writing the report he was preparing and laid down on the living-room sofa. He took the TV remote control, pointed and pressed a button to hear the news.

". . . Today a committee of experts from the Republic of Congo and experts from the USA are visiting the region thought to contain deposits rich in titanium and uranium. Soil tests and satellite photographs will be conducted soon under USA supervision."

Larry, confused and tired from the previous conversation, picked up the remote to change channels when his hand froze at the sound of the word Beni. He turned the sound louder.

"In this cave inhabited by bats, in the Beni region, technicians have recorded a decisive increase in radiation which prompted American companies to begin exploration."

Larry was really astonished now. In just a few days, his head was filled with seemingly unrelated information which, it now appears, is very much related to everything else he is learning.

He tried to concentrate on the facts. A scientist is injured and decides to speak about something that happened billions of years ago-if it did happen. NASA prepares an unprecedented, secret "star expedition." The Pope, personally, wants to hear David's tale. The American government is mobilized and digging out the strange extraterrestrial structure David talked about without succeeding in convincing anyone until today.

With these thoughts, and tired as he was, Larry fell asleep, all dressed up, on his sofa. It would be nice if sleep, this pause in logical thought, were associated with a pause in further developments. On the contrary, one might say that the combined interest of the scientific, political, technological and even religious authorities had developed its own force and momentum and was moving at its own fast pace. In NASA, uncontrollable rumors had reached the press and the public that had sensed the existence of something extraordinarily important was thirsting for information.

# The Politics
of Science

The top secret program under the code name "The Beginning of the Beginning"—or "B of the B"—was just the cover for a subject of strategic studies. Hardly anybody knew the exact content.

The launches that had taken place with no publicity at all aimed at a very important research, so important that very few persons knew the whole scenario. For security reasons, nine shifts worked on the project, and each one of them worked on the completion of only one small part of the program. This was, of course, an excellent way to maintain secrecy.

Rumors spoke about landing on Europe, Jupiter's satellite, and claimed that an entire lab-self-assembled by remote control on the satellite's surface-was already transmitting confidential information of undetermined scientific importance. It was theorized that a cover-up was in the making because the money had been spent for nothing. Others spoke about the transport of materials of unknown origin that were being analyzed in over fifty laboratories.

The debate over secrecy versus public information raged wildly.

"Too bad that everybody seems to know certain things. It often results in public policy mistakes," was one point of view. The rebuttal, "Blind people cannot defend themselves. Knowledge is power." And another point of view demanded, "Why don't you tell us what's going on? Are we lesser people who cannot understand the importance of things?"

Another curious phenomenon was that a special Papal envoy, a Cardinal, spent his time running from research facility to government offices and back.

This discussion seemed to snowball in the printed and electronic media and even the public spoke with fear and uncertainty about a potential threat. The most pessimistic wondered, "Are we in danger? Is it the end of the world?"

The press corps resembled a priest who was offering Holy Communion to a world that was dying. The news was unreliable and contradictory. "An unidentified spaceship transported material from a point in space to earth. . . "

Somebody, who had heard the news, asked CBS, "Do you think we'll take off so much excess weight from celestial bodies that they will finally fall upon our heads?" Somebody else asked, "Really, what happened to those rocks our Astronauts brought from the Moon?"

Naturally, the discussions slowly calmed down and, for a long time, nothing more was broadcast because audience interest diminished to almost zero.

The subject was not discussed again until the day a Hungarian geologist who specialized in crystallography threw his hat into the ring of controversy. He clearly accused the former Soviet Union of "parochial thinking-that if something does not originate with them it is not worth mentioning." He had been sent some materials that were supposed to have been brought back from the Moon. After extensive studies, the researcher, Milio Kosta concluded the material sent by the Soviet Union had absolutely nothing to do with the Moon!

A journalist who interviewed Kosta finally managed to get

some information. "Mister Kosta," he asked, "Why aren't you publishing the results of your research? Aren't you absolutely sure about them?"

Milio Kosta's reaction was strong. "If any scientist doubted the authenticity of his experiments he would be like the parent doubting he is the father of his own only child." The scientist was shouting mad at the question as he had misunderstood the journalist's real reasons for asking such a question. Journalists often use surprise and manage to find the sensitive point to bring out an interesting comment.

"Could it be that you are not right?" the journalist persisted.

Out of control, Professor Milio Kosta jumped up from his seat and, pointing a finger at the journalist, said, "My research is correct, sir, two hundred per cent. Eight years of hard work, for nothing! It was clearly a criminal act!"

"But, why would they do this? What do you think was the origin of the material?"

"I think the material came from a common Russian cemetery in Leningrad. That was my final conclusion."

"Why a cemetery and not a farm?"

"Because what I found one can only find it in a cemetery or in a dentist's office."

"You haven't yet told me what you've found, Professor!"

"Enamel! Yes, enamel! That's what I found in the "samples." In a very small quantity, but it's certainly enamel. But, it's crazy what they did to me! They sent it to me from the Institute of Scientific Research of Leningrad. They wanted to make fun of me because of the tenacity I demonstrated in demanding the material."

The journalist, who had heard plenty of strange things in his career, was shocked. "You're talking about that substance that covers the teeth?"

"Yes! That's what I'm talking about! In other words, I've lost eight years of my life, working day and night to discover a fraud. I don't know what I will do if I ever meet the guy who underestimated me in such a barbarian fashion."

"And you're absolutely convinced it was not something else that you might have mistaken for enamel?"

The Professor showed the exit to the journalist. "As far as you're concerned, I would advise you not to insinuate such things because your journalistic reputation is in danger!"

Mario Canakis, the journalist, finding himself in a very slow news period, thought he would seek a meeting with the person responsible for this fiasco. "You never know what may come out of this," he thought, "You only find something when you're looking for it."

He visited the nearest University. He went to the Geology and Crystallography Departments, and then to the Soils Study Department.

After an exchange of endless fax and e-mail messages, he managed to find the solution. The head of the Leningrad University Crystallography Institute/Space Research Centre was the famous scientist, Vladimir Lisenco. He became Canakis's target.

Canakis learned from a reliable source that Lisenco had misappropriated funds for research that never took place. He had even sold to the Americans almost nine-tenths of the samples Soviet Cosmonauts had brought from the Moon. Soon Canakis secured an address for Lisenco who was now living as a respectable Swiss citizen in the most luxurious Martinique Hotel, in the French Antilles. Yet, the journalist finally found him on the beach of Grand Beach Hotel, in the Dutch section of Saint Martin's island, very close to Phillipsburg, the capital city.

"Tavarish Vladimir Lisenco?" the sly Canakis asked the sunburned, middle-aged man who weighed at least 230 pounds. "Da. . . !" the comrade replied, obviously in an excellent mood. He tried to look up. "I don't think I know you," he said in Russian.

Canakis laughed and said in French, "Comrade is all I know in Russian! Fortunately, the French you've learned in Geneva is much better than my Russian."

"Are you American?"

"I'm an American national; my father was Greek, my mother Colombian, and I was born in Granada-by accident."

"I've visited there! Great medieval monuments!

"Not in Spain. I meant the island of Granada, the island that is a little bit lower on the map, left from where we are."

"Ha, ha, ha!" Despite the humor, there was no news. That's why Canakis attacked in a more direct way. He had to take his victim by surprise.

"Your enemies say that you've sold the stuff for five million Swiss francs to us Americans. Is it true?"

Lisenco became immediately serious, sat on his fat behind, lit a cigarette and said, as if talking to his son, "The place where they'd put it and where it was left, nobody was interested in examining it. It was useless. So, I thought that for the sake of science. . . "

"Now I see," Canakis said pretending agreement. "For the sake of science and a little bit of your own. . . OK!"

"Of course," the other man smiled.

"You thought giving it to American scientists, they would put it to good use. Congratulations. You are clever! That would be the best motive for an honest man like you. But, were there any lesser motives?" he asked with a smile.

"At my age, I need some good times. I thought that, once I offered something to science, science had to comfort me, financially speaking. I only got two million Swiss francs in installments. The rumor about five million isn't but a myth.

"When other scientists asked you for samples, did you send them the right ones or whatever was handy?"

"Listen, son, I am not an impostor. Anyway, only one of those who asked for samples finally got the authorization. You see, bureaucracy was. . . "

"Do you remember who it was?" the journalist asked looking straight into Lisenco's small, bright eyes.

"Milio Kosta, the most famous of all of us; a real nerd, a very difficult man and a terribly obstinate scientist. I don't think any one else is as detailed in his work; he is a workaholic. Such a perfectionist, but with very few social graces. I remember I'd sent him samples from all the missions and, indeed, those that morphologically presented some interest."

Canakis had his trap ready. "You trapped the poor guy, Mr. Director of the Institute! You trapped him and forced him to work like a slave for eight years for nothing!"

The enormous Vladimir stood up, his face in an angry frown. "I forbid you to insult me! I am very sincere when I am talking to you. Instead of thanking me for that, you accuse me of having trapped the most famous geologist, my own colleague Milio Kosta! Never on earth would I do such a thing! It would be a crime!"

"Well, listen to exactly what he has to say about it!" Canakis took the recorder out of his bag and turned it on.

The April sun was not strong enough to explain the sweat coming down Lisenco's face. His eyes were filled with questions. Obviously what he was hearing was deeply confusing. He quickly looked for a pill in the pocket of the short-sleeved shirt next to him and swallowed it without water. The color of his face betrayed that his blood pressure had shot up in no time. When Milio Kosta's speech was over, Lisenco was crying. He was crying like a baby.

"Never! Never! It's a lie! I've never thought or done anything like that! Somebody must have changed the samples, someone in his own lab. Certainly some rival, in order to discredit him. I never did a thing like that! Never! I swear!"

Canakis would have liked to make him swear on the two million, but he pitied him. Now he was certain that, in front of him, stood a little man whose interest was to take care of number one. But he was not one of those who like to harm others for the fun of it. He was not a sadist.

Things calmed down only after he reassured Lisenco he believed the Russian was telling the truth. They left the beach in a friendly mood and Vladimir asked his new friend to join him for dinner in the "Green House" restaurant. Good food and good wine uplift the spirit and bring people closer. Then, as the evening was coming to its end, Canakis asked something that had nothing to do with the subject they had discussed earlier.

"Vladimir, how is it all the Soviet officials were chubby and remain chubby?

"Listen, my friend, it's really a paradox. And, the only way to know is to do some proper scientific research, the object of which would be "the relationship between obesity and the Hammer and Sickle." They both laughed to tears.

Canakis was to have taken an American Airlines flight to Miami at 2:22 p.m. on May first. He was convinced Vladimir's assumption that a rival had changed Milio Kosta's material seemed reasonable, even likely. So, this entire trip had been for nothing? He now had to make something up, in order to justify the expenses. He had told his news director, "I'm preparing a big surprise for you!" Yet, it was Vladimir who, unintentionally, had prepared a real surprise with his legondary sincerity.

He was already in front of the clerk at the travel agency where he went to pick up his ticket and a boarding pass. The clerk pre-empted Canakis's request.

"The Carnival-aren't you going to Saint Martin's Carnival tomorrow? You can leave tomorrow, at the same time. It would be easy to change your ticket."

"All sorts of things can happen during a Carnival festivity," he thought. "In Rio about 200 people are killed. Here, according to the most pessimistic expectations, about a dozen persons would die to celebrate Labor Day. Strange place! Labor Day and Carnival at the same time! Crazy!"

The hot sun greeted Labor Day. By noon, the temperature was over 100 degrees. The hotel was filled with travelers from the other islands, St. Bartholomew and St. John, who had arrived in colorful costumes to take part in the Carnival. At the reception desk, Canakis asked to be connected with his friend's room.

"I am sorry, but you must be making a mistake. There is no Vladimir Lisenco here," the receptionist answered.

Canakis was surprised. "But, you, yourself told me yesterday where to find him. In the casino, I also saw the temporary charge card the hotel issues to its guests and I saw his name on it. He was in room 510 with a view overlooking the parking lot. Are you trying to drive me crazy?"

The employee shook his head, annoyed, to emphasize that "No, there was no such guest at the hotel. Please, sir, I have work to do. So, please, let me do it!"

Like lightning, Canakis raced up the stairs to the fifth floor and knocked on the door. Nobody! He asked the black employee on the floor if he had seen the fat man.

"Yes, very early in the morning. He went down with a suitcase," he said in Ebenistes, the peculiar English dialect of the natives.

"Did he leave for the airport?" Canakis asked, as he was running down the stairs.

"No, he was taken by a helicopter towards the sea."

Indeed, Canakis remembered that he had been awakened by the noise of a helicopter taking off at five o'clock in the morning. Yes, now he remembered. It carried the emblem of the American Coast Guard! A kidnapping? Why? What interest could the American State have in the retired Vladimir? What was the reason?

Of course, if Vladimir were a voluntary guest of the government, a few dollars would be enough to close the mouths of the staff. Obviously, they missed one.

Mario had a terrible night. His sleep was repeatedly interrupted by nightmares. At last, the sun was coming up!

The Carnival was wonderful. For three hours, happy groups of people in costumes had the time of their lives. He was only bothered by the frequent and overbearing advertisements for Heineken beer that tended to diminish the feast aesthetically.

Lisenco's disappearance puzzled Canakis. Should he cover it in his newspaper story? He would probably have to ask his news editor who, in turn, would ask the CIA in order to avoid a monumental error. They would have to cover themselves.

Canakis had an alibi. The story he was going to file could possibly wait a few days.

Reaching Miami, Canakis thought he had to phone Milio Kosta to inform him about the meeting with Vladimir and to assure him he believed the accused was innocent. He had to find the snake in his nest, in his own lab.

"I would like to speak to Professor Milio Kosta" Canakis said to the secretary that answered the phone.

"The Professor left for Houston, Texas, today."

"How can that be?" Canakis asked, surprised.

"An invitation for a conference, a round-table discussion, from a group of American scientists."

"Do you happen to know the subject to be discussed?"

"Just a moment! I have to look into the papers that are in the other office." Several minutes of real torment passed and then the line was disconnected. He called again. No answer, as if the number no longer existed. This case was cloaked in mystery. In the morning, they suddenly grab Lisenco and, almost at the same time, they "invite" Milio Kosta to Houston. Something strange is ticking in NASA's heart in Houston.

"I'm going to find out what's going on even if I have to spend my last cent," Canakis said to himself with determination. He rushed to the ticket office.

"When is the next flight to Houston, please?"

"You will just make it if you hurry."

# Unexpected
# Journey

L arry Keith slept for fourteen hours straight. The tension of the past two days had literally shaken his health and had drained him emotionally. He needed the renewal that sleeping brought to him even though he had nightmares.

In his dreams, the Archangels, carrying spears, battled huge armies of winged devils and slaughtered each other at the front door of Larry's home. His house was transformed, for the occasion, into a tall castle with myriad towers. The noise of the fax machine woke him up.

Still overcome by his dreams, he staggered into his office and found a long message, six pages, from Theodore, David Mason's engineer friend.

"That's very kind of you, Mr. Papadopoulos, but only after I take a shower," Larry said as if the man could hear him. Larry soon felt relaxed and ready to work as he lounged in a clean pair of pajamas and with a cup of freshly brewed coffee. He began reading the fax containing Papadopoulos' report that had been sent previously to ministers and scientists.

"Sir, it was genuine surprise, a strong sense of protest and justified resentment that we, myself and David Mason's other collaborators, felt when we were informed of the rejection of the thesis Traces of an Unknown World of Extraterrestrial Origin, submitted by this wonderful man and highly trained scientist.

"Here, in Africa, we often become familiar with occurrences that can only be explained or understood through parapsychology and metaphysics. From time to time, underground explosions occur in Beni's region and, every seven years, children are born with strange genetic malformations of unknown cause.

"My company was involved in a construction project and tried to find gravel by digging 36 feet deep, in a 500 square foot area. During the excavations we failed to find any gravel. However, we came upon a surface that shined like green gold. At first, because of the color, I was certain it was malachite, in other words a mineral copper. To confirm, we called in a mineralogist who descended into the pit. Suddenly we heard a hollow sound and the poor man lost his senses, probably because of fear. At the hospital where I visited him, he tried to convince me that he saw winged demons, resembling humanoid bats, moving around and flying from one mountaintop to another.

"The mineralogist's breakdown was quite original. So much so that he wrote down on a piece of paper the chemical type of the substance that covered the bottom of the pit. Only problem, the elements were completely unknown to us. The mineralogist died at the end of the week and we never saw the paper again. Until the very end, the poor man tried to convince us that he was not crazy.

"The rejection of David Mason's thesis slowed down all efforts by the local Belgian authorities to investigate what had occurred. I consider you, gentlemen, personally responsible for wasting a perfectly good opportunity to investigate a situation that showed the potential to draw world attention."

Theodore also stated many other points in support of his

friend, David Mason, but they were of no particular interest to Larry.

"He writes very well," Larry thought. "Like a prophet, I could say. Yet, bureaucracy might keep this unread for decades. So, at that time, a mineralogist had an experience similar to David's experience. That was very interesting!" Larry dialed a number on the phone.

"Is that you, Mr. Papadopoulos?"

"No, I'm his son, Basil. We sound alike, I know. . . "

"Indeed," Larry agreed. "Could I. . . "

"I'm sorry, sir. Who am I speaking with?

"Larry Keith."

"Oh! My father left a message for you, before leaving."

"He left? Where did he go?"

"He'll be away for about ten days. He went to Rome."

"Maybe to visit the Pope. . . "

Papadopoulos' son laughed. "My father doesn't really have much in common with priests! You must have said that as a joke."

"Not really, but I would like to know the purpose of his trip, although I'm aware that my inquiry may not be very discreet."

"I don't know if you're informed. . . my father is honorary president of the World Committee for Restoration of Monuments and Works of Art. His presence was necessary at the annual meeting of the European Committee, in Rome."

"Have you spoken with him on the phone? Has he arrived?"

"Of course, he has. He has even addressed the meeting."

Larry felt better. For a moment, he was afraid he had lost one of the most serious sources of information and the only eyewitness. "Could you, please, read me the message?"

There was a pause, then silence. "Hello? Hello?" The line went dead. Larry tried calling back ten times. There was no answer.

"Europe! Nothing works right over there," he thought. "I'll call back tomorrow morning. If I can't find him, I'll search in Rome."

Next day, the reception at Memorial Hospital was impressive. Wherever Larry went, starting at the parking lot and all the way up to his office, staff and patients congratulated him. Everyone was informed, in detail, about what had happened. In his office, he found a bouquet of eleven roses with a golden paper heart instead of a card. He dialed her mobile phone number. He wanted to thank her.

"Barbara, my darling, I thank you so much! Aren't you afraid leaving me for so long? Aren't you afraid I might get into trouble? Thank you for the roses! My love, I am really sorry and really grateful for your understanding." She was his woman, the person that reaffirmed his existence and loved him very much.

"I've thought about it, Larry, in a business manner. And I calmed down. I said to myself it's better to have ten percent in a running concern than one hundred percent in a business that's up to the neck in debts."

"My entire investment is in your beautiful hands. I hope you won't let me down. . . So, how is the search for Okapi coming along? Have you found any traces of it in Uganda?" Larry asked with genuine interest.

"Larry, we've been informed that two couples of those rare striped antelopes have been seen very far from here, almost close to Kenya's borders with Congo."

Larry jumped out of his chair. "Kilimanjaro?"

"Here we call it Roentzore. Congratulations, Larry, I see you're making progress in geography, too! I hear now you also have dealings in parapsychology. . . I'm sorry! I have to go now!"

Larry had just enough time to say, "I'm sending you a long message! I might come and see you!"

"Liar!" They exchanged loud, passionate kisses and the conversation was over. Barbara Haim, Larry's love, was part of the group organized by the National Geographic Society to locate and help preserve a rare species of beautiful striped antelope, the Okapi antelope, that hadn't been seen in over 15 years.

What a diabolic coincidence! The Okapi, unbeknownst to Barbara, was getting close to Beni's region, at ground zero.

Since he had eight days at his disposal and his meeting with the Pope was cancelled, it was an excellent opportunity for him to stretch his legs, to participate in an organized safari in the African jungle, in the company of his sweetheart, Barbara. It would be a great surprise.

At the embassy, where he inquired about the necessary paperwork, he was greeted with a series of obstacles. Excuses for inaction.

"You should consult the Ambassador. We do not handle these matters."

Larry was mad. He asked to speak with the embassy's first secretary in Washington.

"Pierre Calango speaking! I'm listening!

Larry protested but the secretary did even attempt to explain, not even once.

"Let's cut to the chase. Who am I supposed to speak to for information? Please. . . "

"The CIA." And the line was disconnected.

At the time of the call, Alexis Nefski, Larry's assistant, was also in his office listening to the conversation. Alexis was a very intelligent American of Bulgarian origin.

"If I understand it right, Professor, you wish to communicate with Eastern Congo."

"You understood it right, Alexis. So, is there anything you wish to suggest?" Larry baited him without any effort to hide his irritation.

"You should, perhaps, get in touch with our Department of Defense," Alexis answered without hesitation.

"You must be kidding!" Larry said.

"Since yesterday, Professor, the region south of Kilimanjaro and east of Bounia is under American control.

Larry collapsed into a chair. He could not believe his own ears. "We have occupied a part of Congo? What are you talking about?"

"Occupation was not the goal of the military operation.

Everything was done with permission by the government of Congo. It is temporary. The purpose is commercial exploitation of, and future exploration for, mineral deposits in the region by the two countries."

The professor remembered the TV broadcast he accidentally watched before falling asleep on the sofa. "Michael strikes again!" he thought. "Michael doesn't joke. When the going gets tough, he sends in the marines."

Alexis felt uneasy with what he heard. He understood very little, but considered it in his best interest to extricate himself from this strange situation. Later on, he would have the time to learn all the details.

Following instructions Larry had given earlier, Dorothy, his secretary, came in bringing the necessary information to call Theodore in Rome.

"That's great, Dorothy!" Larry took the paper with the phone numbers. He also did not miss a chance to glance at Dorothy's elegant silhouette and seductive walk as she sashayed out of the room. But he still had no clue that this girl was madly in love with him and extremely dangerous.

"I would like to speak to the honorary president, Mr. . . . "

"Oh! You're very lucky, sir! Ten minutes later and he wouldn't be here!"

"Is he ill?" Larry asked worried.

"He is not used to being sick, sir. Indeed, he says he doesn't have the time to get sick. You know, Mr. Papadopoulos will die, yet he'll never get old. He declared this, yesterday, in his speech."

"Hello. . . Hello! Mr. Larry Keith, I presume!"

"I am very glad I've managed to get you on the phone. I've received your message and I'm really grateful. I need to have your opinion on that metallic 'floor' at the cave in Beni."

"It was a roof of sorts-a very small part of the roof of a spaceship. We did not mention it in our report but we tried to drill a hole in it unsuccessfully. We couldn't even make a scratch, although we used heavy power tools. My opinion is, deeper in the bat cavern, perpendicular to the ground, there was a hole leading exactly under our target."

"Didn't you try to get there through that hole?" Larry inquired with great anticipation.

"Of course, we did! Unfortunately, the ten workers we sent in never came back."

"Why?"

"Because, four minutes after the tenth worker's entry, we felt the cave shaking. Three explosions followed. We ran to save the workers, but there was blue smoke with an overpowering odor rising from the hole. It forced us to abandon the cave with the bats and our efforts to rescue the workers. All said, we lost our co-workers and we gave up on the digging; we covered the pit and left. Manuel Calango's father was one of the victims."

"I imagine your disappointment!"

"I wrote all this on the message I left for you. My son didn't give it to you?"

"I was unable to talk to him long enough. You see, our telephone communication was suddenly interrupted."

"The death of the ten workers was what stopped any further research. David Mason and I could have been thought responsible for the accident which would have meant potentially severe punishment; it could have been considered a criminal offense."

"I understand. My secretary told me you were leaving. I guess you are going back to Belgium or to beautiful Athens."

"No, Professor. I wanted to inform you about it, but it was sudden. Guess who invited me."

"Would I dare hope for an empty Coke bottle again?"

"This time it shall be full."

"The Pope in person. . . Am I right?" A long pause followed . . . "Theodore, do you hear me?"

"You're something else! I bet you can read the contents of a letter sealed in an envelope. How did you guess?"

'Ted. . . May I call you by your first name?"

"Of course!"

"The Pope will invite you and me and anybody who has anything to do with David's File."

"He also invited you? Then, we shall meet there."

"Yes, he did. And, I see my invitation coincided with yours. However, for some reasons I cannot discuss on the phone, I must not go. The Holy See seems to be extremely worried about something that has to do with Beni."

"But, I think they invited me for my work. I had suggested all genuine art objects should be withdrawn from all the museums and placed away under perfect conservation and security conditions. Then perfect copies, with a statement of authenticity should be placed in public view. I think it's the only way to avoid any future destruction or theft of priceless treasures."

"Sincere congratulations, my friend. I find this suggestion of yours very original and it is certainly practical. But I would like to ask that if the Pope questions you about Beni, you should pretend you don't remember anything. Otherwise, this matter shall grow larger and beyond our control, endangering David's life and, possibly, yours and mine."

"The Vatican? Impossible! I think you're exaggerating. I'm afraid David's stories have affected you. . . I don't think the Church. . . "

"I hope you're right and I'm wrong. Anyway, it's important you are informed."

Theodore's naïve attitude did not please Larry. It was probable his wish and ambition to be decorated by the Pope would loosen his tongue and he might tell everything he knew about the buried spaceship or whatever that thing was. As far as his proposal concerning the monuments, it was very avant-garde and unlikely to be accepted.

The world was turning upside-down, but Larry had made up his mind; he would meet his darling Barbara in the jungles of Eastern Congo. Until his next meeting with David Mason, he would try to forget who he was and what his job was all about. "Take it easy, Larry," he admonished himself.

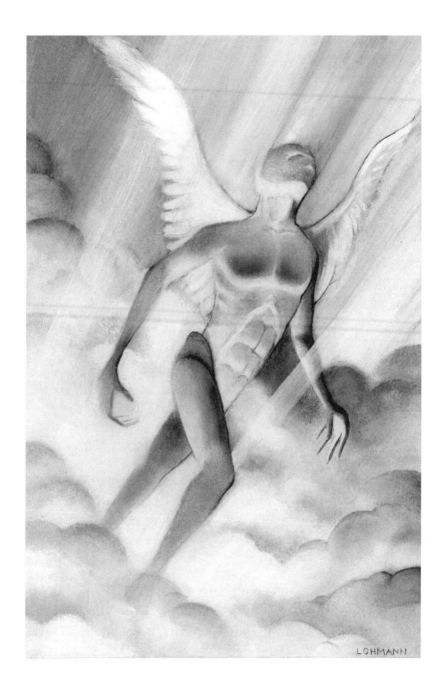

# Cloning

"**D**avid Mason carefully hid the recorder Larry had smuggled into the hospital room. Now he was ready to record the rest of the extraordinary events and, particularly, as Larry had asked, the story about the fate of the swarthy demons. After he had some rest and felt his strength returning, David was determined to fulfill his promise to Professor Keith. David positioned himself comfortably in bed, pressed the recorder's on button and closed his eyes.

"The primary concern of the MANTA after they'd assured their hegemony over KEROPS, was to get rid of every possible threat to their rule. Their eternal enemies were in a literally miserable condition. With their wings made useless, they were trapped in their inaccessible shelters. The dark, handsome creatures were unable to secure food regularly and reverted to cannibalism. This was, of course, the worst solution possible. To begin with, they decimated their own group and, at the same time, cannibalism destroyed their cohesiveness as a group. They were afraid of each other and all contacts were suspect. Emaciated and terrified as they had become, they easily succumbed to the first hostile operation of the Angels.

"Victory, the sweet triumph over their historic enemies, was a very important moment in the development of the Angels' tribe. Victory celebrations lasted for days. The Angels could not erase the dark memory of the valley of death from their collective past, and thus their revenge had to be monstrous. Science became their accomplice. First, they put to death all their dark rivals except for the newborn children.

"Larry, instead of an act of genocide, the Angels reversed the conditions because they had devised a particularly evil plan to wipe out all vestiges of the culture and history of their enemies. The Angels' plan provided for the kidnapping of the swarthy babies and arranging for them to grow up in a manner the Angels had prescribed. In this fashion they would create a new tribe characterized by a completely different behavior and culture.

"In modern times on earth, this is something the Turks did to the non-Muslim populations they conquered. They kidnapped babies, brought them up as soldiers and organized them in a separate army that went to battle against their own people. Those were the terrible 'Genitsars.' Barbarossa was one of them.

"When the swarthy babies became grownups, they would know absolutely nothing about their origins. They were to be indoctrinated by the Angels and inspired to feel proud of serving the Angels all their life. They felt grateful for not being hungry and unemployed! All heavy manual work, such as construction and agriculture, was the slaves' exclusive 'privilege.' The naturally weak Angels had, this way, found the solution to realize each MANTA's most ambitious plans.

"But the numbers of Angels and slaves increased in geometrical progression, while arable areas remained the same, few and poor in yield because of constant cultivation. As construction of big cities accelerated, the shortage of arable land worsened. Hunger returned and was soon decimating the Angels and their slaves indiscriminately.

"Larry, my friend, I am certain you thought about birth-control. The evil MANTA Archangel, on the other hand, devised a really extraordinary solution. He neither sterilized nor slaughtered the slaves. Just the opposite, he obliged them to reproduce faster, because his plan required the availability of infinite working hands!

"MANTA had noticed that most of the plants on the planet looked like hollowed bamboo stock. When they were dry the wind blew them to the water and they drifted over the ocean. For years, they stagnated on the surface of the water until they deteriorated completely and became rotten. MANTA ordered the slaves to pile up earth on one of those cemeteries of floating vegetation. That created a solid surface, able to withstand the weight of walking creatures. But, where one can walk, he can also sow.

"As you can tell, Professor, that was the creation of the first floating field I've surprised you, I'm sure. You couldn't predict something like that. Moreover, this floating field did not need to be watered by mechanical means. The oceans consisted of fresh water and the fields absorbed water from below. Through these self-watering, floating fields that could be moved around as necessary, the Angels had discovered the total and definitive solution to their most serious problem.

"Millions of slaves-expressionless, voiceless, tireless, never protesting-worked day and night to create as much arable land as possible. Of course, the building methods were primitive. In the 200 years that followed, equivalent to 1,000 years on earth, huge bells constructed of non-oxidized metallic material replaced the layer of vegetation.

"The floating surfaces eventually grew to enormous size, and all the Angels migrated to their new floating country. Even their cities were transformed into floating areas thus solving their sewage problems. But safety constituted perhaps the most important factor. The Angels never forgot what had happened to them in the 'valley.'

"The slaves were mostly employed in the mines and in the maintenance of the waterfalls. The less intelligent were slave-farmers. The Angels selected them according to that criterion because these slaves were closer to the floating cities. Of course, there were also the lucky ones, those who worked only as serving staff.

"Time, again, had its own plan. Eventually, the problem of genetic specialization began to develop. Scientists had to intervene again. For dozens of years they had studied this challenge and had reached the conclusion that they first had to solve the genetic problem of the Angels. The solution was radical, revolutionary and did not differ from a new way to create the world according to scientific criteria.

"The MANTA leading them during that period studied the plan and congratulated the head scientist. He was enthusiastic about the solution. It was important that a real miracle should happen, a radical change towards perfection. He would be the 'Creator,' the tribe's 'Founding Father,' the one who would renew planet KEROPS.

"The plan consisted of the creation of beings that would combine the perfect intellectual, physical and aesthetic features. Science was, more or less, proposing the creation of Super-Angels, or 'Supermen' as one might say! The new elite race would have the beautiful features and the muscle power of slaves, but it would also acquire the Angels' intellectual sharpness and rudimentary pink wings, the latter serving only practical considerations.

"Production could start immediately through cloning. Suppose that, for each living Angel, another one would be created with the new features I've mentioned, using a slave's uterus. Some years earlier, through experimental procedures, geneticists had reached the conclusion it was possible to do so.

"Of course, the use of hermaphrodite slaves for cloning, meant the end of the ascendancy of the 'birth-givers' in the social ladder. Floating maternity home-ghettos were immediately created. Of course, nobody had asked the slaves' consent, but as a reward for their part in race rejuvenation, instead of calling them slaves, they renamed them OMOH. Also, during the first year that followed birth-giving, an OMOH would work only part-time in the fields. This was a kind of bonus for what he'd offered to his masters.

"No matter how much biology had progressed, no matter what reason-endowed creatures did, no matter how much the MANTA may have studied the details of the plan, nature would again show its independent power. In some rare cases, due to atavism, the descendants of some slaves had intellectual capacity that could be compared to that of the Angels, since both races had a common DNA stem. One of those bright, swarthy slaves happened to work in the National Library and had secretly learned to read.

"One night he remained hidden in the electronic library and had no difficulty in finding and reading all the information about the terrible truth! He now knew how the swarthy Apollos were reduced to becoming the living robots of his masters. He made up his mind. He would take revenge. His thirst for Justice was drowning any logical thinking. With great difficulty he managed to secure employment on the unspecialized staff controlling the balance of the Angels' floating capital, PSIKATH. It had a population of 5,430,000 inhabitants.

"On the anniversary of the 'Slaughter in the Sunny Valley' surveillance was rather loose because there were no enemies and no dangers. The slave, the swarthy Spartacus, took his revenge. He opened the master switch that controlled the floating bells and maintained constant pressure. Slowly but steadily, a floating surface of 1,100,000 acres, with all its public buildings and industrial areas, began sinking. Of course, there were safety valves and auxiliary super-pumps that had been installed for emergency purposes. The sirens went off and their wailing warned of the impending danger.

"The capital was saved, but there was a multitude of victims. The culprit was found and genetic scientists were in charge of selecting an appropriate punishment.

"As I'm recording those events, it's as if I am really describing the images that I see in front of me even with my eyes closed. They are like TV spots with clear explanations. Last night, Larry my friend, I was awakened by a nightmare. It's as

if I was in an octagonal booth with weak purple light. I first
heard a whisper and, then, a guttural voice speaking an unknown language that, curiously, I could understand.

"During the nightmare I heard the following. 'Stranger. . .
Up to now, the mission you have been charged with by the
transmission department has been fulfilled in a satisfactory
manner. If, for any reason, it is interrupted or distorted, or if
you are late you will immediately die because the micro-pyra-
mid lodged in your brain will self-destruct.

"Every single part of the mnemonic sphere that injured you
is a 'chip,' as you call them, that contains the narration of our
entire history. It is set up to transmit the events in chronologi-
cal order. It is impossible for you to reach the end before
transmitting what preceded. If the chip that is in your brain is
not discharged of its content within a prescribed length of
time, it shall explode and neutralize you.

"By the end of the narration, as a reward for the superior
services you have offered to my people, you shall receive a
present for the world you belong to. I want to give you a general advice. In the animal kingdom, at its highest level, two in-
terdependent species with the same dreams about the future
may not exist. It is predestined that one of them shall disappear.

"Larry, I didn't mention this at the beginning of the tape,
because I still hadn't made up my mind whether I should do
so. I feel I'm in constant danger, my friend, that someone will
decide I am mentally disturbed and lock me in an asylum. I
think it's still too early to publish the last MANTA's message.
Let me first finish the story and then we can decide.

"You see how much I trust you, Larry, my friend. I consider
you a father or a brother. From now on, I shall do whatever
you advise me to do. I have just received an order that I must
pronounce. So, I go on.

"When the rejuvenation project was met with success and
the 'old models' followed the path of recycling, the planet was
under the domination of the new tribe called AENH. They
didn't need birth-givers any more. Female ANEH gave birth,

through sexual encounters, to descendants. Exactly the way we, humans, do. After this monumental success of theirs the genetic scientists moved forward to the second phase, the reformation of the OMOHs.

"Spartacus's attempt to sink the capital had terrorized everybody. The AENHs' order to the genetic scientists was clear. Complete reformation and, at the same time, adaptation to various professional needs.

"They had noticed that the mines needed strong, small sized workers, with protected vision, thus with small eyes. Also, workers at the bright side of the planet would be better if they were strong and completely black in order to withstand the radiation of the twin sun. The supreme order was issued and, in the span of only two generations, two separate tribes were created that were no longer hermaphroditic. Just like the AENHs, they were programmed to have no feelings, no judgement and no sense of time. They were real robots but with flesh and blood.

"When their population reached a specific number, the Angels added substances to their food that destroyed their ability to reproduce. An implanted receiver woke them up in the morning and guided them by giving instructions directly through their nervous system to their brain. When an OMOH's performance diminished and reached levels below medium, thanks to his 'electronic guide,' the OMOH went by himself to the recycling booth. Thus, the possibility of a 'Spartacus phenomenon' was eliminated once and for all.

"In the recycling booths, bodies were turned into cubes used for feeding the OMOHs. A complete recycling! You can see the AENHs imposed cannibalism for purely economic reasons! Nothing was wasted. If, my friend, you still insist on calling them Angels, you'll be faced with my complete disagreement.

"I see the tape is running out and I am very thirsty. I will send this tape to your home with the beautiful Natassa."

Natassa was a beautiful and sexy girl, a "VIP escort." She used to be a nurse and, for the occasion, Memorial Hospital very cleverly arranged to put her into David's arms so that he could live normally. At the same time she was the Hospital's informer. David thought that she was a real nurse and believed that he had charmed her with his personality.

At first, Natassa worked professionally, but lately her behavior had changed. Something inside her pushed her into David's arms, and money had played no role in this. She was no longer following instructions, only the messages of her heart and the tenderness that had bloomed for David. She instinctively felt something very serious was to come out of this strange story and, probably, her beloved David would be the victim. For the first time in her life, she was worried about somebody else!

"My dear Natassa, would you please take this tape and give it personally to my friend, Professor Keith?"

Natassa mocked an army salute. She stood straight up, saluted and said, "At your command, boss. . ." and she disappeared.

# A Father's
# Helping Hand

Jonathan, Larry Keith's father, a veteran Marine, realized his son loved him very much, but he didn't quite believe or trust the information he had.

The son had once cross-referenced information provided by his father and realized that the information was inaccurate-doctored up to cast a different light on the subject. When Jonathan hung up the phone, he was sure his son considered the information he passed on was exaggerated or outright wrong. Stubborn as Jonathan was, this hurt him deeply. So, he decided to play detective since he had plenty of time and enough money.

The first and most innocent step was paying a visit to his friend, Harry Owen, who lived halfway between Cape Canaveral and Tampa. Harry lived alone and had repeatedly invited Jonathan but the marine avoided him because Harry talked too much. "But Harry was an excellent chess-player," Jonathan thought to himself, "so I will find some peace." Perhaps he could also find something interesting through all of Harry's chat.

Very often, Harry had told him on the phone that some of his friends were NASA technicians who lived in the same neighborhood.

Jonathan's main aim was to "interrogate" his friend and to get information about the future space project. Certainly the relatives and friends of the technicians must have leaked something.

"Harry, is that you?"

"Damn you! Don't tell me you remembered me! Keith, it is a pleasant surprise." Harry had called him by his last name, a common way of addressing each other in the military, so Jonathan was relieved that Harry was in a good mood.

"Listen, old buddy. I feel terribly lonely. I've called my son Larry on the phone and I realized that I wasn't that welcome.

Jonathan knew that Harry had problems with his own children. He used this little lie to win easier acceptance.

"Leave those dirty kids all by themselves and come immediately! I've bought myself a jeep. I want you to drive it and tell me what you think about it!"

"I'm on my way! I'll be at your place, I hope, by 5 o'clock tomorrow evening! Get the chess set ready!" Harry Owen was very happy. He suddenly had an old friend coming for a visit. It was also a great honor, because Jonathan was considered an important person.

Harry was going to impress his friend by showing him he had important "connections." He picked up the phone and in the next 24 hours he put together a party. Two former astronauts, now fathers of candidate-astronauts, four ground technicians and an electronic operator working at the Central Coordinating Office accepted his invitation to dinner.

Satisfied, Harry laid back in his rocking chair and fell asleep. Jonathan's car woke him up with its coded signal, "ta, ta, tatata, ta!"

They fell into each other's arms and tears of happiness witnessed that friendships based on bloody combats and sacrifices remain solid.

Hugging each other like brothers they walked into the house and, for quite some time, they gazed at each other, obviously moved.

"It's been five whole years! Aren't you ashamed of yourself?" Harry asked with some bitterness. Now that Jonathan realized his friend's love for him, he was feeling guilty. " I'm a real son of a bitch," he thought, "I want to use him, while he . . . ."

But, when he saw the dinner guest list, Jonathan regained his composure and toughness in the face of duty. "First my country and then all the rest," he always said and he meant it. Now, he would make the supreme sacrifice; he would submit to chatty Harry for an entire weekend.

It was 10 o'clock in the evening and, Jonathan's target guest, from the Central Coordinating Office, had not yet arrived. It was NASA's brain, the source of information, orders and reports. Of course, everything was top secret and the likelihood of learning something out of this was minuscule. Suddenly, the door opening was filled as Dino Brahe made his appearance. He was about 40 years old and his brown eyes sparkled.

"Strange!" Jonathan thought, "How can such a young man with such a position decide to visit veterans of another generation?" Before he had the time to complete his thoughts, Jonathan had the answer.

"Harry, I've heard you got some Retsina wine from your trip to Greece! That's why I'm here!" Everybody laughed and offered him the head seat at the dinner table. Harry had a good sense of humor and always came through in his introduction of the guests.

"Dino Brahe is the descendant of a famous family of astronomers. Only, his ancestors were plain Peeping Toms, they watched the stars. . . while Dino, here. . . takes part in making love, too!"

The guest stood up with his glassful of Retsina.

"I'm among American heroes tonight and proud of it! I think you have the right, more than others, to hear for the first time something very pleasant."

In his customary manner, Jonathan rubbed his hands under the table with secret satisfaction and anticipation.

"You live nearby, so you certainly hear the launches. It's the first time secrecy is so important, because NASA's mission is of huge importance." You could hear a pin drop as everyone waited to hear the rest.

"Permanent installation in space is necessary because we must, finally, learn who we are and where we are headed." He seemed to have noticed his mistake and stopped there. He immediately changed the subject.

Harry brought out a tape he had bought as a present for Dino. It showed dancers demonstrating all "Syrtaki" postures as well as those of another dance, the "Kalamatianos." Yet, this changed nothing. For Jonathan Keith, the night was no more than boring as he realized he did not manage, although he tried many times, to get a single scrap of important information from Dino. Stories about the past that he had heard many times, and Greek dances left him completely indifferent.

At about midnight, the gathering was over. Dino invited them, if they wanted, to witness a launching that had been programmed for the next day, at 7:00 a.m. He was drunk, and most of the other guests also had plenty to drink.

In the bathroom, Jonathan noticed a folded piece of computer paper on the floor. It carried the stamped inscription "TOP SECRET" and "NASA/Geology Department" on the left corner. Jonathan washed his hands and picked it up. It was the description of the discovery of an opal mineral that interested the world's scientific community. Two British geologists, Desmond Clark and Anna Grason, had discovered it at a rocky site close to Kilimanjaro. Despite their long experience in the field, the two were unable to classify their discovery.

It further stated that "the laboratory at the Natural History Museum had just completed an analysis of the stone and concluded it 'did not resemble any known mineral on earth.' Its composition was unknown.

"The electronic microscope had helped them establish that the stone's structure, that slight iridescence reflected when the stone was moved, was composed of microscopic, fluorescent grains, pyramid in shape. Molecular analysis had shown that the stone had no relationship with any organic or inorganic material on our planet. The British geologists even avoided naming the stone. Research is continuing. Signature, Dino Brahe."

Jonathan exited the bathroom and quietly went to the fax machine where he made a copy of the document. He immediately went to the dining room and threw the piece of paper under the table, close to where Dino was seated. Soon afterwards, the party was over and the boisterous guests left as a group.

Several knocks on the door made Jonathan run to the guestroom where he pretended he was asleep. The persistent knocking and the ringing of the doorbell woke up Harry, who dragged himself to the door. A Military Police officer entered the house, followed by Dino Brahe.

"I'm terribly sorry, Harry, but I think I've lost something."

"Don't worry, pal, my home is at your disposal. You'll certainly find it somewhere."

"Where were you seated?" the officer asked Dino. He pointed at the head of the table. The officer kneeled and looked under the table and, with relief and enthusiasm, picked up the piece of folded paper. The document was safely placed in the officer's bag, and they left hurriedly after offering repeated apologies.

"Quite a fuss for a dirty piece of paper," Harry said and dragged himself back to his bed. Jonathan, while pretending he was going to bed, waited until the house was silent. When he was certain his friend was sleeping, he went back to the office and transmitted to his son, Larry, the text he had copied.

Next morning, only Harry and Jonathan showed up at the 7 a.m. rendezvous at Cape Canaveral.

"Welcome, boys!" Dino greeted them with a smile. "This is where I give the orders so, to make up for yesterday's disturbance, I shall get you into the flight control room through the back door. It's a historic day! We are about to send up the biggest payload yet, a humongous package. It's wrapped inside what looks like a huge circus tent."

"What's the use of this booth?" Jonathan asked vaguely, trying to contain his emotions.

"They need space. We are about to create an inhabited base. We will send thirty booths like this one and they will be connected to each other. When operation "Selini Village" is completed, then the world will be informed and will be amazed at the USA's space technology." Jonathan knew, thanks to his excellent classic education, that "Selini" was the Greek word for the Moon, but he feigned ignorance.

His friend spoiled everything when he asked, "What does this mean? And where is it going to happen? At what height?"

Dino, realizing he had said too much, felt secretly happy that his guests failed to understand that the permanent base was to be installed on our natural satellite, the Moon.

"Well, guys, one can't know everything! The public will probably know the S-Village operation in two or three years. The height is, for the moment, classified."

Indeed, on the screen, a rocket ten times the volume and five times the height of the familiar rockets, was already on the launching pad. Eighteen propulsion rockets containing fuel were ready to blast off and offer the necessary gigantic power to transport and place the first "human circus" on the Moon's surface.

"Seven, six, five, four. . . zero!" Although the launch pad was five miles from the control room from where the guests observed the action, they felt the vibration when the 18 rockets spit their fire and lifted the secret mission off the ground.

The launch was completed. Elegant in its simplicity, the silhouette of S-Village was on its way towards the earth's inhospitable satellite. Ten minutes later, when everything seemed to be progressing smoothly, Dino approached them again. The accolades he received from Harry and Jonathan seemed to slightly loosen his tongue.

"Unfortunately, guys, I've got to leave. There's an urgent meeting I have to attend."

"But, you've just brought to an end such a difficult mission. You should be given a few days off for R and R," Jonathan pressed on, soliciting more comments.

"Ha, ha, ha!" Dino laughed. "Time is money, my friend!"

"At least a few hours of rest. I consider it inhuman. No break at all!"

"Mister Keith, you're basically right, yet, it's urgent! Russian and Hungarian geologists and some others have done their own research and their conclusions worry us. For that reason I've got to go to Martinique to see exactly what is going on."

"Bingo! All this was butter on Larry's bread," Jonathan thought, with a great deal of satisfaction. He said, indifferently, "That's strange! You. . . a man sending stuff to the stars, you're interested in geology! What could that have to do with your work?"

Dino smiled and answered casually, "Even the stars throw rocks at us, my dear friends!"

Harry and Jonathan thanked him and drove back to the house. Taking advantage of Harry's absence in the garden, Jonathan sent a second message to Larry. "Subject: Geology, S-Village."

# Present Danger

The most important sky cartographers were holding a three-day meeting at Chicago's Adler Planetarium, by Lake Michigan.

European scientists were here to brief their American colleagues on challenging conclusions that they had reached as they were completing the recording of the celestial bodies, with a very small margin of error.

Several years ago, the Big Bang theory of creation was about to be rejected because some astronomers had proven that some stars existed before the great explosion!

In the amazing work completed by the Europeans, answers were provided to many questions in a project named IPPARCHOS, after the first Greek astronomer. Yet, they would also consider some very unusual cases that had been observed, and they would ask the Americans to help explain them.

In the crowded semi-circular room, somewhere on the sidelines, a middle-aged, very masculine man had gathered his staff. One could immediately understand that he expected to hear something very important. Neither he nor his staff had any nametags. He had to be a highly placed person, something more than an astronomer is.

Discreetly, a member of his team who seemed to be his right-hand man checked his mobile phone to get the incoming message. Then he approached his boss.

"There is a message at the Westin Hotel stating that Larry Keith went to Africa, to see his girlfriend." The boss jumped out of his seat and gave instructions.

"He must be stopped in Nairobi! He's certainly going to Beni and Kenya is on his way there. They should persuade him to come and see me immediately. Things are moving too fast. I need him." He sat back in his chair. Silence followed the announcement that the president of "IPPARCHOS" was about to speak.

The president of the Space Congress, an astronomer and president of the American Society of Astronomy, took his place, and with a well-known American informality pointed his finger at the middle-aged man and his staff. "Let's first address the American Government's representative, the Secretary of Defense, Mr. Michael Donovan!"

The Secretary almost had a heart attack! He was terribly surprised and had every right to be so. He didn't know that, in order to justify expenses, the government had revealed his presence at the meeting.

"Of course," the president continued, "we most probably will not challenge him professionally, although a space mystery about which you may hear might be of interest to him."

The participants laughed with this pleasant introduction. Near the end of the five-hour meeting, a very slim, yellowish man, with acne on his face and a slight hump on his back, took the podium. "Our colleague, Bo Ritzberg, from Sweden's Goteborg University, will now report on a strange observation," the president announced.

The Secretary emptied his third glass of Coke and put another stick of gum in his mouth. He was bored. But the words "strange observation," an unusual phrase for a scientist, made him pay attention.

After posting symbols, numbers and coordinates in the sky, the scientist said, "This planet altered orbit when it acquired a huge artificial satellite." The words "artificial satellite" drew a reaction by all the participants. It was only natural. If a planet had an artificial satellite, then, the creatures that accomplished that miracle should be exceptional and superior to human beings, at least as far as technological progress was concerned. When man is compared to another creature proven to be more intelligent, this creates a psychological problem. It does not set well.

The phlegmatic Swedish scientist, indifferent to the reaction his words caused, continued. "There is an important contradiction here, for me. Some brains accomplished something that even we, with our advanced technological equipment, have not been able to do. Yet, they had to be very careful about the effects of such an operation.

"For me, the problem: Why didn't they choose to put smaller satellites in orbit? This would prevent problems created by the propulsion power required to launch a satellite of such dimensions. My opinion is that the change in orbit caused such geological disaster that it meant the end of any living creature."

The chairman of the meeting, who noticed the participants' negative reaction, intervened. "If what Bo Ritzberg said was coming from anybody else, I assure you I would be among the first to react. Do not forget that we owe him the solution of seven, up to now, enigmatic questions.

"I happen to know the details of the study of the planet previously mentioned. Chronologically, those events took place 200 million years ago and they have but a slight theoretical importance. It is well known that our colleague is a perfectionist and, if I were an astrologist instead of being an astronomer, I would impute it to the sign under which he was born . . . he is a Virgo . . . "

This was a pleasant way to end the meeting, but not for

Michael Donovan. The following day he asked for a synopsis of Professor Bo Ritzberg's paper to be brought to the President's Suite on the executive floor of the Westin Hotel on Michigan Avenue. He later met the Professor for lunch at the roof garden of a high rise building.

"Up here, we're much closer to what you study," the Secretary said to break the ice. "Indeed, Bo Ritzberg was not very happy about the invitation; first because he was rather a loner and, second, because he could not see any common interests between himself and the Secretary.

"From up here, one can better 'control' the city and spot suspicious characters," Bo answered. "You observe things down below, from an upper position. We do the opposite. So, our ways never meet."

Michael did not give up. Attack is the best defense. That's why, even in this case, he used the German method of Blitz Krieg

"If it weren't an artificial, but a natural satellite, what would your alibi be, Bo?"

Even a shot into his head would not shake up this fragile man as much as that question.

"Natural?" Bo repeated confused.

"Of course! Imagine there's an explosion on the Himalayas and Everest flies off."

"Do you realize what you're saying? Are you serious? It's as if we said Maradona was playing soccer with an artificial leg!"

Michael immediately commented on the remark. "Maybe you're certain he doesn't have one, because you saw him in action. Yet, if you'd only seen the outcome of the game, as you did for the planet, you wouldn't swear he does not have an artificial leg."

"You are playing intellectual acrobatics and you are bound to fall off your rope sooner or later."

"Professor, the reason I invited you was to discuss certain things without prejudices. Not to have a quarrel with you."

"You're scaring me . . . I feel as if I was interrogated between smoked salmon and the main course."

"I'll go straight to the heart of the matter, my friend. My primary question needs a direct answer. That satellite, artificial for you and natural for me, was it, or was it not, the size of Australia?"

"Australia! Australia!" Bo was surprised. He let the fork drop on his plate. The question confused him.

"In my paper, I mention, 'The satellite had approximately the dimensions of Australia.' But how do you know? In the synopsis I've sent you, I don't mention anything about it!"

"I've got my sources," Michael said, and then remained silent.

He covered his face with both his hands. "My God!" he was thinking, "So, it's true! Crazy David Mason isn't that crazy, after all! We must do something quickly!"

"A last question. Your planet . . . was it ten times Earth's volume?"

The Swedish scientist couldn't take any more of this!

"Did you hear me?" Michael asked, insisting on an answer.

"Ten times . . . Yes, ten times. Yes, it was when it existed, but . . . "

Michael pretended he was feeling poorly and left immediately. Thousands of alarm bells were ringing in his head as the elevator raced non-stop to the ground floor. He felt the heavy load of responsibility. He was the only man in the world who was absolutely certain that David Mason gave the world valid information. Yet, that information had to be screened to conform with the greater goals of the state. Expediency is the name of the game. By all means, Mason had to be muzzled! It was urgent!

When the Secretary arrived at his hotel, he sat down to reorganize his thoughts. "Let's take the facts from the beginning! Where are we now . . . I've stopped Larry Keith and I am bringing him close to me. Theodore Papadopoulos also has to be brought here before meeting the Pope. Barbara Haim has to be taken away from Beni. We've also got that crazy old guy, Keith's father, poking his nose into other people's business. I've got to know where he is and what he's doing! I almost forgot! We also have the geologists! Another crazy story! They were to meet in Houston, Texas, for safety reasons; yet, these brains changed their minds and decided to meet in Martinique! If they were only on American soil where I am able to move freely . . . My God! They're driving me crazy! How can I catch up with them?"

He felt he was on the front line and had ordered a counterattack! He was in charge of coordinating the attack, and his staff did the rest. Fax equipment, e-mails, and mobile phones—everything was on fire! Attack was but a matter of hours away!

# The Confirmation

When Christopher Colum-
bus came back with no
gold and no Chinese people, nobody was interested in the exotic fruits and the strange tools of the natives he had brought
with him.

When the astronauts returned from the Moon, very few
were really interested in the useless bunch of rocks they
brought back.

A superficial analysis showed that there was nothing precious there, so there was also no reason one should spend
much time on those stones. Fortunately, among the numerous
scientists, there are also the "nerds," unpleasant or anti-social
individuals whose goal in life is to torture their brains, perhaps
to forget their loneliness! Two American geologists belonged
to this segment of the population: Dean Peterson and Enrico
Pinelli.

When they received samples of the Moon rocks, they began an extremely detailed analysis. For three consecutive years they worked separately but neither one managed to reach a clear conclusion. By the third year's end, the two met, got acquainted and decided to collaborate. It was rather difficult to persuade the government, through NASA, that it was likely that something exciting would come out of this research. If truth were told, they themselves did not believe so either. Yet, what brought them some satisfaction was the fact that they had been entrusted with the most rare research object, whose origin was celestial!

Of course, the Russians had also returned with "Moon material." The Russians took a similar approach. But in addition to the Russian scientists, a Hungarian was included among those who studied the samples. His name was Milio Kosta and he had recently launched a protest because he thought the samples allocated to him were fake. Intemperate by nature, he refused to moderate his behavior. He lived under an authoritarian regime that depended directly on the USSR, but that did not prevent him from protesting in public.

American Airlines' Boeing-747, chartered by NASA, landed at 2:22 p.m., at the airport of Fort-de-France, the capital of Martinique. This exotic island, part of the French Antilles, situated between Dominique and Saint Lucie, was the homeland of Empress Josephine. Unfortunately for the natives, Napoleon occupied it so that his wife would be considered a French national.

This view of history is supported by local attitudes. Josephine's statue in the city's central square is permanently decapitated even though the statue has repeatedly recovered its head.

On the flight there, the list of passengers was an impressive version of "Who's Who" among the world's foremost authorities that had dealt, directly or indirectly, with extraterrestrial minerals.

Vladimir Lisenco, the chubby Russian who was responsible for the Russian samples, and skinny Milio Kosta were the first to get off the plane. The two British who had found the strange stone, Anna Grason and Desmond Clark, followed. Finally, the Americans, Dean Peterson and Enrico Pinelli, deplaned. Behind them was an old man whose fake moustache provided a poor disguise for Jonathan Keith. In the reception area, Jonathan was disappointed to find Dino Brahe and Michael Donovan waiting for them.

They almost saw him. Fortunately he managed to hide behind corpulent Vladimir and was first to reach the passport control area.

Of course, the cunning journalist Canakis, Lisenco's shadow, waited for them, too, and immortalized them with his camera. Yet, before he had the time to take another shot, two CRS men, from the French Security Police, very rudely took his camera and confiscated the film. They escorted him to a waiting car that had bars on the windows.

Fowler, Barbridges and Hoyle, known as the Shumacher Team, would not be absent. No official press team or independent journalist had been invited. It was an informal convention sponsored by NASA to help American scientists become informed about research conducted in other countries.

Five speeding limousines took National Route 5, avoiding the capital city. They took the direction of Rivière Salée and reached La Pointe de la Chery. The Hotel was built on this wonderful site. The Novotel-Diamant was the diamond of luxurious hotels. It had 180 magnificent suites and a Convention Hall that would put to shame most American or European Convention Centers.

The guests, who, except for Vladimir Lisenco, found themselves in this earthly paradise for the first time, were overwhelmed. A group of local beauties dressed in colorful native costumes greeted them at the entrance. The manager, Jean-Jacques Hacx, welcomed them and served a glass of sugarcane rum that was a local product. All this happened to the accompaniment of Creole music.

After the formalities, they crossed the bridge that spanned the pool and walked towards the suites with a magnificent view of the La Pointe de la Chery bay and four splendid sand beaches. The list of surprises was still not over. Inside their suites, a plate filled with gorgeous exotic fruits awaited them, placed next to the work schedule. It was a rather busy schedule indicating the first meeting was to take place that very same evening. It would be a working-dinner.

By 6:30 p.m., everyone had already taken his seat around the oval table that was adorned with a wonderful variety of exotic flowers. Canakis had placed a microphone somewhere under the table. He had managed to persuade the CRS officers to release him, as he had no idea about the importance of the guests or about the meeting.

The French Secret Service is not known for stupidity. On the contrary, they have an excellent reputation for their intelligence and effectiveness. The Intelligence Service indeed discovered the microphone and in order to mislead "foxy" Canakis, placed it elsewhere. He would listen to a recorded discussion that reached the conclusion that "nothing important was happening and there was no reason for them to go on with the meeting." In addition, the "discussion" ended with the participants saying they would, nevertheless, discuss some classic research projects of theirs and exchange opinions on the pension problems of retiring scientists.

The journalist felt really disappointed while he listened to the discussion. It was at his own expense that he had followed Vladimir Lisenco to Houston and then to Martinique. He was literally broke now. All of his hopes were dashed the moment he heard they would talk about retirement problems. Of course, the meeting seemed very short because the tape only lasted three quarters of an hour.

"When one admits his defeat, words are of no use, they just prolong the pain," he thought. "Research failed. It's time to go! It's over!"

Under the discreet surveillance of the CRS, the disillusioned journalist paid his bill and left in the hotel's jeep, headed straight to the airport. Fortunately he had an open ticket and he could take a flight leaving in three hours. His bad mood following such a monumental flop could only respond to one medicine, strong liquor.

He was at the bar, drinking a cocktail drowned in rum when the TV news went on. At the same time, the passengers of American Airlines' Flight 603 to Miami were called for boarding.

Mario Canakis paid the bartender and followed the other passengers towards the gate when he thought he heard on the news that "the scientists' first meeting was still continuing!" He boarded the plane and took his seat, feeling a little dizzy. "What meeting? It's not the only meeting going on in this island? It could be the City Council's meeting . . . "

Unlike Canakis's microphone, Jonathan Keith had luckily placed his microphone between the orchids, right in the center of the table. An argument was raging between the American scientists and Milio Kosta, the Hungarian.

With a stubbornness unusual for scientists, Dean Peterson and Enrico Pinelli were trying to persuade the other participants that what their colleague had isolated and called "enamel" had just been mechanically produced under particular temperature and pressure conditions. Milio Kosta was aware of Vladimir Lisenco's reassurances and oaths that the material was genuine. He brought transparencies on which he pointed out electronic images of dental enamel and the enamel from Moon minerals.

The Shumacher Team maintained a neutral attitude. The participants were really impressed because the two images differed very little. The British, Anna Grason and Desmond Clark made their case pointing to comparative transparencies of the diploid. This is a bone with little girders, surrounded by the two cartilaginous surfaces of cranial bones in vertebrates. They compared this image to those of the rocks given to them by NASA scientists. The scientific argument between the

Hungarian and the British, on one side, and the Americans, on the other, lasted for quite a while. Of course, it was a very polite argument.

Looking at the hard evidence, the Americans' sense of fair play prevailed and they finally admitted that their own research obviously had not reached the conclusions it should have. Indeed, they admitted that they had never believed in the organic origin of the fossils.

Prejudice kills scientific research. Their research aimed at defining the inorganic elements and agreed with the research conducted by Barbridge, Fowler and Hoyle.

They promised that upon their return home they would change their direction and bring it in line with the Hungarian and the British scientists. At the end of the meeting that lasted much longer than predicted, the participants decided they would consult paleontologists-anthropologists.

Silent, in deep thought, constantly playing with his pen, Michael Donovan listened to the extraordinary news and wondered about the best solution. His presence at the meeting had only one aim. "Michael, the only thing I ask you is not to mess up the world," the President of the United States told him on the phone, immediately after being informed about the developments.

The participants were already gathering their papers in order to depart when Michael Donovan stood up and asked them to pay some attention to what he had to say.

"Gentlemen, on behalf of the President of the United States, I ask you to follow my instructions in order to avoid a worldwide upheaval because of what you have revealed here, today. First, each one of you should coordinate his research with the other participants in order to not waste precious time. Secondly, I wish to inform you that, in the very near future, a convention sponsored by the United States will be officially organized in Cancun, Mexico. There, you will have the pleasure to announce the results of your authentic, original work.

Dino Brahe spoke immediately afterwards. He agreed with the Secretary of Defense.

The only one who disagreed was the Hungarian, Milio Kosta, who spoke with great difficulty. "Why should the world be in trouble? Only the professionals dependent on religion and religious groups will worry they may lose their monthly income."

The Secretary reacted immediately. "I do not wish to muzzle science. I wish to postpone all official announcements until you reach final conclusions. Imagine the public disappointment and suspicion towards science if the final results happened to be different from those you have presented today."

Dino Brahe and Michael Donovan went straight from the meeting to the Secretary's suite and made plans for a course of action. In the laboratories of the British Natural History Museum and of the Natural History Museum in Budapest, special commandos would alter the samples of Moon rock used in the experiments. The commandos would add a substance that would clear the rocks of any crystallographic structure of animal origin.

Before dawn, the fax in Michael Donovan's bedroom woke him up with the message: " OK, boss! London-Budapest."

Jonathan saw the two government officials leaving in a hurry and understood, before consulting the tape, that things were getting very hot. The tape's content literally put wings to his feet. The next day, he would leave to meet his son at Memorial Hospital. To be safe, he had sent a copy of the tape, by airmail, from Port-au-Prince to his own address.

"Passengers coming from Martinique are kindly requested to go to Customs Control . . . " When he reached Customs, Jonathan Keith was surprised. Dino Brahe was there, smiling.

That ironic smile clearly meant that Jonathan's presence at Novotel-Diamant had not been a secret. "Above every bright guy, there's another one who is brighter," Dino whispered in Jonathan's ear.

The luggage control employee searched Jonathan and gave the tape he found to Dino. Wily Jonathan pretended he was terribly confused. Dino Brahe should not realize he had another copy, the one on its way to Texas.

"Ok! You may pass, now!" the Customs employee declared and Dino Brahe, after a sarcastic glance at Jonathan, walked towards the office.

"Things are getting tight," old Keith thought. "I'd better go home rather than meet my son. Anyway, I'll have to wait there for the tape." He was very pleased with himself for mailing a copy.

"Why are Americans so interested in this matter? They must be hiding something more important."

The substance used by the commandos on the rock samples required twelve days to be effective and untraceable.

That's probably why Milio Kosta felt rather dizzy while attending the farewell dinner. Shortly thereafter he lost consciousness. At the hospital, the American doctors that accompanied the group reassured the participants there was no serious problem. The diagnosis was salmonella. It had caused dehydration due to diarrhea. In a few days, perhaps . . . twelve days, the professor would be able to go back to his country. What a coincidence!

"Salmonella" was not required for the British. They gladly accepted postponement of their departure to go on a ten-day cruise to Mexico's Cozumel Island. The convention organizers, of course, paid the expenses.

All of the participants, except for Vladimir Lisenco and the team of three who were considered unproductive, would participate in a second and decisive meeting in a few months' time. Many important persons would be invited to this official meeting. The aim would be to put an end, once and for all, to the rumor according to which David Mason's stories had anything to do with the origins of life.

The tough patient from Budapest, despite his fever and dehydration, had declared, "I shall do you a favor and comply with your advice, but I now declare that no one shall stop me from making announcements and express my personal conclusions at the end of the next meeting."

Mario Canakis, in order to reorganize his energies, preferred to stay at the Airport Hilton in Miami. He dared not show his face to his news editor. He sent a deceiving fax, an article with the impressive title "Vertebrates Once Existed on the Moon." Using the sender's information on the fax, his editor sent him the following thundering message — "Dear Mario, the news according to which vertebrates once existed on the Moon caused endless laughter to all of our newspaper's staff. The same news also caused the management's irrevocable decision to remove Mario Canakis from the correspondent's position."

To top it all off, another message reached Mario an hour later informing him that he could go to the National Bank of Miami to settle his account with the newspaper. If ever a man swore to deal only with the ephemeral for the rest of his life, that was Mario Canakis. This story cost him his career. Despite all this, deep inside him, his instinct told him he was on the right track.

# From Safariland to Brussels

The landing at Nairobi was rough. By mid-May, high winds from the Indian Ocean were recorded over nine on the Beaufort scale, and made landing problems part of everyday experience at the airports of Kenya, Seychelles and Saint Maurice.

Larry Keith felt as if he was an ice-cube in a shaker. The suffocating heat lashed his face and soaked into his pores the minute he stepped off the plan. It felt like stepping into a Turkish bath. As in any city that attracts large numbers of tourists, everything seemed to be in a state of irritating disorder. People moved about hurriedly, with no clear destination. Those who wore official hats had a serious expression on their face and a heavy accent.

Larry had been waiting for an hour in the line for passport control. He suddenly found himself in front of a credit-card telephone. He did not hesitate a single moment. Surprise was a good idea, and calling her would also help if Barbara were going somewhere difficult to reach. If he missed the chance to meet her, it would be an unpleasant and a painful surprise for him

"Barbara, honey . . . !"

"Larry! How are you, darling? What's new?"

"I'm here, my love! Almost in your arms!" He paused, then said, "I'm calling you from Nairobi!"

"You are kidding! Wait for me there, my Larry! I will be right over to pick you up . . . "

The line was disconnected before Larry had a chance to tell her the name of the hotel where he had a reservation.

"That's strange," he thought. "Barbara is so careful about details. Now why did she do that?"

He moved forward and finally managed to reach the passport control officer. He handed his papers to the man. The officer, working at a slow pace, examined the passport thoroughly. "Larry Keith," he repeated in a loud voice. Then, he took a thorough look at Larry and moved closer to his colleague. He whispered something. Larry could not hear a single word. Next, the officer stamped the passport and returned it to Larry.

He followed the crowd down the hallway that led to the baggage claim area. Nearby he noticed a man in a long, white, medical jacket whispering to a police officer. Larry picked up his luggage. At last, he was free to hurry to the Sheraton Hotel where he had booked a room. He desperately needed to take a shower. His clothes, soaked in perspiration, clung to his body as if glued.

"Please, allow me!" Larry turned around and saw the man in the medical jacket.

"May I see your vaccination certificate, please?" the doctor said with an air of authority that would not accept any objection.

"But . . . I don't have any! Nobody told me . . . "

The doctor seemed more gentle, now. "You are right. Three days ago, there was no such requirement. But today . . . "

"What happened in the last three days?" Larry asked, unable to hide his annoyance.

"A typhus epidemic, Mr. Keith!" the doctor replied.

Larry was surprised to hear the doctor call him by name. Combining this with the suspicious manner in which the officers checked his passport, he became genuinely frightened! He recovered his composure immediately.

"I'm sorry, doctor. Exactly how is it you know my name? How is it possible you know it without looking at my papers, my passport or identity card?"

The doctor had made a blunder of the first order. The only explanation he could offer—instead of replying—he disappeared. Just as abruptly, he was replaced by a high-ranking police officer:

"If you do not have a vaccination certificate you may not enter the country. This, of course, is for your own safety. It is the law."

Larry Keith insisted. "May I call the American Embassy?" he asked.

"Of course, sir," the officer agreed. He led Larry to the Commander's office where Larry dialed the Embassy phone number. He was beside himself. Each second he waited seemed an eternity!

"The Ambassador is not here, sir. I am the Embassy's third secretary, Mr. Keith!" Larry recounted the incident "Please! Shall I put the police officer on the phone so that you can tell him to let me go to my hotel?"

Without waiting for an answer, he handed the telephone receiver to the officer. After a five-minute discussion, the officer informed Larry he would spend the night at the Sheraton. However, the next day he had to leave the country on the British Airways flight to London.

Whether he liked it or not, Larry had to agree. All the while he was wondering why and how the doctor knew his name. The third secretary also had called him by his name! This was very unusual! There had been a set up somewhere, but who did it . . . and why?

As usual, Larry had booked a room at the Sheraton Hotel to be sure he would get all the comforts he needed. At the reception desk he asked questions about the epidemic, but nobody seemed to be interested or even knew anything about it. When he asked the housekeeping maid about it, she looked at him with disbelief. Nothing was mentioned in the evening news! "No fuss so that people won't panic," Larry thought. "The less developed the country, the more sensitive to health concerns."

The shower rejuvenated him. Because he was not allowed to go out, he had dinner in his room and went to bed.

It was five o'clock in the morning when the phone rang. He answered with his eyes still shut. "Larry Keith . . . whom am I speaking to? . . . Barbara? Is that you? Where are you calling from?"

"The reception desk! I'm coming upstairs!" Larry smiled with happiness. After all this time he would finally meet again the first and only woman he had ever loved. At last, he would hold her in his arms and forget about this complicated and dangerous story.

"Larry!" . . . . "Barbara!" For a while they stood there, in each other's arms. Then, they sat on the bed, hand in hand, looking at each other with adoration, like two lovebirds. Only a typhoon that suddenly and violently unites the earth and sky could be compared with the passion they felt as they reached the mountaintop of desire. The struggle of the two bodies for saturation of all senses reached its climax quickly, and the two lovers were left spent, next to each other, savoring the calmness that followed the storm of passion.

'Larry, my love . . . "

"Barbara, why can't we be together for ever?"

"Larry, I agree with you, but now that my head is a little bit clearer, I want to tell you something."

Larry turned on his side to face her and observe her reaction. "Really, Barbara, how is it you're so far away from your place of research? And how did you find me? I hadn't given you any address. I hadn't had the time to do so on the phone."

'First of all, I know you cherish comfort, and Sheratons have become an eccentricity of yours. As far as the other question, it's much more difficult to answer. Really it is."

"What do you mean?" Larry was unsettled.

"Larry, something very serious is going on. Almost the biggest part of UELE, the northeastern province, from Bounia to the borders of Kenya, is under military occupation."

"Do you suspect what I am suspecting?"

"I'm sure this case you're handling, this David Mason case, has drawn reaction from different places. Things are going faster and faster, they are snowballing. From what I've heard, I believe that the Americans will try to unearth the object in Beni's cave of the bats, something they may have already accomplished, or they will try to destroy it. Because I know you're interested in this and because I love you very much, please get up, get dressed, get your suitcase ready and let's get out of here." Barbara was already getting dressed.

"And where are we supposed to go?" Larry protested

"To Beni," Barbara said, and continued her preparation. I think you're the only well informed person. Your presence at an event of such importance is necessary and, of course, useful."

"Barbara, I'm quarantined. Authorities said that tomorrow . . ."

Barbara interrupted him. "The story about the epidemic is all bull. I've arranged everything." She looked at her watch. "In two hours, we should be out of Nairobi."

Barbara left the room first and Larry followed. Fortunately, the man guarding the floor was not there. They climbed out through a fire escape that led to an alley. They ran to the black Volvo that was waiting for them with the motor running.

"To the heliport!" Barbara ordered.

"What do you mean, Barbara?"

"I've thought of the possibility of drawing attention either by plane or by car, so I've asked the company I work for to let me use one of the helicopters they use to observe animals movements. My friend François will pilot it."

"Oh, I forgot to introduce you. Larry Keith, François Dumont, an acrobat of the jungle! He is able to lasso a giraffe from the air. All this, while he's in the helicopter. Lately, he has learned to drive, too."

"Don't pay any attention to her, Larry. She's exaggerating. But, I do have difficulties with giraffes that have a short neck!" They laughed at the driver's joke.

They crossed the border in an area by the foot of Mt. Kilimanjaro but not without a small adventure. The border guards saw the helicopter and suspecting an unauthorized crossing, they shot at them causing minor external damage to the chopper. Fortunately, according to François, the damage would not endanger their landing scheduled to take place close to Bounia, not far from the cave. But they all knew in their hearts that security forces were able to bring them down at any moment, if Nairobi wanted to mobilize the Air Force.

The helicopter carried National Geographic Society's "Wildlife Mission" signs and they hoped that the military would not want to create an incident. Still, the authorities were well aware of National Geographic's legitimate activities, especially during such periods.

When they reached the Beni region, three tracer bullets informed them they had to land as fast as possible for customs inspection.

"I think I must comply!" François said. "We are not dealing with border guards here. It is the American military. It's almost certain that if we do not respond, they will stop us with a Super Cobra helicopter and turn us into molecular dust."

Barbara quickly handed Larry the false papers she had prepared for such an occasion. She stuffed the real papers in an empty battery.

Larry was astonished. "Barbara, you are really surprising me! Are you a CIA agent? Are you keeping some secret? In any case, you're unpredictable! When did you have the time to prepare all this?"

"I'm all yours," Barbara said with charm, but did not answer the real question.

Landing was uneventful, and three American soldiers proceeded with inspection.

"Barbara Haim!"

"Yes!"

"François Dupont!"

"Oui!"

"Patrick Morrison!"

"Yes!"

"I'm truly sorry," the officer said, "but you'll have to stay here in Beni, for the next three hours."

"And why is that?" Larry asked with deliberate indifference.

"They just completed an operation and, until further orders, nobody can travel in the area.

"But why?" Barbara asked, knowing a man's tongue gets looser in front of a beautiful lady.

"All the information I've got is that they've found something archaeological and they're digging it out."

"Archaeological? In Africa?" Larry said as if the idea was preposterous.

"Yes! And it's huge. They say it is 450 feet long and 96 feet wide. Some say it's a UFO. Imagine! Aliens came to get bananas and pineapples and got a flat tire! They even made tunnels, underneath, to get out of here. They found some skeletons. It might be extraterrestrial skeletons. Ha, ha, ha!"

Larry remembered Theodore and the ten unfortunate workers. Where could Theodore be now? "How far is it from here to the place where they found the archaeological object?" Larry asked.

"About three miles." The officer had hardly completed his answer when a ball of fire shot into the sky followed by noise resembling a loud groan. The ground shook with an earthquake that read six on the Richter scale. The fireball traveled west and soon disappeared. Other explosions followed like a series of canon shots and clouds of black smoke and fire filled the air within a few minutes.

The guards ran towards the direction of the fire. Unexpectedly, they were free of the guards. It was time for them to go, too. The three looked at each other in silence, boarded the helicopter and flew in the direction of the explosion.

A gigantic ditch had been created and it was obvious that the object of unknown origin had been skillfully trapped. Maybe it was programmed to self-destruct as soon as sacrilegious hands were about to violate it. Seeing that any delay would be useless, they headed towards Aba, a city on the Sudan border. They wanted to get to Khartoum as fast as possible, to the international airport. When they reached Khartoum, Sudan's capital, they lost no time in the city and went directly to the airport.

Thanks to the never-failing international language of bribes, Larry and Barbara bypassed passport and baggage formalities. They thanked François for his precious help, and bade him farewell, giving him a substantial bonus for his work. The couple easily found two business class seats for the United States, via Rome, on the next Alitalia flight. Exhausted after their eighteen-hour voyage, they fell asleep until the airplane landed in Rome. They had a one-hour layover.

Larry explained his thoughts to Barbara in a few words. "Now that the only authentic, first-hand information source they had hoped to find was destroyed, they will, unfortunately, turn to David Mason with much greater interest."

"I think you're right, Larry. I may add that—call it a woman's intuition—I think David is in immediate danger. It might even be too late."

"I agree! He is in mortal danger," Larry concurred and covered his face with his hands in an attempt to concentrate. "I dare not think about the consequences if anything happened to David." It was urgent that Larry plan a course of action without delays. Time was precious and shouldn't be wasted aimlessly.

"The phone! How did we forget it . . . we must call!" Larry cried out. "I remember the hospital number and the extension."

He pulled the telephone from the back of the seat in front of him, slid a credit card through the side of the phone and dialed the number.

"Memorial Hospital! May I help you?"

"Connect me with room 620, Neurosurgery, please!" There was no immediate response; then, "I am terribly sorry, sir, there is no answer."

Larry hurried to identify himself before the operator got off the line. "I'm Professor Larry Keith and I want to speak to David Mason. It's urgent!"

"Unfortunately, I cannot help you."

"But why?"

"These are the instructions I have been given."

"Can you at least tell me if he's all right?

The operator kept the line open as he mumbled something and, finally, Larry heard him say in a conspiratorial tone, "You've often helped me, Professor, about relatives of mine. And I'm grateful to you. You probably don't remember me, personally, but I think I now have a chance to be useful to you. Ingratitude, you know . . . "

"I know, I know!" Larry said impatiently. "I'm listening. How can I speak to . . . "

"Miss Popov."

"Natassa?"

"Yes, Professor! She gave me a phone number in confidence, and since I'm aware of her relationship with . . . "

"Ok . . . Ok! Now give me that number!"

"0032-223-4988."

"In Belgium?"

"Let me tell you, Professor, that is real love! Nobody can deny this. You see the entire hospital has been talking about it. She kidnapped him!"

Larry did not wait to listen to the operator's gossip. He was satisfied he had managed to get some information about David. "Undoubtedly Natassa was with him or, at least, she could inform them about David's new address. The hospital operator got instructions . . . from whom? And all this secrecy . . . It means I'm also on the list of persons to keep an eye on,"

Larry thought. Without losing any time, giving an excuse that they were facing a family tragedy, Larry and Barbara changed direction and flew to Brussels on American Airlines.

From Larry, Barbara had learned about Natassa's change of heart and her passionate relationship with David. She was absolutely sure that Natassa had persuaded him to change his strategy, to stop giving information and to disappear with her. Thus, they would live quietly, far away from publicity, content and happy, even in Brussels's rainy climate. She agreed with Larry. But something inside her told her Brussels was not just a love nest. It was a shelter against outside threats.

Landing at Brussels' Zaventem Airport was quite different from that at Nairobi. The pleasant surprise of a sunny day in Brussels changed into an unpleasant encounter when the taxi driver told them the price of the fare. Nevertheless, they were rewarded by the sight of Metropole Hotel, the Belle Époque's little palace in Bruker Place.

Before they unpacked, Larry grabbed the phone and called the number in Brussels. "Hello! Hello!"

"Who is it?"

"I would like to speak to Miss Natassa Popov." The party hung up.

"Let me try it," Barbara said with a smile when she realized that Larry stood there without alternatives.

"Do you think they don't answer to a male voice?" Larry asked.

"Hello . . . Information Operator? I would like to have the address corresponding to number 02/234988, please . . . What did you say? Jean-Baptiste Colyns, Boulevard 142 1060? Is there a second number to that address? Yes? What is it? 343 1766! Thank you!"

Larry was in awe. "How stupid can I be . . . " he murmured.

"As usual, I absolutely agree with what you say," Barbara said, falling into his arms.

Jean-Baptiste Colyns. It was one of the main streets in the suburbs of Brussels. Barbara forgot to ask for the name, but they knew from the operator that the house was listed only under one name. When they arrived, they saw a small inscription by the doorbell: Basil T. Papadopoulos — Ingénieur Civil.

Larry was not surprised. From the beginning he thought David would find shelter at an old friend's place — a friend like Theodore, Basil's father, who actively helped David at the beginning of his tumultuous career. Theodore had the third floor of the building to himself. It was arranged so that he could live near his children and grandchildren without being in their way.

The welcome Barbara and Larry received was unprecedented. Theodore took them into his arms, kissed them three times according to the Belgian custom, and introduced them to his children. Larry tried to ask about David, but Theodore avoided a direct answer.

'We've got time. We've got time. Don't hurry. You'll get old too soon! We'll talk about all that, after coffee." When the greetings and introductions were behind them, they had lunch and then sat down for a demitasse of Greek coffee.

The family patriarch said, "Our mutual friend, David Mason, felt lost and missed your warm friendship, Larry. Three days ago, with no medical authorization, he had some visitors who made him sign a false statement."

"What do you mean?" Larry asked.

"The first ones . . . "

"You mean there was more than one visitor?

"Of course! Five committees visited him in one single day! The first group, David thought, were churchmen.

"Priests?"

'No! It seems they were legal advisors representing religious societies. Maybe even sects!"

"Incomprehensible," Barbara said. What does religion have to do with this matter?"

"A great deal, indeed, Barbara," Larry replied. "You see, I didn't have the time to explain all this to you. David's story unveils new devils."

Theodore took his turn again. "So, they pressured him in the name of God and our faith to sign a statement that everything he had said was the product of his morbid, sick imagination, concocted in order to make some money from the publicity. Naturally, at first he reacted strongly and threatened them he would appeal to the Human Rights' Organization. Then he saw that they became more and more threatening and got really scared.

"Did he sign?"

"What else could he do? They clearly told him they would not tolerate anybody alive like him, anybody who tried to undermine the religious faith of everyone on the planet.

"So, they threatened to exterminate him."

"Yes! That's why he signed. And as if this weren't enough, others followed, talking and acting the same way. They came from organizations and government offices. David signed whatever they asked in order to get rid of them. He had to save his hide."

Larry, disappointed by what he had heard, sank in the deep armchair. His head was buzzing. "So, everything is over. But, if he did what they wanted him to do, why did he leave? What was he afraid of?"

The perceptive old man, Theodore, saw Larry in that state and smiled.

"Don't throw in the towel yet, Larry. First listen to the entire story, in detail, and afterwards you may feel as sorry as you wish. Unless, of course, you decide to retract."

"Why? Is there something else?"

Theodore began narrating the story as it happened. "The day the blackmailers announced they would be visiting, Natassa, that foxy female, advised her beloved David not to sign anything."

"But, he did sign!" Larry said sadly.

Theodore smiled. "I'm almost ninety years old and still I can't pretend I understand the way a woman's mind works . . . I beg your pardon, Barbara!

"A woman's soul looks like the abyss," says a Greek song. "It contains both heaven and hell. When she wants somebody, when she loves somebody, a woman becomes a supernatural being! Our friend followed Natassa's advice to the letter. David signed but, as suggested by Natassa, the signature he put on paper was not his! It was just a nice smudge."

Larry stood up. His face shined with joy. "Fantastic! You mean, what he signed is null and void? Great lady, that Natassa!"

"My daughter," said Theodore to Helen, "bring an empty bottle of Coke to my friend and give him the prize he's finally won!"

Of course, they would realize the fraud when they compared the signature with those on David's papers and applications, and David would be paying with his life. They both knew it and had made arrangements for a successful escape to Europe. Two of Natassa's friends agreed to travel using the names David Mason and Natassa Popov. They went to Los Angeles the very same day, hoping that the pursuers would follow that trail.

"So, they also implemented a diversionary tactic! Really, where do they live now?"

"My brother owns an empty villa on Boulevard de Waterloo. For years, it housed the Argentine Embassy.

"You mean we may visit him?" Barbara asked joyfully.

"Of course. But first I think we have to take some precautions."

"Why? It must be peaceful there. What's the problem?"

"Haven't you heard?"

"What?" Larry asked.

"The explosion at Beni brought the matter back before the public and newspaper reporters are looking everywhere for you. Some say you were killed at the explosion. They say you were there incognito. Others say you died in the epidemic in Nairobi. The most reasonable ones, nevertheless, believe you've kidnapped David so that your assertions about him would not be discredited.

Barbara sighed. "Fortunately, at Hotel Metropole we used my name, Mr. and Mrs. Haim. So there's no Larry Keith. Of course, I also gave your phone number."

"Great!" Theodore said. "Then I'll make sure that tonight we will all be together. First, though, I have to ask if they are able to receive us."

Larry jumped up and interrupted anxiously. "David has health problems? Hasn't he recovered completely yet?"

"Headaches. He complains that with every day that passes, his headaches become stronger. Even aspirin or any other strong analgesic is not effective."

Larry bit his lip and covered his face with his hands. Once more he had to concentrate to bail himself out of a difficult situation. The others, respecting his problem, left him alone with Barbara and retired. He remained like that for ten minutes. Finally, he put his hands down and, as if in a hypnotic state he said, "Barbara, pains have started. He's got to deliver."

Barbara was worried, too. Her lover's words were unintelligible.

"Who's about to deliver? That's crazy talk. I'll do what Natassa did! I'll grab you and get you some place where you'll have nothing to worry about. Let's say, the Seychelles."

"Barbara, there is a microscopic, delayed-action bomb in David's brain. If it's not neutralized by David himself, by transmitting the information he has to give, the bomb will explode. That would be his end!"

"I don't understand a word you say!" Barbara said worried. "What you say makes me nuts!"

"Barbara, the fragment that got into his brain is a microchip programmed to destroy itself if it's not unloaded. Perhaps it has warned David about this."

Barbara anxiously tried to calm her lover again. "Larry, my darling, how can it be that you came up with this sudden explanation about David's condition? What you are saying is nonsense! A microchip in the brain! This has never happened before!

"But it has, Barbara." Larry explained, caressing her hair. "There is a precedent, a geologist to whom the same thing happened. And, as he probably failed to react properly, he died instantaneously."

"You mean that David is in danger because he has not delivered his story for some time now?"

"Yes. Fortunately, I gave him a tape recorder, to help him in case of a problem, in case he had to reduce the intracranial pressure. Let me see!"

Larry looked in the small handbag he always carried with him. He found the tape Natassa had given to him before his departure for Nairobi.

"I want to listen to that, too!" Barbara said, with obvious interest.

" I haven't had the time to listen to it, Barbara."

She took the tape and pushed it into the recorder that was under the TV-set. Theodore discreetly came into the living room and sat beside them. They were all curious to hear what David had to say.

First, the tape talked about the MANTA dynasty and their system of laws. Suddenly, there was an interruption. In an altered voice, David went on with an important announcement—"Whoever you may be, I warn you that if, for any reason, even a justified one, this transmission-narration is interrupted or delayed beyond some definite deadline, if the meaning is distorted, you shall instantaneously die! The activated microchip, the 'Pyramid of Knowledge,' depends upon the pace of discharge. If it does not unload completely, it shall destroy itself, causing the death of the host! End of transmission."

They looked at each other, distressed. The clearly threatening warning addressed to David left no doubt and, of course, no possibility to rest.

"We've got to find David as fast as possible! His life is in enormous danger!" Meanwhile, Theodore had wasted no time. He dialed David's number on the cell phone:

"David, is that you?"

"Yes, Theodore! Only . . . as you know."

"I've got your medicine by me . . . filled with tapes . . . "

"Is Larry there? I can't believe it!"

"Yes, David. He's here. I won't let him speak to you, as we

don't have time. We're coming immediately. He's got his own Natassa with him — Barbara."

"I'm waiting for you," David said with genuine enthusiasm and hung up. "Darling, we're not alone, any more. Reinforcements have arrived . . . This headache is killing me! Please, hurry, I'm dying!"

# Ьuman Recycling

Larry and Barbara used Theodore's key to enter the hideout in Brussels without announcing themselves. They found Natassa seated on the floor with her arms wrapped around David's knees. David, his head leaning back on the armchair, his eyes closed, was narrating his story.

Natassa jumped up and pressed her finger against her lips indicating they should be silent.

"I almost lost him! That's why we began unloading his brain before you got here," she whispered.

Four tape recorders were installed to immortalize the historical description of this irrational world that nobody knew whether it existed in the past or was to exist in the future. If what David was narrating was going to happen in the future, then he had surpassed Nostradamus. They sat down to listen to the narration. David continued in a monotonous, but clear voice.

"To make the events clear to you, I shall make my description frank; some might say crude. After the impressively radi-

131

cal reforms achieved by technology and biology, the AENH race of creatures was a purely genetic creation, their dream, perfect creation. They were handsome, powerful, long living and intelligent.

"The MANTA were always at the pinnacle of the hierarchy. In other words, they were the class whose duty was to guide 16 billion creatures. In order to achieve the most excellent MANTA possible and to avoid succession problems, biologists checked them when they were still in their mother's womb. If they did not meet defined criteria, pregnancy was interrupted.

"If more than two very remarkable MANTAS were born, they let them grow up and selected two from the bunch. The others underwent extraction of their superior faculties, by pharmaceutical means, and became one of the AENHs. Another option was to leave the second MANTA in a state of lethargy. This way, there was always one MANTA, one or two successors and one in lethargy, as a possible replacement.

The two slave races were programmed to deal with nothing else but their specialized work. No initiative was possible for them. Their DNA had been blocked carefully to achieve the desired effect. Meanwhile, an electronic chip that was embedded in their bodies woke them up and guided them to go to work and back at strictly predetermined schedules. They were even relieved of the onus of dreaming.

"And what happened when they died?" Theodore asked. He was preoccupied by this existential question because of his own age.

"They didn't die," David replied to everybody's surprise. He immediately explained that they didn't die because of the very existence of DE.A.T.H.

Larry was worried about David as he listened to his friend's incoherent words. But before he could express his concern, the explanation became clear. When, as the AENH said, an OMOH-slave reached his limit in life, that is, an age at which performance automatically decreased, the internal chip guiding him led the slave to a building called DEATH.

"DEATH? What exactly do you mean?" Barbara asked with an expression of fear on her face.

David, without changing the tone of his voice, spelled the word and its meaning.

"DE.A.T.H. The letters have their own meaning. 'DE' stands for 'Debris;' the 'A' for Access; 'T' for To, and 'H' for Hew. DE.A.T.H. meant "Debris Access To Hew."

"The OMOH that reached the pre-determined condition, like robots, without any trace of fear, stepped onto a moving sidewalk that carried them to a drop into the factory. The next stage was their dismemberment and the transformation of their bodies into pyramid-like forms whose sides were about two inches long. No workers were involved in the process. Those protein units, enriched with substances resembling our vitamins and tranquilizers, were put into small individual bags, ten pieces in each bag, and were distributed to the OMOH for lunch and dinner at various working areas.

It was only natural that a description of the methods and behavior of the hellish Angels towards innocent creatures brought indignation and disapproval among the listeners. Some became ill by what they had heard. Barbara felt dizzy and passed out. With Natassa's help, Larry carried her from the sunroom to the first floor bedroom.

David, on the other hand, had taken one dose of a cocktail that created a hypnotic state, and did not react at all. He did not even open his eyes. He just went on speaking to an audience that consisted of four microphones and Theodore.

"This was cannibalism, David," Theodore said. "Something similar was described in the book *2001,* although it wasn't as horrible. Really! How did their conscience allow that? Their religion? Had they no inhibitions at all?"

"Their behavior, Theo, didn't differ from that of cannibals. They, themselves, though, were civilized. This means, to the AENH, the OMOH were just useful animals, as oxen are to us. And, we've got some animal lovers but no ox-lovers. Don't you think this is very pragmatic? They had no 'slave lovers;' they were sincere killers. You spoke about their religion. But, even ancient Greeks offered sacrifices, hecatombs, to please the Gods. The AENH had no God as we mean it.

"To them, the creator was an entity that did not impose any limitations. And, let's not forget, they reproduced only themselves. They made two copies of themselves. The first was born brainless. They sacrificed it and turned it into a personal bank for parts which they kept in their own home. Of course, the first copy was created right after their birth. Thus, they had the possibility to live twice as long. The second copy was created right after their death."

"After their death?" Larry asked. He had just walked into the sunroom. "But then they didn't have the satisfaction to see they achieved some kind of immortality! Anyway, this is a rather morbid method, don't you think?" Larry insisted.

David was surprised. "Of course, after their death. I think it's reasonable. Otherwise, the cloned creature could have demands on the belongings of the original. There would be a problem. But if they took a cellular nucleus from the original body and created a copy, there was absolutely no legal problem."

Theodore took a deep breath. "Where are you Hitler, Attila, Sultan! This is the moment of vindication! The Armenians' slaughter, or the SS camps, look almost normal compared to what we hear!"

David did not answer. He continued with his gruesome narration. "The dead Angel's embalmed body was transferred to KOX's Sacred Crater. This was the name of the crevasse that had been created when ANOL separated and became the planet's natural satellite. It was 750 miles long and six miles deep. Its deification was abolished after their vertiginous technological progress, yet, perhaps due to some inner need, they wanted to keep a connection with their pagan past. The body was simply dumped into the crater; no ritual was involved. The crater had finally become a garbage dump rather than a cemetery. But there were no relatives to cry over and take care of a grave. This was how they came to the world, through their only relative's death. They never saw him dead to feel sorrow for him."

Theodore, who adored his children and grandchildren, could not take any more of this. "The kingdom of absolute solitude and madness. This is what this terrible world you're describing should be called, David! This was Hell itself!"

Maybe because the cocktail's effects had passed or because Theodore was actually yelling, David answered. "State of the eternal, individual self-sufficiency. This was, in our own free interpretation, a description of that state. They had no flag and no guns—those were a MANTA privilege. Biologists had not managed things so that there were no enemies any more, nor could they be created. Microbes did not exist, only recycling fungus. Death was only the result of mechanical degradation or of obstruction created in the brain's circulatory system.

"The population of the Angels did not change in number while slaves diminished or increased according to needs. Once, geologists discovered a Morantiggus deposit—that's what they called it—but the site didn't allow the use of machines or tools. So, they created pygmy workers and named them 'Cut-Eyed' because they only had incisions between their eyelids in order to protect them from stone fragments.

"Cut-Eyeds also had another peculiarity in the lumbar region. They had a black, extended mark, which hosted a hypodermic teledevice that transmitted stimuli to make them execute orders. If they did not obey, the immobilization that followed was equivalent to a sentence to death, by hunger."

Barbara reappeared, to everyone's great relief. Larry, afraid that she might again break down, managed to change the course of the discussion to less emotional subjects.

"David, my friend, in the tape you've sent me you mentioned things about the cities and the fields."

"Oh, yes! Well, I shall cover those two subjects in a few words. I ask you, though, to pay attention to what I say so we don't have to repeat this subject. That would cause us to lose precious time. For your own awareness, personal joy and happiness, I am pleased to let you know that my headache is gone!"

Everybody applauded. It was very comforting to know that the danger for self-destruction of the microchip was postponed and David had escaped his demise once more.

"What I am about to describe has to do with flotation. The floating soil on which cities were built had exactly the same configuration as any beehive with cells in its honeycomb. There were surfaces connected with each other by bridges that looked like a geometrically arranged wire netting. The surface of one floating part was connected to six other hexagonal shapes with three large bridges at every edge. The surface of one hexagon was equivalent to the Manhattan section of New York. The bridges assured the net's cohesion. They were mobile so that, at any time, they could isolate or move the hexagonal quarter. It was something like a floating Venice whose every quarter was a hexagonal floating part.

"People were transported by floating vehicles that resembled our own motorboats. They were all electronic, though, because they had no liquid fuel. They had plenty of electricity thanks to the waterfalls. The reason they preferred a means of floating transport was to spare energy through buoyancy, as batteries were very heavy.

"When those cities reached a specific size, hexagonal parts were separated from the central mass and, thus, the center of another city was formed. This, of course, happened until the population of Angels stabilized. For safety reasons, the water-cabs and water-private-cars were under absolute electronic control of the planet's Intelligence Service. If a departure was considered criminal or suspicious, then the boat sank through a remote self-destruction device.

Natassa could not bare this "David, stop! It's time for us to have a drink. Aren't your lips dry?"

Only the voice of his beloved could take David out of his voluntary hypnosis. He opened his eyes and smiled. "Oh . . . Hello! If I knew you were all here, I would have interrupted the headache-therapy for you." He sat up comfortably to enjoy his friends' company.

Barbara felt she had to speak. "The conditions under which I've met you were peculiar and now, suddenly, I am listening to all these tragic stories."

David nodded knowingly and replied. "My dear, I must confess that what I've said before might come directly out of my own mouth, but I had nothing else to do with it. Indeed, some of the things I've told, I should hear them again myself because I did not have the possibility to evaluate their importance. I don't want you to misunderstand me, if I don't answer you sometimes. It's not my fault. You should blame it on my guardian and dictating Angel!"

Larry appeared absent-minded. He was preoccupied by something serious. Barbara noticed, approached him and asked for the reason of his mood.

"Is it me, darling, with my foolish questions?"

Larry smiled. "No, Barbara, it's not your fault. It's the last Archangel of Hell, the MANTA. Fortunately, he can't hear us now, because certainly he went to Hell. I was thinking, David, he'd charged you with a mission that not only assures its people glory but also enriches our own knowledge. Of course, he didn't do that to help humankind. On the contrary, I believe he wouldn't mind exterminating it if it caused him any trouble! I'm sure about that."

Theodore could not believe his ears. "What are you trying to say, Larry? Are you thinking about the developments of genetic engineering? You wonder if we might also end up doing something like that, if we followed Doctor Richard Seed?"

Larry motioned no with his head. "Not at all! I'm referring to the use of flotation, the artificial soil. I was thinking that, if the ices on the poles melted, three-fifths of our cultivated land would disappear from the face of the Earth. From what I know, there is no alternative solution. Everybody just talks in generalities about the possible danger!"

They were all hanging on his every word. Larry, thanks to his attentiveness, had drawn out of David's narration a very useful discovery, perhaps the greatest of the twenty-first century. It might be the one that would save the world from hunger! Theodore, as a long experienced engineer, perceived the matter in its correct dimensions.

"My friends, Larry has unveiled the world's third most important invention, after the discovery of the wheel and electricity. I'm convinced that I am not exaggerating at all! If we had those floating and fertile valleys, sown together with anything we wanted, we could study climate changes and move them accordingly so that we would avoid possible disasters."

"How would you water those areas?" Natassa inquired, but Theodore continued as if he had not heard the question.

"Aeolian and solar energy, transformed into electric power, would desalinate the sea water in order to water the fields. And agriculture is not the only potential beneficiary of this. The potential applications of a floating ground are innumerable. Consider floating airports, so that in case of emergency landing, there is an option in the middle of the ocean!"

"Why not floating cities, too?" David added. "Such as those of the MANTA . . . I mean, floating tourist islands," David added. "Imagine, instead of dragging tourists to the Bahamas or the Aegean Sea, there could be a whole floating island that could move each night and, in the morning, would be close to another island! The tourists wouldn't have to leave their hotels!"

"I think you are being carried away by your enthusiasm," Natassa said. "You are forgetting the possible side effects! If what you say can happen, all private companies would build up floating islands and declare them independent states. They wouldn't pay taxes any more. Imagine IBM that has billions of profits, and CNN, not giving a single cent to the US Government! Every tycoon would build his factories on his own floating island and would enjoy a tax-free life!"

Barbara was impressed by the socialist twist that Natassa gave to the whole matter. She wanted to state her own point of view.

"Military bases, if they were floating, would practically be unbeatable, unsinkable. Especially if they were built of small hexagonal autonomous parts loosely connected with each other. They could constantly control everything and everybody! Imagine if, instead of hundreds of landing boats, a huge articulated floating platform were used, filled with tanks and guns!"

"The beachhead would be ready as soon as the strategic island reaches the enemy land!" Larry added, in fact completing what his significant other was saying. "Humankind will turn into a society of snails!"

"This probably demands some explanation," David ironically said to Larry.

"Every rich man, instead of building his home on some dried up island, will do so on a floating lot. Following the weather forecast and his own mood and professional needs, he'll carry his home, exactly like the snails do!"

David, wanting to show that he was no less imaginative, added, "Right! You're probably right! But, in my opinion, there is another possible application. Let's suppose there was an epidemic, a really terrible one, and we had to isolate the infected individuals in order to control the disease."

"So, what do you propose, David?" Natassa asked, a little annoyed because she could guess what would follow.

"We should have a floating island with hospitals, where infected individuals would have to stay until complete recovery!"

"Darling!" Natassa exclaimed pulling David into her arms. "I have the impression you are influenced by what you have been narrating. Don't you think you are proposing the creation of a ghetto? Don't you think your proposal is rather . . . Angelic? I would worry if any member of the Human Rights' Organization heard you!"

Barbara, assisted by Natassa, served some ice cold Stella Artois beer and a tray of appetizers and snacks. The evening was coming to a comfortable end and prospects for David's health were good. The dangers were now far away. Larry and Barbara finally accepted the invitation to be Theodore's guests. They were ready to wish everyone good night when the phone rang.

It was Basil, Theo's son. "Hello . . . Is that you, father?"

"Yes! What's going on?"

"Please call the gentleman from Sudan, somebody wants to talk to him!"

Larry and Barbara looked at each other. Larry hardly had a chance to pick up the phone.

"Are you Mr. Haim?"

"Yes! What's the matter?"

"Nothing important, but I thought I might be useful to you!"

"Could you, please, explain what's going on and who you are?"

"I'm working at the Metropole Hotel's reception desk. I realized you were late and that's why I called the number Mrs. Haim left here."

"I'm listening!"

"Nothing special. After you left, a gentleman came by. He had a photo that resembled you a lot." The sweat on Larry's face showed he was really in a difficult spot.

"Yes, and what did he want?" Larry asked, pretending to be rather indifferent.

"He asked if you were a client, if you stayed here. He also said your name was Larry. Larry . . . Something. I don't remember the forename, unfortunately!"

"And what did you say?"

"Since I didn't know what you'd have liked me to say, I tried to convince him I didn't know you. He insisted. He even tried to bribe me with a large sum of money." Larry had difficulty swallowing.

"Hello? Are you there? He said he would come back again. What am I supposed to do?" Larry's brain worked like lightning. There was no time for diplomatic niceties.

"Wait for me and I'll double what he is offering."

"Thank you but, you know, because you're a guest I wouldn't want to put you in a difficult spot. Unless you insist!"

"I insist! I insist! I would like you to do me this favor. You know, my escort, whose name is Barbara, is that guy's wife. She left him to come with me. I think he's carrying a gun. You should be careful! He's a little nuts!"

"He really told me some crazy things. You're absolutely right! He told me his name was Mario Canakis and that he was an American journalist."

"It would be a real pity for your hotel's reputation if this scandal of ours became public," Larry said to frighten him.

"Oh, you're absolutely right! I hadn't thought of that! It would certainly be a disaster for the hotel!"

"And you would lose your job, my friend," Larry added.

"Are you going to be late?"

Larry took Theo's Mercedes and vanished. When he reached Brucker Place, where the hotel was situated, he parked the car in a side street to avoid detection. With the stride of a carefree, jovial tourist he reached the hotel's revolving door. A brown-haired and exceptionally restless man, carrying a camera and bags, and wearing a cap from St. Martin, was gesturing and talking to the receptionist.

The receptionist realized Larry had arrived and Larry made sure the receptionist saw that he pulled his wallet out of his pocket. As soon as the receptionist got rid of the journalist, he greeted Larry with unusual politeness. In a few seconds, the receptionist had the pleasure of pocketing—against his objections, of course—a respectable bonus.

"I think I've discouraged him. Only, he'll spend the night here, in the hotel," he told Larry. Ten minutes later, Larry paid the hotel bill and loaded his luggage into a cab. As a precaution, he decided against using the Mercedes.

"Boulevard de Waterloo!" he ordered the driver. "Quick! I'll show you exactly where, as soon as we're in the vicinity. I don't remember the number but I know it used to be the Argentine Embassy!"

Larry was contemplating how close he came to meeting the journalist. "The world has become too small; it's impossible to hide. Fortunately, bribery has retained its traditional value and power!"

# Unexpected Ally

When he arrived at the villa, Larry noticed a cab, with the motor running, was stopped very close to the main entry. He paid his driver and went toward the parked taxi.

"Who are you waiting for?" Larry asked the driver.

The taxi driver quickly informed him he had picked up a man at Brucker Place, probably a reporter, who had to do a brief interview and return to his hotel. Larry was anxious. Every hope of keeping David isolated was suddenly collapsing. He was now certain that a journalistic storm would hit them and destroy such a serious and responsible work. He was also sure it would bring about the chip's self-destruction in David's head and his friend's death. Humankind was to lose its one and only unexpected link with another world, incredibly more advanced technologically, yet monstrously governed.

With such dark thoughts floating in his head, Larry went into the villa. They all were in the living room. Yet, the atmosphere did not reflect Larry's bleak thinking of a minute earlier. David Mason calmly attempted to speak first, obviously inter-

143

ested in introducing the stranger. But, before he opened his mouth to utter the name of the latest addition to the group, Larry interrupted.

"Mr. Canakis, you were very good at the Brussels' taxi-race! What I would really like you to tell me, though, is how you've managed to get here as, I must confess, I was confident I had lost you."

The journalist, after exchanging a handshake with Larry like two boxers in the ring after the game, replied, smiling in a typically casual, American manner. "It was the Arabian method. If one pays, my friend, everything is possible!"

Larry hastened to add, "Even if one pays, my friend, everything is not necessarily possible. It is only possible if you find yourself an honest blackmailer!"

David took it upon himself to inform Larry about what had happened and asked Natassa to pay the waiting taxi driver, as their new friend was to be his guests' guest for the night.

"Our friend, Larry, obviously came with bad intentions because he hadn't realized we neither were conspiring, nor were we undermining anyone's peace or security. I think we've persuaded him that our intentions are good. We've also convinced him about the difficult position we're in, because the authorities are poorly informed. He told us he would help us as much as he could in exchange for exclusive information to publish. In other words, he will be our representative to the outside world — our public relations consultant."

Canakis sat on the carpeted floor—in the style of a genuine, educated, young American—and seemed deeply preoccupied. Larry, David, Barbara and Natassa waited for him to speak. They had not told Theodore, as he was certainly already asleep at his son's home.

The reporter was puzzled because it was the first time he had spoken to the protagonists of the drama and was trying to assess the information in his sharp mind.

"My friends," the journalist finally decided to break his silence, "you're locked up in a closed circuit and have no idea of the tremors you've caused. You also can't imagine the degree of fanaticism with which states and religions are fighting you. They are looking for you discreetly because any publicity would result in significant upheavals in society. David's fake signature on the declarations they proposed created a real mess in the different government services. Forgery is considered a crime in my country and, you understand, it's one more thing for you to worry about."

Their faces got pale. Until then, they were unaware, they could not imagine, the passion and religious zeal with which everybody was trying to muzzle them.

"Suffice it to state what happened during the past four days. On May fifteenth, the monks of Burundi, Kenya, and the Republic of Congo held a secret meeting, which I was able to attend. No procedural matters were discussed. Their arrows were pointed at your heart, David."

"You mean, they're going to kill me? What did I do to them? I really don't understand!"

"If they could, they would have already done it. They tried to trap you a couple of times but you escaped unwittingly. You are a lucky man."

"But . . . what have I done to them?"

"David, when you talk about a developed civilization that 'got rid of religion' because it considered it was not quite a serious matter, this is a deadly threat to the professionals of this area. If this also happened on earth, it would mean their disappearance as a group. Don't you understand that? They're losing their jobs."

"But, they don't believe a word I say, Mario! Why should they be afraid?"

"This means, David, they know much more than we do about this affair. The military and the monks agreed to blow the 'thing' up without first examining it. Imagine how irrational they are. Imagine their blind fanaticism."

" Was the explosion at Beni arranged?" Barbara asked.

"Of course, it was! Only, something unpredictable occurred. The core of the unidentified object, instead of exploding, was finally launched into space and, according to one version, was headed for the Moon. Some say it was programmed to destroy itself. Others say it was programmed to automatically return to where it came from."

"To the Moon? I suppose that is a fairy tale!" Larry said.

"I wouldn't presume to enter another person's territory," Mario said. "In any case, this unpredictable development relieved your terrorized persecutors of the most serious piece of proof. In Martinique, there was a geologists' convention. They were all specialists in rocks from the moon."

"That's another crazy story!" Natassa remarked while serving coffee. "What does one thing have to do with the other?"

"Although I'm not sure, I think I smell something. I also believe, please don't think I'm crazy, but I feel like Galileo at the Inquisition. There must be some serious relationship."

"Tell us, Mario, what improbable you think is more probable?" David asked.

"My friends, I suspect they found evidence of life on the Moon. What were paleontologists doing with biologists and geologists in Martinique? That was enough for me to get suspicious!"

"But the earth does not move," Barbara said in laughter. "Even if there was life on the moon, in our case, this leaves us completely indifferent. Larry, do you see any connection?"

Larry scratched his head, rather embarrassed. "Our foes are troubled minds. They see ghosts everywhere, ever since the Iron Curtain fell. They've got a big problem!"

"What's that, darling?"

"Barbara, the biggest problem, for a mathematician, is not having anybody who expects solutions from him. Likewise, the secret services lack a substantive issue, so they artificially create a tense environment to feel they're useful and to justify the money they budget. They pretend to defend religion and the principles that rule our life, when, instead they're trying to exterminate us. These people, by nature and profession, suspect everybody. They are afraid of their own shadow, and they are afraid they may lose their jobs. For them it is second na-

ture to threaten us with extermination and to actually implement their threats."

"You mean even physical extermination," the journalist intervened.

"I agree with you. You see, they try not to leave any traces
that would, in the future, uncover the threat they see. That's
why we must immediately take precautions. I think we must
move now."

"Why all this haste?" David asked. He seemed completely
exhausted. It was natural he would be. It was five o'clock in
the morning.

Mario insisted. "No, David! I know you're really tired and
had much more trouble than anyone of us had because of the
constant intellectual tension. But, don't forget, all of you, that
a cunning blackmailer who suspects something very big is
tracking us! One thing is for sure. He is not sleeping! Our
survival depends on our endurance!"

David went into the office and sent an unsigned e-mail message to Theodore. "Your friendship, legendary hospitality and
your support will remain unforgettable to me. My aunt, in
Melbourne, is dying. We'll talk again soon." As a diversionary
tactic, he wrote the previous day's date.

"I think we have to leave our friend, Theodore, in peace
now. He is so old that, if anything happened to him, I would
feel guilty that I contributed to his death," said David.

They quickly packed and, riding in two taxis, abandoned
the villa. They agreed to go by car to Paris, and, after resting
in a motel for a day, to recharge their internal batteries and decide how to find a secure hiding place.

"We are just like the five fingers of the hand," Larry said.

David added, clearly moved, "But the precious ring on this
hand will be our incredible friend, Theodore Papadopoulos."

As they were making the turn at Boulevard de Waterloo,
they saw a motorcade with four black cars. The first one belonged to the Corps Diplomatique and had an American flag.
Two police cars were behind it, and last was an old model
Opel with a swarthy, middle-aged driver that smoked like a

Turk. His original name was "Judas." God blinded him from recognizing them. If he had seen them and had alerted the convoy, the hand would have been mutilated once and for all.

Larry used his mobile phone to call Zaventem Airport and booked a one-way ticket for Melbourne, using David's American Express card. One must admit the trick was rather obvious, yet they would win a little time over the men hunting for them. Each minute was precious to them.

They ordered the taxi drivers to take them to a village close to the Belgian-French border. From there, they would take the first train to the Gare de l' Est, in Paris.

The judge of the Brussels night court had issued an arrest warrant for the Americans, in order to search and arrest all those whom, in the Embassy's opinion, were part of the conspiracy. When nobody answered the doorbell they broke in, thanks to the swat team they had with them.

Michael Donovan was in charge. He happened to be in Brussels for a convention on the eradication of terrorism. They searched everything in minute detail. Fortunately, the message left by David had the wrong date, which misled Michael, who knew that David really had an aunt in Australia. He didn't know any details about her, though.

"We have had such an exhausting time for nothing," Michael said to the informer. "You lied! It wasn't today! They left yesterday! The birdies flew off together, with the thousand dollars you were supposed to get! Now get lost, you snitch!"

When Mustafa-Judas left, Michael sat on the sofa, deep in thought, and assessed the situation. "The most reasonable possibility is they feel hunted and they've quit everything. They're afraid to venture outside. Those were his thoughts, yet, because of his professional skepticism, he would not close this case until everything was cleared up the way he wanted—the death of the protagonists and collection of the reward money.

At least, he had cleaned up the geologists' affair; although, in this case, no matter how one tried to do the right thing, there was always something dirty, a suspicion, an underlying threat. That damn Hungarian is really stubborn," Michael thought.

They had not yet reached Paris when David again started complaining about his headache. This time, though, the symptoms were not the same. He now was vomiting ceaselessly. That really worried Natassa, who had specialized training in neurosurgery, where she served for years.

She had absolutely no doubt. Her beloved David exhibited all the symptoms of intracranial pressure syndrome, whose most frequent cause was a malignant tumor. That was the reason why they did not go to a motel. They preferred a hotel, near the Champs Elysées, the Elysées Etoile, so that David could get some rest.

When Natassa informed the others of her opinion about David's health condition, at first, there was panic. " You should take him to be examined, in a hospital, immediately," Larry said. "Even if someone recognized him, they would certainly not bring a sick man to trial! The American Hospital is here."

The one who was directly interested in the diagnosis, David, was following the discussion from the room next door. He was moved by the concern they were all showing for him, and not wishing to lengthen their agony and panic, he opened the door connecting the two rooms in the middle, and surprised them.

"Even if I had a cancer, MANTA would not allow me to die before my mission was completed. I exhibited the same symptoms before, at the beginning. I'm sure it's a signal, indicating I must quickly unload my pyramid. Those Angels have too many dealings with this pyramid shape! Now, get over your gloomy mood and get the recorders ready! I feel as if I could explode at any moment! My head is bursting inside like a pressure-cooker, with no exhaust pipe and no whistle!"

They felt encouraged. They knew David had more information than they did. Anyway, when he was with them, he always was a big mouth and did what he wanted. Natassa testified to that and she claimed to be a dependable witness. They all laughed at her realistic outlook.

# Ultimatum from Space

Natassa gave David the Mythos Cocktail solution, as doctors at Memorial had named it. It was a substitute for, or helped facilitate, hypnosis, according to the needs. Hypnosis, if prolonged, could have unpleasant side effects. The substitute, Mythos, certainly had none.

At the beginning, David needed additional hypnosis, but as time passed the cocktail seemed to be enough. Maybe Natassa's beautiful eyes did the trick.

When they looked for the tape recorders, they realized, to their great chagrin that they had left one of them at the villa. So as not to upset him, they said nothing to David about it. He was exhausted. He could barely move without Natassa's help. The violent pain had become unbearable. In the past 24 hours he had vomited ten times. Fortunately, he managed to keep the liquids he drank in his stomach long enough, and there was no immediate danger of dehydration.

Everything was ready for a new recording that would relieve the pressure on his brain. "We're listening to you,

David," said Larry who was going to play the role of the facilitator again.

A harrowing, ear-piercing scream came out of David as soon as he closed his eyes. The hotel was almost empty that Sunday afternoon or guests would have called the police, Larry thought.

"The whole planet seems in mourning. Planet KEROPS weeps. The Angels, including the MANTA, feel lost! Terrified. Planet's complex information systems had just carried the fatal news, the sentence!" Larry was shaken to see tears running down David's cheeks. He thought something was going on

"Keep cool, my friend. Don't forget we're dealing with criminal masterminds. What's making you so emotional about them?"

David moved his head sorrowfully, "When there's an earthquake, you feel like a little child that has lost his mother. Because, for you, your mother is a symbol of permanence, the one you can hold onto to avoid falling. And what a mother is to a child, the ground is for a planet's inhabitants."

"Oh, I see! An earthquake shook the ring? But, the Angels had floating cities; they weren't in danger. So, let's not exaggerate!"

"No, Larry! There was no earthquake! Something more terrible happened. Something that resembled nature's condemning sentence! A real disaster of Biblical proportions!"

"Was it the plague? Did climate radically change? Tell us!"

"The original Angels would find it easy to withstand such disasters. The impending catastrophe could not be faced successfully. It was a sentence of annihilation and it was total. Completely! Astronomy was perhaps the most developed science among the Angels, in addition to the general scientific progress involving genetics and technology. The study of space was very advanced and space scientists were held in high respect. From time to time, usually every ten years, they published a detailed communication presenting research results. This increased knowledge among the Angels, who were always eager to learn things. This time, fourteen years had passed and astronomers could not agree upon publishing their latest discoveries.

Larry objected to listening to all this. "I've got the impression, my friend, you're off the subject. What does all this have to do with sympathy tears for the Angels?"

David, paying little attention to his friend, went on talking. "The MANTA, the absolute ruler of planet KEROPS, became concerned when the astronomers invited him to participate as Chair, at the Astrophysics Convention. It was the first time he was invited. Furthermore, they did not even bother to present him with the convention's agenda. He was planning to castigate this behavior when the time was right.

Canakis, seated on the floor, found the discussion of no special interest, and leaned his head on the sofa and soon began snoring. Larry was furious when he noticed. "Don't you think that a little coffee might invigorate us?" he yelled, on purpose, to awaken Canakis. "Tell me, David, are you sure the urgent message that caused your symptoms had to do with the Astrophysics Convention? Couldn't we bypass it?"

Meanwhile, Canakis who was emerging from his stupor, remarked he found Larry's observation very interesting. "Did they find evidence of life on ANOL?" he asked, showing signs of particular interest.

Barbara laughed. "Dear Mario, the idea of life on satellites or the Moon and, now, on ANOL has become an obsession for you!" David bit his lips and hid his face behind his hands. He avoided answering, sipped his coffee quietly and closed his eyes again. It was certain he had not heard a word of the discussion among Larry, Mario and Barbara. So he remained disinterested and calm.

David continued. "Addressing the Chair, the President of the Astrophysics Society got immediately to the point with no general introductory comments. 'Leader MANTA,' he said, 'the countdown has begun, as far as life on our planet is concerned.' This rendition is a paraphrase, but expresses accurately the meaning of what had been stated."

"What do you mean?" asked Natassa as she wiped the sweat off his forehead.

"Natassa, and all of you, my friends, I wish from the bottom of my heart this never happens to us."

"What is it? Try to be clear, David," Barbara pleaded. "What happened at the Convention? What did they say?"

'In 49 earth years, comet ZX03 that passes by our planet on regular intervals every 12,032 years shall collide with KEROPS. This will be the rendezvous of death for us."

A complete silence followed these words. The astronomer continued. "According to statistical analysis and countless verifications through the most complex means we possess, the fatal rendezvous is not just a mere probability. It is a well-established prediction.

"Maybe for the first time in the MANTA Dynasty's history, the leader did not offer an immediate solution. He got up slowly, as if his body weighed twice as usual and spoke. 'I am aware of the accuracy of your experimental research. I know this deadly threat will come true, with the hyper-collision between KEROPS and ZX03. Already, during its last appearance in the sky, the historians had described unusual phenomena. Instructions had been given to pay particular attention to this celestial body that will be the silver bullet.

'It is reasonable to expect a leader to react, to give solutions. Yet, this is not an ordinary problem. And, at first glance, it seems to have no solution. I shall ask you to be most discreet about this matter. You will consider it top secret. No information should reach the mass media. Publish a routine information bulletin expected by the Angels. That will pacify them until I finally give the authorization to announce the truth. One never runs to a dying man to announce the date of his death. Yet, one never stops trying to save him.'

"No follow-up meetings took place. They all retired, disappointed with their leader's attitude. He seemed beaten, insufficient . . . so small!"

The team waited for David to continue. Larry seemed distraught.

"This is a very inglorious end", he said in a colorless voice. "At least this will eliminate your headaches."

David reacted with sarcasm. "I would not destroy an entire planet just to cure headaches! Unfortunately, everything comes to me in the order they want and I don't know what the outcome will be. Larry, my friend, what I'm absolutely sure about is that AENH's history is not that short. So, there's no reason to be disappointed. The wise MANTA shall think of something . . ."

Larry, acknowledging the stupidity of his remark, tried to make a joke of it. "Even if they died . . . they would still be Angels . . ."

"Hell's Angels, most probably," David added. He closed his eyes again. "It was impossible to keep it a secret for long. People began reacting. At first they issued statements and resolutions, but hysteria was not far behind. Many remembered the religion of their ancestors. They felt guilty! And, then, there was a religious revival. 'No God, whoever he might be, would approve the biological manipulation of the slaves. It is revenge time. This is the reason why God wants to annihilate us.'

"In order to satisfy an angry God, many began caring about the slaves, who, however, could not react as they had been deprived of feelings and reason.

"Even MANTA's statement, on the occasion of commemorating the Day of the Slaughter in Bright Valley, was short and direct. 'All of my people, scientists and citizens, are summoned to use all their intellectual and scientific knowledge and abilities, all of their wisdom, to find a solution to our problem. The one whose solution is considered the best, and is implemented, shall be your new leader. A new dynasty, that shall be called the Savior's Dynasty, shall rise and have absolute power over you and myself.'

"The following day, through the electronic network, thousands of proposals and surveys were sent for storage in the Hyper-tech central computer's memory. All this was processed at the speed of light and, if practical elements were included, a signal was issued to identify the precise proposal. Because of

panic, only incredible solutions were submitted. The best pro-
posal concerned the installation of rockets at the feet of KOX
Mountains! It was termed Temporary Orbital Modification.
Absolute madness!

"Among the theories filed away for further consideration
were a couple of special interest. Somebody called Levax proposed blowing up ANOL, the satellite, a little before impact
with the comet. Thus, KEROPS's return to the position before
ANOL would save the planet. It seemed reasonable yet, after
the astrophysicists studied the proposal, it was rejected because the deviation would be null and provide no hope for salvation.

"MANTA's son, a young man aged 17 in earth years, also
sent a proposal without informing his father, under the pseudonym "Savior." He proposed all the Angels move to ANOL
satellite so that, when the planet is destroyed by the collision,
they would all be saved. But the change in orbit after the collision would be so severe that nobody could be certain that the
new conditions would allow survival. In addition, it was most
probable that ANOL would also be destroyed by the collision.

"The MANTA, who received detailed reports whenever an
interesting proposal was selected, submitted the second proposal for special processing. Though considered inapplicable
at first, this solution drew much attention. There were major
problems to be solved, though. In order to immigrate to
ANOL they had to create an atmosphere. Of course, the satellite had materials and water from the underground lakes that
survived the launch. Moreover, there was already a rudimentary atmosphere. It was practically impossible for the entire
population to be transferred there. First, they would have to
slow down cloning to a reasonable number and that would destroy succession if done hastily. Even with maximum ware-
housing capacity, they could live for a maximum of ten earth
years.

"Lately, the MANTA frequently discussed the problem with
his son. In a moment of inspiration, the son said, 'Father, what
if we combined the two theories? Two negations result in an

affirmation; this is a known law in mathematics. Perhaps, Father, the two inapplicable theories contain applicable and combinable parts.' The MANTA was amused by the youth's optimism. Something inside him, though, was telling him he should study his son's suggestion in detail. The MANTA had the feeling that, some day, a solution would be found.

"The time available for study and experimentation was limited. Some of the problems that emerged needed centuries to be solved! The solution given primary consideration that moment was the construction of a huge spaceship that would be completely autonomous, recycling its own water and oxygen. About 10,000 Angels and 5,000 servant OMOHs would live there. This spaceship would look for a Promised Land and could take all the time it needed. This project was practical, but drew a terrible reaction from the masses.

"Others proposed a huge platform that could carry 1,000,000 souls. The scientists eliminated this option because this monstrous engineering feat was out of their technological reach. Moreover, the psychologists and the sociologists claimed that if something like that happened it would result in the development of major psychoses. The platform would be transformed into a huge madhouse in space."

"You mean, as in Star Trek, let's say," Larry interrupted.

"It was exactly that. This was better as a scenario and extremely pleasant as an idea, more so than a real ark.

"In the ark, though, the OMOHs would take the place of animals and, let's not forget it meant OMOHs with different specialties and colors. I see, David, that likening the spaceship with the Ark is a rather interesting comparison."

David smiled. "After all the dull things I've said, my dear friends and my lovely Natassa, I would like to declare I make no effort to portray KEROPS's history more beautifully or more ugly than it is. When I'm speaking about all this, I'm just a translator and a narrator. Still, sometimes, like when I spoke about the ark, I have to use free interpretation to be understood. I would like you to be tolerant because, as soon as something makes me nervous, I mix up the order of events I narrate.

"The language I'm translating is completely unknown to me. An inspiration of the Holy Spirit allows me to translate rather easily. If I were an agnostic, after what I have experienced, I would claim that something similar also happened to Jesus' disciples who spoke in different tongues."

Larry felt uncomfortable. He felt that David's words were aiming at him. He had to find a way out, so pretending to be jovial, he said, "Let's take a small break from all those sad events! I suggest we go have something to eat! Let's go to the Rotisserie d' Alsace; it's not far away!"

The others agreed. David added, "We'll drink some Kronenbourg to the good health and salvation of the Angels and we'll wish them to behave, some day, like human beings and not like winged demons!"

# Attempt to Negotiate

Since Brussels, Larry Keith and the rest of the team used Mario Canakis' Universal-Phone to communicate with their friends. Similarly, Theodore, a veteran of life's battles and an experienced man in such matters, used the mobile phone of his gardener's cousin from Antwerp! It was a most secure phone system. When they arrived in Paris, Larry woke up the Congo's "old wolf", Theodore, to inform him about everything that had happened. He wanted to warn him to stay away from the villa.

Theo was really surprised; so many things had happened in such a short time. Even Churchill would have been impressed. Never before, had so few people done so many things in such a short period of time. Larry had warned him. "Theo, my friend, it's certainly your turn, now. You'll have visitors."

Theo replied, "Hospitality, for the Greeks, is a divine command. Don't forget . . . Zeus, the leader of all gods, was also God of Hospitality. My home is open to everybody. I'll be in touch so we may co-ordinate our action. If it's possible, send me a fax-summary of David's narratives. You see, I'm hot with curiosity. Of course, after I've read them I'll burn them."

Everything seemed so calm, like the calm before a storm. The new challenge, though, was coming soon.

An incoming call followed Larry's phone call. A woman's voice politely asked Theo to visit the American Embassy. An embassy car would pick him up at home. Fortunately, he knew that his friends had left one of the tape recorders behind. So, he was aware of their level of knowledge. Larry had even described for him the appearance of the snitch from Metropole Hotel.

At the American Embassy he was accorded the welcome of an important guest. In the Ambassador's imposing office, Secretary of Defense Michael Donovan was waiting. Theodore, with the experience of almost a century of living, immediately understood the caliber of man he had to deal with. He had bright eyes, an aggressive aquiline nose, and a seductive smile. In other words, he had all the features of a bright leader. Sure enough, he surprised Theo even before the latter had taken a seat.

"With the talents your son and daughter have, Mr. Papadopoulos, how is it they've never thought of living in the United States?" Theodore knew the Secretary was using the unmistakable argument he, himself, would not be able to resist—flattery. He replied skillfully.

"If my children were to decide to live elsewhere, I'd rather see them come to my home country rather than yours! I think you would agree that it would be more reasonable." Theodore's repartee seemed to have broken the ice.

Donovan leaned towards him, put his elbows on the desk and, with gestures that underlined each word, said, "Dear Theo, you know, as do I, that for no particular reason, a problem has developed that, fortunately, hasn't yet received any publicity. Of course, some reporters have written about small aspects of the story, but I personally consider the case a slow-burning threat, a bomb ready to blow up."

Theo interrupted him. "As you want both of us to be sincere, I would like to know the absolute truth, coming from you. For instance, I'd like to know the truth about the explosion at Beni's cavern. I'm very curious. Anyway, I've got the right to know, because I'm the one who discovered the . . . "

"Sure . . . Sure . . . It's one of the reasons I've invited you here," Donovan intervened without letting Theodore complete his phrase with the word spacecraft. Their discussion was, perhaps, being recorded and, someone might ask for explanations later on.

"We've tried to clean it up," Donovan continued. "As if it were a dinosaur's skeleton, that is with finesse and religious respect."

"Oh . . . that's why there are so many priests in the area," Theo said with a tinge of sarcasm.

"Yes, there are many missions, both Catholic and Protestant. So, I was saying that everything was on the right track, when a sudden gas explosion occurred. It would seem that divine providence had decided to give this matter a final solution."

"So, divine providence destroyed it?" Theo pondered.

Although Donovan seemed bothered by the tone of irony in Theo's voice, he put his cards on the table.

"No, Theo . . . I'll call you Theo, it's quicker. We were the ones who blew it up, although it took off unharmed. We wanted to put an end to the story that, even if it looks like a fairy tale, could possibly arouse man's metaphysical curiosity and introduce a new era of religious wars. We tried to blow it up because we Americans wish to protect the world's peace and tranquillity, at any cost. We blew it up because it carried the seed of a diabolical theory that would attack the social fiber and arouse passions and fanaticism. Don't forget, Theo, the Nazis were telling stories about the lost Atlantis being somewhere in the Northern Sea. And, I suppose, you're aware of the results."

"Of course I am," Theo said. "But, that was completely crazy!"

"Still, despite all the bullshit, they almost ruled the whole world. If they'd won, we might by now, you and me, be working as some SS officer's slaves, in their fields."

"You probably would, but not I. Because of my age, I'd rather be in the traditional Heaven or in my bed, dying . . . Really, now that we got rid of the new, as you say, religion's Ten Commandments you shouldn't worry! What's troubling you? The weapon of the crime doesn't exist anymore."

"Theo, we are not here to fight. We are here to coordinate our actions to neutralize the rest. I want you as an ally. David was and remains your protégé. I respect that, because I'm aware of the whole story that began many decades ago. Also, as I'm certain that you've got contacts with him, I'm asking you to convince him to show up here, with Larry Keith and the women."

"Are there any guarantees?" the cunning Theo asked, pretending to be anxious.

"Of course, there are! You'll receive a document when you are ready to leave here. I guarantee they shall, all four of them, receive new passports; in addition, two million dollars for David, and two million dollars for Larry Keith.

"Don't be so unfair to the ladies. Don't forget they're no more the weaker sex! Any way, all of this seems fine to me. But how are they supposed to settle with the churches that have put a price on their heads?"

The Secretary leaned back and took a deep breath. "So, you also know this? Really, before I met you I didn't imagine you were so well informed. My aides misjudged your talents!"

Theo interrupted him. "You're giving them a new identity and fortune, while the Holy See in collaboration with the Islam groups will offer them eternal life! Could you explain this incongruity to me? If they are to die, how are they supposed to live rich?"

"Theo, we're discussing this very point right now, and I think that our proposal will be accepted. The price the religious groups put on their heads shall be given to David and Larry themselves, not to the informers. This would be in addition to our own offer, under the condition they remain quiet, of course."

Theo wanted to know what the head bounty was. "Total amount?"

"Exactly twelve million dollars! As you can see, it's a respectable sum. Nobody could pretend indifference unless he is an idiot."

Eight million dollars coming from the churches! A fantastic sum! The Devil himself had never been outlawed with such a price on his head.

Despite his age, Theo had some kind of intellectual explosions, what we call inspiration. At completely irrelevant moments, bright ideas came to him, giving solutions where everybody thought there could not be any. The same thing happened now. During the short break they had, for Theo to take his medicine and a cup of coffee, Theo felt only one solution could bridge the different interests and save his friends from certain death.

"Mr. Secretary . . . "

"Michael, to my friends and collaborators."

"Michael, my son, I feel tired. You understand, my energies are abandoning me. I would like you to know before you leave that you've succeeded in convincing me." Donovan smiled in relief. Theo noticed that and continued.

"To be against the Secretary of Defense that controls the whole planet and, at the same time, have all the religions on your back, looks like pure madness or suicide!"

"I absolutely agree with your thinking, Theo. It is indeed useless to hide because, sooner or later, an end shall be given and it would be their physical annihilation. The era of David and Goliath is over. Please, arrange things to finish as soon as possible. I've learned to reward those who help me, and I understand it would be insulting to try to bribe a proud Greek. So, I shall reward your good intentions with some top secret information."

Theo, without showing his deep interest in what Donovan had for him, just put on his good-hearted smile.

"They've found enamel on the Moon, in a mineral, recently."

Theo, pretending to miss the point, just said, "Thanks! I don't understand much about astronomy. He got up with the help of his ebony cane that was a present from a Uele tribe chief. He also picked up the small masculine handbag he had rested on the desk. In the bag was a very sensitive electronic recorder that functioned during his entire meeting with Donovan.

"My son," Theodore told the Secretary, "tell them to take me to the Commission, to my son's, because there's nobody at home now. We'll meet again very soon. At my request."

Near the office door stood a short, swarthy man with a thick moustache and a beer belly.

"He must be the informer," Theo thought and walked by him without showing the anger he felt at that moment.

Before going to see his son, Theo went to his secretary's office and asked to be left alone for a few minutes. He used the gardener's telephone to call Canakis. He quickly asked for the hotel fax number and informed the team that they would receive a very, very important message. He would send it coded, of course. In exchange, he asked again for a summary of the newer narrative.

That same evening, the informer received his "thirty pieces of silver" and handed over the tape he had stolen the night they had searched the villa. Donovan took his companions, the American Ambassador and the Cardinal of Paris, to dinner at the Tour d' Argent.

"Michael, my son, our common interests oblige us to be sincere with each other. You have been telling me in many details about the discussion you had with Theodore Pap . . . "

"Papadopoulos! I don't see why they persist in having such complicated surnames . . . those Greeks!"

The Cardinal continued, "Are you certain, my son, this cunning old man was convinced? Otherwise we will have to take some urgent measures against him too."

"In God's name!" Michael shouted, "In God's name! At this moment, he's the only known connection between them and us. If we destroy the bridge, what might follow could be catastrophic. We'll lose contact! Larry Keith and David Mason are terribly bright and inventive persons. Don't you see that the whole world is hunting them, yet nobody can find them? If they sense that they're in danger, they will certainly use the ultimate weapon they've got — David's tapes. And the consequences will be those of a world war!"

"Michael, my son, I want us to speak with our cards laid on the table, as we are not restrained by official rules. I would like to know your personal opinion, not as Secretary but as Donovan, concerning this affair, given, of course, the information you have."

"Your Eminence," the Secretary replied with an unusually somber expression on his face, I will confess to you, now. Just like in a real confession, I need to be alone with you!" The Ambassador looked at his watch. "Oh! I almost forgot. Please excuse me for not having dessert with you. I have a very important meeting with a government official."

The diplomat's withdrawal facilitated the discussion. "Yes, Your Eminence . . . Just like you in the Vatican, we know it is all authentic. Everything is just like the twosome, Larry-David, says. The injury caused the verbal diarrhea which is nothing but the description of another world."

"A world that existed or one in the future? If things are correct, as you say, then what does the enamel found on the Moon and at Beni's spacecraft mean?"

Donovan scratched his head uncertain how to respond. "Indeed, those are incompatible events. What's strange is that, according to David's description, there are technological achievements that might have revolutionary applications in our own lives. On the one hand they might harm religion, and you've got your reasons to be afraid, but on the other, they can better life on our planet, too.

"The problem is to know how we'll manage to combine the incompatible events in order to form the complete picture of the problem. Then, it could be possible to neutralize this affair in its entirety."

The digestive liquor they sipped had been delicious. It was already about two o'clock in the morning when they walked out on the street. The Cardinal's limo took him to the mansion, and Donovan's aide drove him to the Embassy.

While the two men were enjoying their dinner, Theodore was lying in bed, his eyes wide open. He prioritized the problems facing him, with David's case on top of the list. "If I try to help them, I will succeed in becoming the next victim, and that might extend to my children. Sooner or later, they'll be tracked down and killed. Would it be possible for me to save them by bringing their hunters, suddenly, under the lights of publicity?"

When he was at the Embassy, he was inspired by a wonderful idea that was now beginning to take shape. He had to develop the idea. "If I succeed in this, then I shall succeed in bringing the story of KEROPS to the forefront, and I will be ready to die happy," he thought.

Mario Canakis, this "fruit of uncertain taste" that invited himself to join the band, was the lever that would move the plan forward. Theodore's plan was a journalistic ambush. Canakis would make enough copies of the tapes and send them to the most important international news networks. At the same time, he would publicize everything. He would cover the scientific aspects, without any mention of the wild pursuit. Through e-mail, David's complete narrative would be published as it is.

Theo knew that publicity would guarantee the lives of his friends, but was still not so sure about his life and that of his family. He had to give this plan further thought.

Nobody slept that night! Even the Cardinal did not go to bed after the prayer. He rushed into his office and reported to his superior.

"We have to cancel the bounty we secretly placed on their heads. Michael Donovan told me, and I think he is right, that we cannot afford to be careless. A corpse is a serious matter and we are about to have five of them on our hands. I think, before we reach a new strategy, we should review again, in every detail, all the information we have on them."

"I agree. This is what I have been doing even without your assessment. I consider it my duty, so I have reached a certain conclusion."

The Cardinal seemed to breathe easier. "I am listening."

"What would you say if you learned that David Mason and Larry Keith are crazy about abnormal sex with women?" said the voice of the head of security at the Vatican, to whom they all reported. "What a humiliation! Can you imagine? Such important scientists to be that depraved . . . "

"What do you mean? What are you getting at? How could that help us?" The Cardinal was, indeed, surprised by the manner of his superior and the rough language he was using. "If I understand you well enough, you ask that we make sure that they become morally exposed so that they would lose their prestige."

"At this moment, if they gave a speech, for example, they are credible and respected and, thus, dangerous. There is nothing reprehensible about them. I agree with you! We have to ridicule them, at any price! They would lose their access to the media."

"Wise! This is exactly what I mean. We first have to find them, though."

"I have learned they were in Paris! My informers have spotted Canakis and are following him. But it is not necessary to find them. One of my advisors, who will certainly become Cardinal if he continues to serve the Church so well, has the perfect answer. We will find David and Larry's doubles and film them having sex with underage boys and girls."

"Divine inspiration! The Holy Ghost must have inspired your assistant. What is the Holy Father's opinion?"

"The Holy Father does not wish to be part of secular affairs, especially after the failure of his intervention . . . you know, because of the Secretary!"

"Of course! I apologize for mentioning his Holy name! I don't think I should announce . . . "

"In God's name . . . Absolutely no one is to know. Except for the Secretary of State."

"I believe," said the French Cardinal, "that implementation of this plan . . . "

"Project Venus! I think this name would be most propitious."

"Yes! Thus, we will also not get involved in their murders."

The other man laughed. "This is nothing. Don't forget we shall also save us the reward's eight million dollars. Ha, ha, ha . . ."

"Oh, yes! I would like to have a part of this for the restoration of Notre Dame."

"We will see what can be done about this. God Bless You, Saintly Brother. It is most urgent that we coordinate things with the Americans. I think you should call the Secretary and request his help. We have to find the doubles."

The devilish Security Officer of the Vatican hung up the phone, feeling very content. David, Larry, and Mario did not know it, but they were already the targets of the Vatican. Only if God was with them could they avoid the humiliation that was prepared for them.

# Last Minute Rescue

The MANTA and his genius son arrived at the only possible answer—an answer that they could turn into reality only if they could reach and use the most advanced technology in their possession. It was a nearly impossible task.

Generally, they would need to create an atmosphere around satellite ANOL, as soon as possible, in order to provide a colony for the Angels. At the same time, they would need to dispatch several thousand robots and mechanical rodents to burrow huge holes to be used as shelters for the Angels of Operation Space Immigration.

Of course, at the center of ANOL they would create a spherical cave where they would set up their Military Headquarters and a station for the MANTA, their aides and a selection of the greatest accomplishments in technology and biology. MANTA knew that even if the plan was not completely successful, at least a nucleus of Angels would be saved who would then withstand any kind of challenge. The purpose of

169

the plan was to enable other worlds in the universe to learn about the history and the achievements of the Angels.

When the public heard of the decision on the plan and that implementation of the plan was already under way, they revolted. And MANTA, upon seeing the public reaction, ordered the immediate interruption of the work and the search for another solution acceptable to the masses.

"David," Larry interrupted, "before you begin telling us about the final decision they took, I think we need to clarify certain issues of substance to the Angels. I am afraid that if you move on to technical matters, you will be unable to return to these issues."

David, who in the meantime had halted the narration in order to quench his thirst and to caress Natassa's beautiful face, casually remarked, not hiding his own amusement. "I agree, as long as I can choose the first subject. And this will have to do with sex . . . how about it?" There was a unanimous agreement. There was something that had to be cleared up.

"Sex as a means of mutual attraction for the purpose of pro-creation was completely useless. Reproduction was secured through cloning, and therefore, physical attraction was unnecessary. But the Angels were aware that pleasure derived from sexual contact surpassed in its intensity every other form of satisfaction. So, they did not dismiss it; they just did not have the best solution.

"I imagine the orgies they organized," Barbara said chewing on a golden apricot. "They would be so satisfied that they would fly without wings."

David continued, "To better understand it, it is necessary that I educate you on the physiology and methodology of sex as it applies to all creatures in the universe."

Larry threw in his two cents.

"David, with your permission, I will undertake the lesson on the physiology of sex, regarding the earth, since I am very well informed. Of course, I will make sure my presentation is popularized, but not crude." They all agreed, and Larry began the lesson.

"In the lowest part of the spinal cord, we have a primitive Sexual Center that, in addition to sexual desires, also stimulates and controls functions such as urinating and defecating. So, if this center was out of control, any of those functions would take place instantaneously, including ejaculation. Fortunately, we also have the Superior Centers, the corresponding centers of the brain that block the inadvertent and joyful activities of the spinal centers."

Barbara, who was listening carefully, remarked, "Larry, perhaps that's why when somebody is hanged to die, he ejaculates. Perhaps he loses the use of the upper centers."

"Great example, Barbara. Thank you! This proves exactly what I have said. In fact, Chinese Mandarins simulated a condition that resembled hanging in order to become sexually aroused."

David jumped in to halt the discussion. "Ok, that's as far as you go. Now, it is my turn. I do not know the scientific terms and I know of only one way to communicate this information. I will describe a house of prostitution for the Angels.

"You would be disappointed, ladies and gentlemen. Whorehouses were grand institutions, equipped with the most bioelectric means. The peculiarity was the total absence of prostitutes."

They were all speechless. Bordellos—without prostitutes? That's complete nonsense—like pubs without alcohol. Larry asked David to describe the service provided by these centers to the clients since these places were not familiar to humans.

"Let's say I am a customer and walk into one of these institutions; what happens next?"

David anticipated the challenge. "Everybody has a box that he had rented at the entrance. He was provided with a comfortable lounging chair whose back continued upwards and formed a light helmet, similar to those worn by bicyclists. At about the middle of the chair was a smooth extension, which touched the naked skin of the person using the chair. The customer, reclining comfortably, placed a collar with two bio-electrodes around his neck and put on the helmet.

"Pressing a small lever on the arm of the chair, the customer started the mechanism of sexual pleasure and erotic enhancement. The smooth extension touching the spine transmitted laser rays that caused a temporary interruption of the lower sexual center from the brain. That, naturally, produced a stream of stimuli to male or female sex organs. Simultaneously, the two bio-electrodes touching the head transmitted strong currents that flooded the centers of vision, hearing and smell with stimuli of a sexual nature. As a result, the muscles over the customer's entire body underwent continuous spasms."

Barbara and Natassa were very impressed by David's lively description. Larry agreed that it had to be something incredible, like a bioelectric masturbation. "Didn't they eventually become too used to these stimuli and therefore receive less pleasure?" Larry asked.

"I was just about to say that, Larry. The frequent visits to these institutions resulted in the reduction of erotic pleasure, so the Angels resorted to other therapies, less angelic and more human."

Larry, who was often unbearable with his comments, took the opportunity to have some laughs. "They went back to womanizing," he said innocently. But David was not amused with his friend's comments.

"You can keep on ridiculing, but their alternative was no different than that of humans. Let's be serious. I am talking to you, Larry, because you are a doctor. I am sure you would like to learn something about heart diseases."

"That's where we should have started," Barbara said. "Really, did they do what we do? Heart transplants?"

"What we do, my friends, are child's play in comparison. Angels never used bypass operations and balloons, and even heart transplants had become old methods a few years after they became established."

"You will drive us nuts!" Barbara said. "Then, what did they do?"

"On KEROPS's bright side lived a creature that resembled our crocodile. Only, it had six feet and two hearts. There was a small heart—let's say, an auxiliary one—and an injection turbo, just as some motors have double carburetors. When the animal was in a tranquil state, then only the auxiliary heart functioned, which was identical to the Angels' heart. Its healthy state depended upon the cardiac muscle's sufficient blood irrigation, just as our own does."

"You mean there was a coronary function," Larry added.

"In a way, yes. Yet, there was also a powerful heart. It functioned when the monster that weighed ten tons was in full activity. That heart didn't have coronary arteries, let's say. There weren't even very many blood vessels to feed it."

"But, this is totally irrational!" Barbara protested.

"No, Barbara! You're wrong, because the walls of that heart, the myocard, were like a sponge. The same blood that circulated also fed the heart. There was no dependence on separate blood vessels. Nourishment was direct! Like a sponge!"

"Don't tell me they transplanted that monster's enormous heart?"

"No, Natassa! Don't be impatient, my sweetheart! Don't jump to conclusions. They certainly didn't do so! The biologists had discovered the DNA genes that corresponded to the creation of the young heart and managed to transfer them, as genetic material, to the last generation of the Angels."

Larry eyes were half shut. "But, I think that our turtles have such a heart! How come our own scientists never thought of creating humans with immortal hearts?"

"If cardiac surgeons could hear you, you would pay with your hide," Barbara said laughing.

"I would like to ask, though, if my statement makes any sense, didn't this affect the operation of the other organs?" Larry asked again.

"Absolutely none!"

David stopped talking and opened his eyes. They could all

see he was troubled. "Darling, would you like to eat something? I see you're very puzzled," Natassa offered.

Ever since his injury, David had developed a premonition ability he had from childhood. It had often helped him avoid disasters. Now, something inside him, like an alarm going off, made him feel insecure.

"Guys, don't you think Canakis is rather late? I feel something's going on. We'd agreed to keep in touch regularly, but too many hours have passed and no word from him."

"David, I think that, for safety reasons, we've got to activate the emergency plan to disperse," Larry said. Each one of them would go in a different direction. They would sleep in different hotels. The following morning, at 10 o'clock, they would meet at the Cathedral of the city they happened to be in. They prepared their few things in haste and walked out of the hotel in ten-minute intervals.

Barbara and Natassa, wearing provocative make-up, left separately. One went down the Champs Elysées and pretended to be a hooker. The other one went down Général Vagrams Boulevard. David, after he bought some French magazines at the reception desk, found a spot in a bistro from where he had a view of the hotel's entrance. He seemed very interested in the content of the magazines, but this was his camouflage. Finally, Larry crossed the Champs Elysées Avenue and went into Etoile's Drugstore.

Less than a quarter of an hour later, Canakis arrived, by taxi, at the hotel. He paid the driver and rushed in. He was carrying a large package that did not seem particularly heavy. A black Mercedes with darkened windows parked in front of the bistro where David sat.

"They're following him, for sure. So, they're aware he's collaborating with us. It would be terrible if he fell into their hands." Nobody came out of the Mercedes. They were probably just observing the unsuspecting Canakis, who reappeared after a few minutes.

On his part, Canakis, realizing they were all gone and sensing danger, left the package with the bell captain and pretended he was expecting someone at the bar. He had to concentrate. He was now assuming that some imminent danger had forced them to urgently activate the emergency plan. Uncertain as to what to do next, he noticed two couples that were waiting with their luggage, ready to leave.

He walked casually to the reception desk. He pointed with his eyes at the waiting guests. "Are they going to the airport?" He was hoping that lady luck would smile at him. "Yes . . . a hotel bus will take them there. Do you . . . "

"Yes! A friend of mine is arriving soon."

"Our bus is going to Charles de Gaulle Airport. Where are you going?"

"What a pleasant coincidence!" Canakis feigned enthusiasm. "Thank you very much!" Two minutes later, the bus with its five passengers was on its way to the airport.

In the black Mercedes, the discussion was animated. Canakis and the two couples, was it the entire band or not?

"I didn't expect it would be so easy to spot them," said the Vatican's man. "The computer informed me the two women, Barbara and Natassa are beautiful and tall while . . . " he said into his mobile phone. Father Emmanuel, in the ephemeral world known as Agent H, reached the hotel's dispatcher at the airport.

"I'm bringing five clients from the Elysées-Etoile, but they're strangers and I can't understand them. Where am I supposed to take them?"

The dispatcher at Charles de Gaulle Airport replied with no uncertainty in his voice. "Cut the crap, Daniel! You know very well there are four Australians, not five, and they're leaving on Singapore Airlines. What's your problem? Are you drunk?"

The answer enraged Father Emmanuel. "They've played us like fools," he shouted furiously. "Canakis is certainly on that bus. We must get him! At any price! He becomes more and more dangerous. He wouldn't mind writing an article or a broadcast piece and spoil everything! It's my decision. I am ordering Canakis's elimination! Immediate arrest or if no alternative, death!"

The black Mercedes picked up speed swiftly to catch up with the hotel bus. Through his mobile phone, Emmanuel ordered someone to go to the hotel and find Canakis's package. Its contents had to be checked in detail. They would notify the French police that the package contained illegal drugs, and the police would do the rest.

A few minutes after he got on the bus, Canakis swore out loud. "Damn it! What bad luck!" Daniel, the driver, asked him if he had a problem.

"My wallet! I've lost my wallet with my papers in it!"

"It's impossible for us to return to the hotel, sir, because the plane takes off in two hours and we need 45 minutes to get there."

"But, I'm not leaving! I'm not taking any plane! I'm supposed to meet a friend who is arriving now in order to take him to your hotel!"

There was a collective sigh of relief. Daniel had the answer. "I'll drop you off at a gas station and we'll go on. You can go back by taxi. What is your friend's name and airline? I will notify him."

"Thanks, don't worry about that. I can call. It's a brilliant idea! Thank you!"

As they were stopping at the gas station, the black Mercedes overtook them and sped ahead.

"Let's get to the airport before they do," Father Emmanuel said to the driver. "By the time they arrive we'll have the reception ready for them. Don't forget the orders! Elimination at any cost! We'll all have the same target!" While Emmanuel was giving instructions and feeling good about how things turned out, the driver noticed in the rear view mirror that the hotel bus was not behind them. He hesitatingly interrupted his boss.

"Father, I've lost the target! They must have stopped somewhere."

"They've stopped?" Emmanuel wondered. "Was there an

accident? What in hell is going on? Stop!" The black Mercedes stopped at the curb and the driver lifted the hood up to indicate mechanical failure.

Without knowing it, Canakis had escaped the trap his hunters had set up for him. He was unaware that only he among his teammates was targeted for execution in cold-blood.

From his chair at the bistro, David had watched the marvelous way Mario had exploited the presence of the two couples. But David did not realize that the black Mercedes was following the bus. So, he abandoned his shelter. He thought he did not need to be concerned about his friend's fate. Valuable, trustworthy and cunning, a precious friend, indeed.

David was thinking about the big but light package the journalist had brought to the hotel. He could not resist the temptation. He took a long walk in the neighborhood, window shopping and stopping for a quick sandwich, and then made his way back to the hotel.

He hardly had stepped into the lobby when he saw the bell captain and a middle-aged gentleman opening the package. Unnoticed, he walked past the elevators and into the dead-end corner behind a column that hid him from public view. From there, he could hear what was discussed. He could also see another hotel guest who had approached the two and was watching them intently.

"Sleepers . . . a box with plastic sleepers for the beach," said the middle-aged man with disappointment.

"Inspector, " said the bell captain, "What am I to do?"

"We'd been informed the box contained drugs," said the inspector. "See that it is repackaged and do everything yourself; not a word about the police and the rest. What do these five do, anyway?

"Businessmen, general trade. That's what the papers state." As he was leaving, the inspector mumbled, "If I ever catch the one who played this prank . . . "

David walked up to the first floor and, from the phone in the hallway, asked the bell captain to pick up some luggage from the fifth floor. When he was sure that the man who could recognize him was on his way to the fifth floor, David went to the lobby like any other guest and walked out as unnoticed as when he had entered. Once more, David had the opportunity to admire Canakis's street smarts. With the package, he was creating an alibi that, unfortunately, was no longer useful. They were already following him.

# The Trap

The conspirators' rendezvous was at Nassau. To be more precise, they met at the Sheraton Hotel on Paradise Island, that famous long and narrow piece of land with the most beautiful beaches in the world.

Michael Donovan and Cardinal Patrick met with the movie producer and movie pimp, Aslan Mohammed. The latter was a Colombian national of unknown origins. He was ready to collaborate with anybody, in any dark affair, if it meant money for him. Totally unscrupulous, he had managed to monopolize the production of movies for sadists, sadomasochists and pedophiles.

Michael Donovan knew that Aslan was once the most wanted by the police, but he was the most fitting collaborator for Operation Venus. He had arrived first, with two fellows that, obviously, had never been in the tropical islands before. They seemed lost and their clothes looked strange in the tropical climate. They looked funny wearing ties in that laid back, casual environment.

The two big hulks had obviously been hired as VIP body-guards or executors! Of course, if anyone took away their sunglasses, combed their hair properly and shaved their moustache, he would laugh at the site. They would look like seals!

A few hours later, two other men arrived, properly dressed up for the occasion. One looked like David Mason himself. The other one seemed to be Larry Keith's twin brother. The resemblance was astonishing!

The selection had been done professionally. An ad was published by several talent agencies. "Two hundred thousand dollars for anyone able to find two men with the following features." A detailed description followed. Furthermore, the ad specified that the same amount would be given to each person selected for the TV advertisement. In ten days, about 212 doubles had applied. Two were chosen.

Of course, it was likely that the two lucky ones were in danger. There was a chance they would be murdered after the job was done to eliminate any leaks. People who knew the two finalists could swear they were not in danger for the simple reason that they had been selected for their low intelligence and had come from psychiatric institutions. They were strictly sex toys. The psychiatrist that had brought them had Michael Donovan's absolute confidence. Through proper treatment at the proper time he could transform those obeying creatures into sex-maniacs, human looking beasts. They had not been allowed to masturbate because their hands were tied for the past ten days. They were primed for a porno film.

Seated like good school-students, the doubles, with their hands tied behind them, waited patiently for inspection. With no particular warning, the Secretary and the Cardinal went to suite 413. The door was half-open and, they could see David's and Larry's photographs over the heads of the doubles. It was easier to make comparisons this way. They carefully examined the doubles and then smiled with satisfaction. The Secretary approached the doctor.

"Doctor Polydefkis, you've really done a good job! Your homeland is grateful!"

"The Church as well," Cardinal Patrick added, shaking his hand. "God shall help us to put an end to this blasphemy!"

"Thank you, gentlemen. They are under my absolute control," said the doctor. "They move and act like remote control robots. I guarantee you that!"

That same night, at the Crystal Palace, the hotel with the famous Galaxy suite that costs an incredible thirty thousand dollars a day, the two distinguished officials and the doctor enjoyed the thrill of baccarat and roulette, until dawn. Of course, it was a false enjoyment, as the money did not come out of their pockets but from government and Vatican secret funds.

The fat pimp, who was staying at the Columbia Hotel, used a purple, six-door limo, at 10 o'clock in the morning, to bring his white and tender merchandise to the Sheraton.

Four gorgeous creatures, two girls and two boys, aged between eight and ten, came out of the luxurious car. They were joyful. Manuel Gomez was the name written on one of the seven passports the awful pimp carried with him.

"Take good care of my nieces and nephews," he told the employee at the reception desk. His bulging eyes underlined his words. He immediately laughed to show the two golden teeth he had had repaired when he was broke, in Cairo.

"Suite 414 is booked for the children, and 415 is for you, Mr. Gomez." He dragged his short, fat feet with difficulty and got into the elevator. The doubles in 413, the nieces and nephews in 414, himself in 415, and the doctor in 412. Donovan's and Cardinal Patrick's room numbers were kept secret. To be precise, Mohammed and the doctor thought the two were also staying at the Crystal Palace.

The troupe was already on the stage. The veteran, Aslan Mohammed, would lift the curtains. He had no assistant. The fewer who knew, the better. Donovan, Patrick and Aslan's meeting was short and fruitful.

"Boss, I only want one thing from you. Just keep quiet, because even your presence here is senseless. When I take something over, success is assured, as long as the bonus is assured, as we've agreed! They listened to him without a comment and handed him a briefcase containing one hundred thousand dollars. They showed him another one, containing the same amount.

"Before you board the plane to Colombia, you'll also get this one," Michael Donovan said with a forced smile. Cardinal Patrick just nodded to indicate he agreed.

When the pimp left, the Cardinal asked the Secretary, "Your impressions, please." The Secretary moved his head from side to side. "If Barabas was like Mohammed, Jesus would certainly have been saved."

Patrick could not resist a long, intense laugh. The Secretary's joke was on target. Michael continued, "It will be a good deed to finally rid the world from such a temporarily, useful son of a bitch. I've made up my mind to send him to Hell and, certainly, the Devil himself won't find it easy to deal with him. If we let him live, he'll blackmail us!"

"Do as God tells you, for the world's sake," The Cardinal whispered and crossed himself. "Amen!" he whispered. So did Michael.

Perversions, cruelty and fetishes took their turns on the half-hour video. The videotape surpassed all expectations. If there were a Nobel Prize for perversion, Aslan would have earned it. If that category existed in the Guinness Book of Records, this film would be classified as the most perverse, the most sadistic and most pedophilic orgy of all times. When invited to the show, the Cardinal declined. He did not want to watch a single scene.

"I concur with your decision," he told Donovan.

Michael Donovan watched the entire monstrous tape to make sure it was completed. When he exited the room, he seemed lost. His mouth and his eyelids stuck open. He regained his composure in a few minutes and grabbed the cellular phone to call the two executioners who were passing their time at the Casino.

"Go!" was the only instruction the Secretary gave them. He put the phone in his pocket and without informing Cardinal Patrick he went to bed. The video had made him nauseous, and he was emotionally exhausted.

Some time before the instruction to kill was issued, an ageless old man got close to the two killers at the Casino. Discreetly and at his own risk, pretending to be drinking, he followed them to the Sheraton Hotel. He almost had a heart attack when he came upon his own son!

"Larry, my son," he managed to whisper. But the man he was looking at walked by him without a word. It was as if he had not heard him. Then the old man recognized David Mason, who was following the first man. He instinctively tried to speak to him. "David, please!" Again, no reply.

Puzzled, he looked closer and observed the way they moved and walked. You can only fool a father briefly. The two men were doubles.

"Damn it! Two doubles of two friends, sought by police. This can't be a simple coincidence. Something's going on! I've got to talk to Larry." He walked to the phone and called Brussels.

"I'd like to speak with Mr. Theodore . . . ."

"He's in the hospital."

"I'll try again later." He thought, "I have got to inform them." Armed with a determination and a few hundred dollars, he got the doubles' real names and Manuel Gomez's platinum card number from a clerk at the reception desk.

The next day, when he realized everybody had disappeared,

he packed his bags and, with the information he had gathered, he decided to meet the doubles again, to determine what exactly was their role. "My son may underestimate my talents," he was thinking, "but I have the obligation to protect my only child."

"May I help you?" offered the operator.

"Menomoni Street 122, Saint Petersburg! Can you please give me the phone number?" He waited, in no hurry. He had plenty of time at his disposal. The 747 for Miami was leaving later, at 2:04 p.m.

Jonathan Keith was puzzled by the operator's response. "Do you have a relative in there?" the woman asked.

"Where, in there?" he said. "I don't understand."

"The psychiatric institution."

Jonathan was speechless for a moment. "No! Why do you ask? What does it have to do with what I've asked you?"

"But, sir, the address you gave me is that of a psychiatric institution! Whom exactly would you like to speak with? A doctor or a patient?"

Jonathan Keith was literally lost. "They must have registered a false address. Anyway, I'll check the details. I might get lucky. Who knows?"

The familiar voice came over the public address system, "Passengers to Miami are kindly requested to go through passport control."

# Desperate
# Measures

David's unbearable headache, accompanied by bouts of nausea, troubled David and Natassa once more.

At the Place Odéon, they had found a hotel—an oasis for outlaws—that demanded no attention from its customers as long as one demanded nothing from it. They were very satisfied that, for once, they would have some tranquillity. They settled in as fast as they could because it was urgent for David to unload. Natassa prepared the recorders. David had already folded his hands on his stomach and closed his eyes. The effects of the cocktail had started. Silence occupied the room.

"The Defense Council that had fallen into inaction because there were no security threats had been hastily reconvened. It was only reasonable that MANTA's loyalists would have the leading role. The Council's mission would be very different from the one it had at the time of the rebellion of the slave-robots. Besides those who responded proposing salvation plans for the planet, there was a group of astrophysicists that asked for and got the authorization to meet with the MANTA and his advisors to review an Extremely Secret Report, with the initials EX.SE.REP.

"The group of astrophysicists, considered heretics in their field, had had many run-ins with the authorities. The MANTA met their request with suspicion because they had asked that no other astrophysicist should be present at the meeting. He finally received them at the floating governmental convention building, in an auxiliary room. At the beginning, the MANTA used firm language.

"Gentlemen, it is the first time that I accept to attend an astrophysical convention without receiving a study in advance. I shall ask you to be succinct."

"Hax was a genius in his field. When the MANTA's speech was over, Hax got up, ordered the lights to be turned off, and drew attention to a huge lighted board where complex physics' plans and formulas appeared.

"He cleared his throat and, in the absolute darkness, said, 'Anyone who wishes to have the results of my team's research work is welcome to ask for them. He may study them and let me know if there is any possible mistake.'

"At the MANTA's order, the lights were turned on and he appeared amused.

"What is this study all about, Mr. Hax? What you have shown us is very impressive but rather confusing for non-specialists."

"Hax, maintaining his temper, replied, 'I can state with mathematical accuracy, that this comet can be destroyed three years before it reaches our planet.'

"The MANTA reacted. 'But, my friend, you are just repeating a proposal of the Ministry of Energy. They have suggested we should bomb the comet and, thus, destroy it. After studying our capabilities, this solution was proved ineffective because of the comet's dimensions and shape.'

"Hax interrupted him. 'Worthy leader, Great MANTA! I am not here to repeat old ideas and waste your precious time. The study I have shown you is about the installation of an electromagnetic field on planet EgXP. The killer-comet will pass very close to it, before our fatal rendezvous.'

"Interesting," the MANTA admitted. "Now tell me, Hax, is it doable?" Hax smiled with satisfaction sensing that the MANTA was almost convinced.

"Four hundred spacecraft with MAGNA load would leave under a coordinated plan to crash on EgXP's surface. This has to be done at exactly the moment the comet is two years' distance from the planet. If it is soaked with MAGNA, that planet's mass multiplies by thousands of times its existing gravity force. The deviation that will be caused to the comet, thanks to the new electromagnetic field, shall completely alter its trajectory. Indeed, I have calculated that this modification shall lead the comet to crash onto our sun, P. My colleagues also maintain that the comet will not even be visible to us — such will be the distance between the comet's trajectory and us."

"The MANTA was somber. He carefully listened to a new scientific rescue proposal that, of course, had to be studied and judged 'If all this, dear Hax, is possible, then I sincerely thank you from the depths of my heart. Your very effort itself, the huge scientific work you have performed is worth my praise. Until I make up my mind, take time to think through the details. Congratulations!' He stood up and everybody did the same.

'I shall take the whole study with me. We will meet again in a month in this same place.'

"When the career astrophysicists, Hax's opponents, learned about the proposal, they pretended to be impressed, but began checking it out with a tremendous zeal.

"Yes, the probability is eight percent, but should we risk the fate of a whole civilization? They were looking for a one hundred percent certainty.

"The MANTA's son, that young genius, did not fold his hands after the initial proposal he had made, and did not rest in the kudos offered by his friends. One day, without notifying anybody, he took the scientific work of the Astrophysicists Convention, the one that declared the planet destroyed after its collision with the comet, and went to study it.

"For two months he thoroughly reviewed the study with the help of his colleagues. All the electronic data, supported by many hundreds of thousands of details included in the study, backed the position of the pessimistic researchers. 'Unfortunately, they are right . . . we will not be able to avoid the hit,' he concluded bitterly.

"The reason he did the study was to ascertain the previously reported danger so that the entire planet was not going through convulsions for no reason at all. Now he was certain that there were no mistakes. He was ready to return the study and to abandon further work when he remembered a paragraph in small type, written in the final text.

"He reopened the convention papers and read, 'If KEROPS did not have a satellite, it would follow a different trajectory and would not face any substantial threat. The inter-relationship of the masses constitutes a critical factor . . .'

"The young man gasped at the possibility opened by this observation. Why try to take everybody to ANOL? If ANOL were to be taken away, KEROPS would not be destroyed. So, the idea of using ANOL to escape was embedded in his mind. He pretended he had discovered something and called a meeting of his most trusted advisors, including HAX.

"He announced his plan. 'Everybody, pay attention! We will study the effects on our planet as if our natural satellite were not there any more.' The cunning young man did not mean the destruction of ANOL, but its departure. 'If we destroy ANOL, we save ourselves,' he explained to his astounded father, whom he convinced with the plans he presented.

"His father hugged him, kissed him and allowed him to use his own secret archives for this study. 'I have at your disposal, my son, all the information available on our planet. Information is power. There are no powerful and powerless people. There are informed and uninformed people."

"The works aiming at ANOL's destruction began immediately. They sent 100,000 Cut-Eyed workers who drilled huge tunnels with the assistance of the mechanical rats. They also took advantage of the satellite's natural caverns. Finally, they would place a large quantity of liquefied, explosive plasma in the heart of the satellite. The mixture was the same as the one that caused the dry volcanoes of KOX to erupt.

"At the proper moment, they would fire it so that either ANOL would be launched on an orbit far away from their planet, or it would be destroyed, an event of minor importance on planet KEROPS. That was the theoretical plan. Yet, it was the plan that served to cover the real one.

"In reality, they were preparing ANOL for the big journey.

"Day by day, imperceptibly at the beginning, then more clearly, the MANTA witnessed his son increase his influence upon the planet's administrative network. Wherever he went, the inhabitants received his son warmly, while they observed only a formal respect towards the father. Jealousy is always contagious. It was inevitable, even for the undisputed leader, to acquire a rival in power. The rivalry was perhaps not so much about exercise of power, but more in its essential meaning, that is, affective influence. Influence is soon is transformed into power.

"The coup de grâce to their relationship was given during the speech he gave at the annual anniversary of the Slaughter in the Bright Valley. In the speech addressed by the Chair of the Science Academy, the very old man had the unfortunate inspiration to refer to the father's promise."

"The one whose plan shall save us, is the young MANTA. Lucky father! You must be filled with excitement that the new MANTA –SAVIOR is a relative of yours! We all expect you to fulfill your promise!" The acclamations that immediately followed froze MANTA's blood. Although everybody expected, at that moment, his son to be proclaimed new leader, the father replied cunningly.

'The planet's bureaucracy would literally prevent my son from realizing his supreme effort. When the salvation plan is completed he shall immediately be proclaimed MANTA-SAV-IOR!'

"The son became suspicious when he noticed the way his father tried to avoid fulfilling his promise. Information is power, his father had told him and he was right. The MANTA's son had this big secret he had not announced to anyone, including his father.

"All the theories deal in probabilities. His was no exception. The only way to attain salvation was "THE SATELLITE TO BECOME A SPACE ARK." The son, with his brilliant mind, had already imagined the creation of a new independent world with new priorities and, why not, a new social order—an active society, based on moral principles, not on animal prosperity. He was already informed about the truth, thanks to the secret files. He had shivered while reading about the cruel ways Angels faced their enemies and transformed them into animal slaves. All this must change. Everybody has the right to live.

"The son secretly met with Hax, whose idea had been rejected by his father's loyalists. He also secretly met with the Chair of the Defense Council who, in reality, had control over the immense efforts for ANOL's transformation, it's destruction.

"Genius is the other face of madness. This was true of MANTA- junior. All his activity, from now on, would be aimed at the implementation of the following project.

"ANOL was to be transformed into an independent and safe shelter for several thousands or millions of known Angels who would use it to escape. They would use it as a super-spacecraft. Half of the tunnels had to be transformed into salvation-cells. The other half would contain the reactors needed to propel ANOL far from KEROPS's magnetic field. The MANTA's son and his collaborators would be hiding in the center, as would their staff of trusted leaders and representative samples of slaves.

"If there was a precise itinerary, if all this effort was aimed at travelling towards some precise location, then everything would have reasonable explanation. But, the new MANTA was to launch ANOL-spacecraft having less information than Columbus had when he decided to cross the Atlantic Ocean. The space adventure he prepared for himself and his collaborators was extremely dangerous.

"Of course, his tormented mind had already thought of retaliating against his father and all this useless, rusty society with no moral uplift, no dreams and no ideology at all. If the satellite were launched four days before the approach of the killer comet, Hax had assured him, then the planet would be saved. But, if it left later, then there would be no time at all for the comet to change its course. In that case, KEROPS would become part of the past, it would turn into stardust, taking with it millions of creatures! He had not told anything about that to avoid expected reactions, yet, inside him, he had decided to destroy his father and all those who were around him. Billions of useless souls!

"Hax, not receiving clear responses to important questions and thinking that the new MANTA was not necessarily rational, tried to influence the young man. 'No matter how much you dislike some people, you may not sentence them all to death,' he advised, whenever he had the opportunity to do so.

"ANOL's center would be arranged so that the headquarters, Niak, would be located in its huge, spherical, artificial cavern. This metallic, spherical submarine in ANOL's center would withstand exceptionally strong vibrations and would be outfitted with a cooling system that could reach almost absolute zero temperature in only six minutes. Thus, at launch moment, they would all fall into hibernation. This would be done very quickly to avoid crystallization of the liquid elements in their cells that would cause instantaneous death.

"According to the plan, automatic defrost procedure was to start when, for any reason, the speed started to drop. This

192 / The Last Dynasty of the Angels

could happen after hundreds or thousands of years. After defrost, they would be able to continue with their lives. This scenario had, of course, been studied so that it would provide the opportunity to survive under new and unknown conditions.

"Everybody knew that such a trip of a body with ANOL's dimensions, for an enormous duration, would mean a weight and volume increase for ANOL, due to the accumulation of millions of small meteorites on its surface. This was the reason why they 'planted' many small starcrafts on the surface. Yet, each one of them was equipped with a small mole, in standby position, that would drill a tunnel at a given moment's notice. Thus, the starcraft would become operational if and when needed.

"Information the MANTA continued to receive, either by his son or by other sources, reported on a completely different salvation plan, 'Simple undermining of ANOL aiming at its destruction by explosion when necessary.' What helped conceal the real work was ANOL's extremely rich soil in all minerals one could possibly need to achieve its transformation into a spacecraft. Of course, this multiplied the number of yellow, Cut-Eyed diggers, and Niak's headquarters had temporarily been transferred to the satellite.

"Natassa, I think my brain's cleared up!"

"At last . . . you got rid of that terrible headache again!"

David smiled "I'm afraid, Natassa, that I've transferred my headache to the old MANTA. An informer has just paid him a visit and brought him some upsetting, frightening news."

David, completely exhausted, turned his head to the side and, fell asleep, snoring, in his girlfriend's arms.

# The Roswell Mystery Revisited

The most important plant for the production of Mozzarella cheese in the USA is located in the small town of Roswell, New Mexico. Of course, one learns this when he visits the town. The reason to visit the town, though, has nothing to do with that fact.

Usually, one goes to see with his own eyes the spot where, on a day in July 1947, a mysterious event that left its imprint on the entire twentieth century took place. Fate often plays unusual tricks on us. In a picturesque place, where nothing special had ever happened, the tragedy of a space crash left its mark forever.

None survived the crash of that flying object. A study of the dead opened many wounds and created many questions that have never been answered convincingly.

The presence of Miss Brigitte Marcais in Roswell was absolutely accidental. She was very successful in her studies at Sorbonne University, in Paris, and her father fulfilled his promise of a 15-day trip to the USA. In the TWA aircraft, she met Chloe Moore, a beautiful lady who was accompanied by her father. They were very impressed by Brigitte and invited her to visit their town of 49,000 inhabitants, Roswell.

One of the curiosities in Roswell was G. C. Brazel's field. On a July day, in 1947, on his way to his field, the farmer saw the wreckage of a strange aircraft. Dismembered bodies littered the area around the craft.

Naturally, Brigitte asked where she could get some more detailed information. A man approached her and leading her away from the others spoke to her in a conspiratorial hush. His ten-year-old son would not let go of his father for a single moment.

"You'd better not put your beautiful little nose in this affair," he said in a way that would accept no objections. "This is precious advice. You'd better keep it in mind!"

When the father left, she noticed his son waved at her to follow him. Brigitte took him by the hand and gave him a present. The boy, without prompting, spoke to her confidentially.

"The bodies, lady, were all white, like ours, but bloated. Their faces were like newborn babies. More like embryos. They were all over the field. Like dwarfs. Really tiny. That's what my dad said to the sheriff."

"Did they mention anything particular?" Brigitte asked, but the boy's mother came over and dragged him away.

"Come, Tommy! The sheriff wants you," she said, to scare him.

The boy, who had already pocketed the five dollars she gave him, shouted at Brigitte, "Miss . . . They also had wings, small, pink wings."

Brigitte smiled tenderly. "That boy has a fertile imagination. He'll succeed in life. Is it his imagination, though, or did he hear all this?" she wondered. Deputy Steven Shif had declared he was convinced that the government, for unexplained reasons, kept the evidence secret.

Anyway, the strategy finally chosen by those who wanted to keep that story secret and to stop every serious discussion about extraterrestrial beings was brilliant. They turned the anniversary into a real circus. Commercialization and tourist hysteria buried the crashed spacecraft's case once and for all. Those who depend on the gullibility of others have written hundreds of books. But no writer mentions that the bodies had small wings on their shoulders.

If Brigitte Marcais had not heard with her own ears that the extraterrestrial beings had wings, she would have remained indifferent. Yet, to verify the boy's version, she thought she would seek information from underground sources.

"Mister Freedman?" she asked on the phone, using her most seductive voice. She was calling the man responsible for carrying the bodies after the crash.

"Yes!"

"I remember you from 1989 when you presented the 'Unsolved Mysteries' on television."

"Yes, of course! Thank you!"

"I was impressed that you'd told the bodies had wings!"

"No, never! They never authorized us to say that! It was forbidden! But . . . whom am I speaking with?"

"Who had forbidden it?" The line was disconnected. But brilliant Brigitte was now sure Roswell's extraterrestrial beings had wings.

Her journey was over and she returned to Paris. She had buried the precious information in the recesses of her memory, since it was of no special value to her. Her studies were her priority. She might have never remembered that again, if she had not learned the revelations by a David Mason who clearly mentioned albino creatures with pink wings!

Noticing that, suddenly, there was no information at all about David Mason, she was rather upset and put an ad in the newspaper *Le Monde* and *Figaro* magazine: "Anyone who knows anything about D. Mason please contact me. I possess extremely interesting information."

"Are you Miss Brigitte Marcais?"

"Yes! Who's on the phone, please?"

"David Mason! I think that . . . "

Brigitte had only put "D." Mason in the ad, to avoid traps.

"I am looking for a Daniel Mason, sir, about an inheritance matter, on behalf of my father's office. He's a notary."

"Yes, I know! Your father is Marcel Marcais . . . I'm sorry . . . " Brigitte hung up. He certainly was not the person she was looking for but Brigitte felt the chilling air of fear at the thought that the ones who muzzled Freedman, certainly saw fit to remove David Mason, too. Why?" With that question in mind, she went to bed. It was 3 o'clock in the morning when the ringing phone made her jump out of bed.

"I hope, Miss, your ad is not a trap. You say you've got information. Anyway, I'm looking for someone to hide my friends and myself. Everybody's after us." Brigitte felt convinced this time but for reassurance she asked, "Since we're talking about that, what was the color of the Albinos' wings?"

"Pink!"

"Pink? But then . . . I've found you, at last."

"What do you mean?" Brigitte let David and his friends come to her place, about 20 miles south of Paris.

David Mason's case, as it started with a narration about a strange world, would remain a scenario for commercial exploitation, except that it contained something exceptional. The peculiarity of this narration was that the creatures mentioned were winged and that it was similar to two mysterious cases. When the security authorities and the Church heard about "winged creatures", they were immediately worried for good reason.

First, the 1947 Roswell affair and the small winged creatures that were found and studied; they remembered the struggle they had to make the case disappear and, of course, the money they had spent to keep some mouths closed. Second, they could not forget the story of the extraterrestrial embryo in Puerto Rico.

On Wednesday, September 17, 1997, at La Colectora community located at Santurce, in Puerto Rico, Fred Acevedo Martinez was murdered in his car. During the investigation that followed, a small bottle was found in his pocket, addressed to Roosevelt Roads Naval Station. The bottle contained a five-inch embryo "that corresponded to no animal on earth," according to the statement of veterinarian Dr. Carlos Soto. At the back side of its thorax, there were rudimentary wings!

Eventually, through an agreement between doctors and a government representative, the case was considered closed. To ridicule the affair, someone put key rings, with copies of the extraterrestrial winged embryo, on the market.

Everything was quiet and completely under control for many years, when, suddenly, David Mason remembered his youth and went to check his memories with the help of the most advanced equipment in Beni's bat cave. Trying, after decades, to justify himself, he nearly died. Of course, now, his life was in danger because he had survived his injury and because, without wanting to, he had unearthed new demons. How was it possible for the Church not to react in the face of this challenge?

David Mason clearly mentioned in his narration that the primitive angels were religious. Moreover, they were pagan. Yet, as they progressed, their religious feeling weakened. Without hesitating, he declared that religion, whose foundation is the purely metaphysical explanation of creation and future life, was not the progressing angel's major preoccupation on planet KEROPS.

Philosophers, metaphysicians and astrophysicists had already accepted the obligation to announce their scientific theories. But they never experienced enough interest from the population.

One theory, David's visions, proved right since winged, humanlike creatures had been found at Roswell and an extraterrestrial winged embryo had been discovered in Puerto Rico. All this cast a threatening shadow over the future of religion on Earth. It was logical, then, that the authorities were very sensitive about anything that undermined the beliefs that kept society together.

If people woke up and saw things from the winged creatures' point of view, that moral principles do not really have to be imposed by the state and by religion, it would lead to a revision of values with horrendous social and religious consequences.

Brigitte Marcais, a gorgeous young lady with big green eyes, opened her door to receive the five hunted friends in her home. She dazzled them all with her beauty.

"How dare you be so beautiful among such human ugliness?" Larry said, forgetting the traumatic effects of his remarks upon the very jealous Barbara.

"I've never been in such complete agreement with my friend," David added, as the telephone rang in Larry's pocket.

"No names! I'm calling from the tropical islands. They're brewing something here! I've seen doubles, identical to you and David. Also, some kind of movie was made at the Paradise Island Sheraton Hotel, in Nassau. Be careful, son, I see you're in great danger!" The line was again disconnected before Larry had the time to answer.

"What's up?" they all asked, worried. They had noticed Larry's face changing as the telephone call progressed.

"It was my father. He's in Nassau and saw two doubles of us."

"My double too?" David asked.

"Yes, David! They are preparing something . . . something evil. But, what?"

Brigitte who, by nature's caprice, was not only very beautiful but also very intelligent, said, "They are certainly using doubles to accuse you of something illegal, let's say a bank holdup . . . "

Barbara, who still had not swallowed Larry's compliment to Brigitte, reacted. "This would be good if we were poor. Thank God, we've got our ways. There is no motive to accuse us of something like that."

"Slow down! It was just an idea. They are probably not setting up a holdup, they might . . . " Before Larry finished what he was saying, Brigitte completed his phrase. "Murder! They want to charge you with murder so their chase becomes legal."

The telephone rang in the room next door. It was Brigitte's father.

"I want you to watch a broadcast on Channel One, in three hours, without the others. And, I'm expecting your assessment. "Her father's voice was cold and, perhaps slightly hostile. "Strange," she thought, "why all this mystery about the others not watching with me?" He did not even call her "my little girl" or "little girl," as he usually did.

She returned to the living room. David was speaking on his mobile phone. "Theodore, our pursuers have found two doubles of ours and are certainly preparing some surprise. I'm calling so you will be prepared. You see, information always helps."

Natassa's opinion was right. All their friends had to be informed to pre-empt any surprises. She also predicted, "I think that because we have disappeared, they're about to stage a false interview in which David's and Larry's doubles will confess that the whole affair was nothing but a publicity ploy to assure success for future books and movies." They all agreed that was highly possible and then settled down to enjoy the coffee brewed by their hostess.

A few days ago, Operation Venus had been completed successfully and the porno-film had been distributed to the mass media. On the Internet, it was filed among "Sex Scandals." So, the "Sadomasochistic-pedophilic-porno-movie," with "David", the biologist, and "Larry", the famous doctor, in the leading roles, was now available for anyone to view.

This blurb introduced the film: "Days and deeds of the heroes of deceit who tried to gain publicity through lies. The hidden camera of a peeper accidentally reveals the parallel life of two scientists whose vices are an affront to human dignity." It was also noted that charges had been brought against them and the heroes were wanted for pederasty and sadism.

There was a good price on their heads. The notification ended as follows: "The dangers to our society are obvious when bad examples are given by the leading members of the scientific community. Anyone with information should contact us either through e-mail, telephone or fax." Numbers were given in each case.

"Despite our disgust, we consider this film's transmission necessary in order to realize the degree of degradation in our society."

The Churches also transmitted comparable messages.

While all this mud was being slung in the mass media, the five friends were enjoying Brigitte's caring attentions. They were not even suspicious of the evil threatening them. In exchange for the hospitality and also in order to inform the others, David put the last tape in the cassette player.

They listened silently. Of course, the one that was really shocked was Brigitte because it was the first time she had heard the text. She was filled with questions. "My dear friends," she remarked obviously moved, "from personal experience and after direct contact with the eyewitness's son, I've learned that Roswell's aliens had rudimentary pink wings. I would like you, if you can, to assure me your Angels did, too."

David answered, crossing his arms on his chest as he always did when he was ready to deliver an important declaration.

"When they were two primitive tribes, the one on KEROPS's bright side and, the other one, on the dark side, not only did they have wings but those wings surpassed a 12-foot spread. Their flying speed was tremendous! They swooped down like lightning upon their victims. This is mostly true for the swarthy tribes.

"Thousands of years later, when science developed, the race

of Albinos dominated through cloning and selection of genes, and created beings with small wings. They used to cut those wings regularly, for aesthetic reasons, just as we shave."

"Both of the tribes did? The slaves too?"

"Yes, the slaves too. In fact, they didn't cut their wings because their final dimensions were small and did not interfere with their work."

Brigitte was trying to absorb all this new information and make some sense of it. After awhile Barbara interrupted her thoughts.

"Guys, something is very wrong! If the plan for salvation doesn't change, their planet will be destroyed and the space-craft-satellite will be lost for eternity in space. I don't know when, but I'm sure this is happening at the end. Don't you think so?"

"Oh, no!" David answered abruptly. "My story could concern the future. Nobody can be sure it's a historic document. In the MANTA's message I received, there were no dates. Perhaps, the MANTA's a prophet that simply describes what is to happen to his tribe and tries, by the way, to avoid our own destruction. On the other hand, maybe my stories are allegories, just as in Saint John's *Book of the Apocalypse*."

Larry Keith, the most romantic of them all, said, "David might be right. Perhaps the MANTA is an improvised Messiah trying, through parables, to make us pay attention to our own future. It might be a parable like 'the creatures of darkness and the creatures of light,' the evil and the good. Then, the good ones win but they use it the worst way. Controversy rears its head among them that leads them to self-destruction. I go a step further. The knowledge of biology was bad for them. This could also happen to us. Cloning is impressive, but what will the social side-effects be?"

"Which government wouldn't like its country's work-force to be absolutely obedient? No strikes, no raises, no family allowances." Natassa shocked everybody with her thoughts. She indeed showed what the real questions were. Someone had to do that.

Barbara said, "I wouldn't want to live in such an inhuman world."

Brigitte was disconcerted. "My friends, I think you're headed in the wrong direction. All this seems very possible yet, it's not certain. Let's not be so pessimistic."

"And why not?" Larry asked surprised.

"Because Roswell's aliens had wings and, according to the last information I've got coming from you, David, they correspond to the Albino tyrants with the pink wings. It is impossible to say when all this happened. What I don't understand is why they're after you."

Natassa picked up a case and put it in front of Brigitte. "In here,

You will find sixteen tapes with David's story. When you're alone, listen to them and reach your own conclusions. Of course, to be absolutely safe, we've placed four copies in four safe deposit boxes. Thus, whatever happens, the story will be saved. After you listen to the tapes, we'd like to know your opinion."

Brigitte seemed to remember something "Hey, guys . . . My father called earlier and told me to watch something on the Internet. Come with me! I am glad I remembered." The only thing she had forgotten was she was supposed to watch the broadcast alone.

Unable to utter a word, for 80 minutes they watched the despicable orgies of a porno movie whose heroes . . . Alas! The heroes' resemblance of David and Larry was astonishing! The atmosphere was cold. Brigitte felt overcome by terror. Only now was she able to explain her father's behavior. Did he know that pimps were hiding under that fairy tale about space? Was she sheltering "pedophilic criminals" and would have to face the consequences?

Regularly, a message appeared on the screen saying the two

were wanted. Perhaps, the call from Larry's father's phone was fake, a ploy. If things were like that, then she was dealing with an organized gang of bright criminals! Brigitte suddenly stopped the show.

"Our enemies' inventiveness is limitless," David said, falling into an armchair. He observed Brigitte's nervousness.

"Certainly, my dear, you've been influenced by this movie and, if I'm not mistaken, you don't trust us that much anymore. If you have doubts, imagine your father, who is, at this moment, watching those orgies. Moreover, he's not informed about the existence of the doubles."

Larry stood up. "I'm sure Mr. Marcais has already called the police. The danger of arrest is imminent. Brigitte, this case with the tapes is a gift from us. You'll be able to realize the tremendous world interest David's narration contains. If you're convinced, you'll help us."

"We trust you, that's why we are telling you where we'll be. We'll go to Binche, a small Belgian town. This is where they celebrate Carnival with white feathers."

Brigitte bit her lip. She did not know what to say. She preferred to remain silent.

They piled into Brigitte's station wagon and left immediately. Brigitte hardly had time to shut her door when the CRS surrounded her house.

"When did you see them for the last time?" the chief asked.

"But, they left two hours ago! They said they'd go towards Lyon."

"What are they driving?"

"A black Mercedes with Austrian license plates." It seemed they believed Brigitte. They went away after taking a good look to be sure that none of the criminals were there, blackmailing her to say what she said.

# Escape
# Plan

An assistant to Hax thought it was not right for the planet's leader to ignore all of what was going on as far as the satellite was concerned. Thus, during a mission trip, he managed to speak to the old MANTA after he persuaded his personal advisor to allow a meeting.

The Law was clear. "If the planet's vital interests are at stake, anyone who can help or provide information can establish direct contact with the Supreme Leader."

"I am . . . " he mentioned his code numbers and was immediately received.

"What good wind brings you here, my son? The old MANTA asked.

The informer, after making certain no one else could hear them, said, "The satellite is being prepared not for self-destruction but for launching. I've seen the plans. I am absolutely sure."

The MANTA laughed. "My son, you should consult a specialist. What you say seems crazy." The MANTA knew about

204

his son's practice of inserting a spy-microchip in all of his assistants. He had certainly already been applied on ANOL. He noticed that all his advisors had a scar precisely under their ear. He had tacitly approved of that because it pleased him that his son took additional security measures.

The discussion with the spy had already been transmitted. This was why, before the MANTA reached his desk, Niak's smiling face appeared on the screen.

"Father, I've heard the spy and we had a good time laughing with Hax. As far as we are concerned, Father, when we get water and your blessing, we're out of here . . . Ha, ha, ha!"

It followed that even the old MANTA was deceived. "It seems I'm getting too old and too suspicious," he thought, obviously relieved.

In the farmhouse where the five friends were hiding, David had to start the transmission immediately. The headache and vomiting were more frequent than at any other time. He took a deep breath, drank some Stella Artois beer, and continued.

"The turbines that were to be filled with the explosives had already been installed on the satellite so that, by launching time, it would act like a whirlpool with extended wings. The 'Cadrano' system that supported the headquarters assured the center of a completely independent equilibrium, backed by gyroscopes. Talking about gyroscopes, I must add that huge ones were installed securely on ANOL to assure a journey without uncontrollable whirls. Mad Niak had arranged that but kept it secret. It was confidential information that nobody had noticed before the danger of destruction became clear."

Larry became more and more curious "You mean, he wasn't a lunatic?"

David moved his head to indicate negative. "Not only he wasn't a lunatic but, I have to say, he was the most risk-taking and adventurous of the MANTAS. He was only crazy about adventures."

"What was the information, David?" Natassa asked, to force Larry to stop his irrelevant questions.

"During a research project, an astrophysicist had discovered a planetary system that, most probably, could be colonized by the Angels. Life-conditions seemed tolerable."

"So, he wasn't leaving without a precise target, as everybody thought by then."

"Exactly! He wanted to create his own society on new principles and in another place. He had in mind the Creation of a new model society according to his imagination and beliefs."

"But . . . he could have taken his father's seat and fulfilled his wishes on KEROPS, without adventures and risks."

"Yes, but, first he would have to kill billions of Angels who would have objected. History would never forgive him if he did something like that."

"Time was passing, the preparation continued and the fateful day was approaching. The MANTA's son kept his father informed by giving him false details. 'We're almost ready, Father! By the time countdown begins, I'll be near you.' Together, they were supposed to press the lever that commanded ANOL's destruction.

"It shall be the biggest fireworks that ever existed," the MANTA told his son during their last meeting.

"When one is young, has dreams and is lucky enough to afford to make them come true then, at the beginning, he looks like a lunatic, drunk with glory. Slowly, as in an explosion, everything becomes more reasonable. Things are modified and applied with less fanaticism and radicalism. That's what was happening now.

"As the escape day approached, Niak was having second thoughts about it. He obviously felt guilty! 'Why shouldn't they be allowed to live?' he finally thought. 'My Angels and I will build, if we can manage to do so, a new society, more just. Let those here rot in their ancient and barbaric social order. Why should I be the killer? I shall let them commit suicide.'

Larry interrupted him. "Did Niak change his mind so easily? Up to now you were saying that . . . "

"No, Larry! Niak only changed his mind once. It was when
the moment approached to depart from his own world. Thinking had led him to more correct choices. 'If my suicide-mission
fails,' he thought, 'because probability is only 17%, then, my
entire generation shall disappear. And the reason shall be me.
Maybe, if I'm lost in this utopia, someone like me will be born
and follow my tracks. He shall lead a rebellion on KEROPS. I
have the right to disagree, but I don't have the right to make
decisions about the future of a superior race that may be
unique in the whole universe. What I'm trying to do is an ex-
periment. I'm giving nature the ability to help me try something new. Luck sides with the brave!'

"Reasonable!" Larry declared. "Of course, you are transmitting Niak's thoughts. Because he's the one dictating
through the pyramidal microchip."

"Either he or a descendant of his. I'm not sure about that.
What you know, I know," David said and sipped some Apolli-
naris. "The old MANTA had never undertaken a destruction
operation. This is perhaps the reason why he had left ANOL's
operation to his son. He didn't want to tarnish his record.

"My son, you are beginning your career, your training in
power, by a mission of super-destruction! I wish for you that it
is your first and last one!"

"Niak's answer was surprising. 'Father, if the planet's salvation demands only one super-destruction, only then shall I accept what you've said.'

David suddenly remembered another conversation the old
MANTA had with his son, before they had found the solution
of blowing ANOL up to save the planet.

"I apologize that I have to make a digression that is imposed
from above. It's about a father-son conversation that took
place many years ago.

'My son, you have no idea what it cost us to build underground shelters on ANOL and on our planet to preserve
everything our civilization has produced. There are copies of

208 / The Last Dynasty of the Angels

everything we have achieved, and prototypes of the computers that can be activated and ready. I am sorry because if we are ever lost, no one shall ever know about our existence and progress.'

"The son, although much younger then, proposed and, finally, managed to perfect the system with microchips. The chips in this system, concentrated by thousands in compact masses, would wait for the occasion to spread and be a reliable source of information for future generations. The one who would consult these chips would experience some kind of Holy Ghost inspiration. He would learn, in every detail, the Angels' achievements in technology, biology and every other field of their history. That was the young man's bright thought. He foresaw that, even if everything were destroyed, the new inhabitants of the planet would fall into the trap of the microchip system. In order to draw attention, it was presented in a very impressive container, a kind of bait. It was a bright transparent sphere."

"I've let you speak, David, as I know you're trapped into something that looks like that. I hope your troubles will soon be over."

David, as usual, nodded, filled with sorrow.

"The end doesn't seem to be near, I clearly feel that. So, let's not waste time. Niak, meanwhile, had arranged to install in his spacecraft an opal sphere with microchips as well as full copies of all the cloning and biology labs. The connection between them was so well established that they were always ready to function.

"Also, without telling his father, he had created slaves on ANOL that differed from the spineless slaves-animals. They had a rudimentary, yet sufficient intelligence so they could communicate among them about simple matters. Niak had provided the genetic material that had been used, but its origin was unknown.

"The biologists proposed those new creatures, the NOVO-OMOH, as they were called, to have many new features. They had a face that changed according to their mood; Angels did not do so. When one reprimanded them, drops ran down from their eyes and they uttered complaining cries. Before sexual intercourse, they were not hermaphroditic; the mates attached their lips to each other's for quite a while. Moreover, when their stomachs were filled, they shouted in rhythm and jumped and twisted their bodies. It was the dance of joy. All this was rather funny for the Angels.

"Often, to break dullness, the Angels brought some of them into their houses to laugh at their comical behavior. They had rudimentary wings that did not interfere in their jobs. A percentage of them were born with no wings at all. They just had small humps on their back. Niak had noticed that partners remained faithful to each other in their sexual choice. He had made up his mind to take some of them with him but, also, some of all the other specializations.

"A shipment of 5,000 high technology computers with high reasoning aptitudes had been distributed over all the important places on the satellite. The small spacecrafts that had been planted on the surface were each equipped with four independent computers that, for safety reasons, were installed in private, long booths, carefully designed to resist vibrations.

"Niak had arranged the installation of 10,000 freezer-boxes in the headquarters. The privileged officers, and some samples of the new, liberated slaves would enter them, before the launch. The first check of all systems done in the central, spherical headquarters was satisfactory. Everybody reacted correctly at the proper moment and took the indicated positions.

"To connect the satellite's caverns, they had created radial, deep wells. On the walls of those wells there were freezer-boxes similar to the 10,000 that were in the headquarters.

"There were about 1,800 wells whose construction was complete. Each one of them could shelter 500 Angels. In total, 9,010,000 chosen ones would constitute the space-ark's crew. Huge water and food storerooms were built. None could predict for how long they would depend on them. Recycling techniques would be of great help.

"Of course, the food was to be transported in secret from KEROPS and the danger that the plan would be revealed was immediate. If anybody on KEROPS realized huge quantities of food were transferred to ANOL, a plausible answer was not possible.

"Niak had the 140,500 food containers in eight floating ports. They were declared as 'highly explosive material' and were labeled with the words 'PLASMA. Destination, ANOL.' The 'D' day approached and astrophysicists were holding meetings almost every day. The old MANTA rarely missed any of those meetings. The outlook was optimistic and the mathematical estimates, when ANOL's presence was eliminated, came out to be optimistic. If the satellite were not there, the comet would pass far from the planet. Of course, no one could assure that there would be no destruction. Still, they wanted to save their planet, even if seriously wounded.

"That day, the old MANTA had nothing else to do. So, he decided to observe the loading of the containers labeled explosive, on the screen of his personal computer. He always enjoyed admiring his people's technology achievements. The whole loading and transport procedure was executed mechanically. The perfect, giant robots had the needed computer-brains to fulfil their mission.

"The old MANTA had almost fallen asleep when, on the screen, he could see a container that had been transported incorrectly fall and crash on the platform with earsplitting noise. The old Angel woke up, but was still very tired. 'Fortunately, there was no explosion,' he thought and turned the device off and went to bed. If he had not turned the device off, he would have seen that thousands of canned food boxes were spread around the destroyed container!

"If the accident were more important, the controllers would have intervened, and they were not joking. They would certainly understand something was going on. They were the old MANTA's SS, only their name was Peace Guardians or 'Pgs'.

"All preparations were in their final stage. On KEROPS, following the MANTA's orders, all the floating cities were lifted 30 feet up, by addition of compressed air in the floaters. The reason was obvious. The smallest modification the planet should expect would be the creation of multiple tidal flows as the comet passed by. Of course, if they only depended upon this precaution and did not hide in KOX's deep canyons, nobody would have been saved from total destruction.

"The slaves had already been transferred in the galleries of the old mines and in the catacombs where the swarthy angels once lived under primitive conditions. Their food and the DE.A.T.H installations that were installed and functioned automatically were all assured."

Larry could not bear to see Barbara with her eyes bulging and feeling dizzy. She had remembered the first narration concerning the production of pyramid food.

"David, you don't have to remind her," he murmured.

David did not even notice her reaction. He was absorbed in what he was narrating. Maybe something very important was to follow.

"During a coordination meeting the old MANTA had with his son, he made an observation. 'I have noticed', he said, 'KEROPS's food production has increased in a manner that does not correspond to the orders we usually have.'

"Niak was always properly prepared. 'Ha, ha! And what if the comet's passing destroyed food production for ten years? What are you supposed to eat, then?'

'What are WE supposed to eat,' the old MANTA corrected and grew moody.

"Niak had finally made the fatal mistake. Without wanting it, he had excepted himself. He knew the old MANTA was cunning and this small word could cause an explosion—the explosion of Revelation! And, if that happened, the plan to escape would have to be called off. 'Maybe not', he thought.

'The last alternative would be for us to eat with the slaves,' Niak said, trying to make a joke.

'My son, in six days everything has to be ready. I am aware that the work I have charged you with is no fun. The thousands of workers that you have taken on ANOL must start their return home.'

"He stood up and, with authority that would tolerate no objection, said, 'In fact, now that I am thinking about it, this returning should have started some time ago.'

"He pressed one of the two screen-buttons of the central computer. He asked for the data concerning ANOL's personnel statistics. The data immediately appeared on the screen. The old MANTA jumped up in his seat.

'It's impossible! 1,010,000 workers are on the satellite?'

"Niak went pale. The old MANTA had never told him there was another computer, independent from the one he knew, yet using the same screen. The computer's activation was accomplished through a secret button, the one the old MANTA had pressed by mistake. The MANTA pressed the second button, that of the known computer. He took a look and, in a glance, realized the deceit."

'Your computer says 101,000, my son. Don't you think urgent explanations are needed? Some zeroes are missing.'

"Thinking operates at speeds that surpass imagination. Time had run out. Niak had to find the correct way out, immediately! 'This is the end!' He thought, 'if I get caught now, everything's lost! With no exception! The comet will crash upon KEROPS and the satellite together.' Certainly, by the time he would stand trial, precious time would be lost. For safety reasons, each time he went from ANOL to KEROPS, he literally imprisoned his 10,000 officers in the central room. If anything happened, nobody would know how to fire ANOL to relieve KEROPS from the comet's crash.

"So, this was the moment of truth.

'Father, there's no time. I shall only tell you one thing. Pay attention to me! There's an explanation to everything. If you manage to understand my plan, you'll certainly forgive me!'

"The father, solemnly, approached his desk. He sat down and, without a word, raised his hand, ready to give the alert signal. With a lightning-fast move, Niak took the defense weapon very few had the right to carry on the planet. This weapon transferred an incredible quantity of energy into the opponent's body. The victim remained in a cataleptic state for a whole month. So, Niak did not hesitate at all, not for a single moment, and used the weapon against his father.

"The old MANTA immediately collapsed on the floor. Niak went near him, assured his father was out cold, and gave the alert signal.

"In fractions of a second, the room was filled with Pgs. Niak pretended to be desperate but lost no time at all. He knew that, in less than ten hours, the coroners would discover their leader's state was caused by the weapon and not natural causes. No law provided for the MANTA's replacement if he was the successor's victim."

"I feel exhausted," David said and opened his eyes. "I feel almost as if Niak had shot me. He stood up to walk a little. They had ordered Chinese food to be delivered to them, as it would be dangerous for them to go to a restaurant." David really looked exhausted that day.

# Temporary Alterations

⁂

Their friend, Canakis, was not one of those guys who sit around doing nothing. His photograph had not been published, either through the Internet, or through any other news media. Thus, he could move around easily. The same was true about the two women. "We must find a solution," he said again and again, "David and Larry must be able to go around freely!"

The present situation was not very different from imprisonment. The heroes' obliged confinement would, sooner or later, end up with an unconditional surrender. In situations, though, where no one is able to give a solution, divine providence manages to do so.

Canakis spent a few hours one night in a brewery in central Binche. He could not help but listen to a conversation, perhaps because one of the persons was speaking unusually loudly.

"But, I'm telling you, I saw Claire and didn't recognize her," said the 20-year-old man, talking to a younger girl.

"I passed her on the street, we literally bumped into each other, she looked at me, smiled and, when she realized I hadn't

214

recognized her, she said, laughing, 'Aren't you ashamed? I was your girlfriend for two years and, now, you pretend you don't know me.'"

The young girl, rather jealous as it seemed, answered him, "She's forty years old . . . She's old and not beautiful any more. You did well . . . "

"No! On the contrary! Claire looked much younger, fresher, newer . . . than ever! I swear!" They both started laughing.

Coincidentally, they saw Claire coming towards them. Claire, walking like a supermodel on the stage, approached and took a chair at their table.

"If this isn't a coincidence," said the young man. "We were just talking about your transformation, Claire."

The older woman declared, "That's progress, kids! No wrinkles, no crinkles! One must never surrender. I fought and won, as you can see."

"What do you mean?" he asked.

"I went to the plastic surgeon, René Fontaine."

"You had plastic surgery?" the young man asked.

"Not at all! What surgery are you talking about? I just had some collagen injections! I clearly told him I wanted to change my looks and I didn't care how much it would cost or how painful it would be."

"They say he's rather peculiar, a little deranged, is it true?" the jealous one asked.

"Absolutely, guys! All the time he was working on my face, under local anesthesia, he drove me crazy with the strange stories he was telling me. Nobody's perfect!"

"He did it to help you forget the pain, certainly. It's a well known and very useful trick."

"Not at all. His bookshelves are filled with science-fiction books, not medical works. I don't know, crazy he may be, but I know how good he is in his work."

"How long does the new appearance last?" The young girl asked showing embarrassing curiosity.

"He gave me a one-year guarantee but he told me I had to be careful about my weight."

Canakis immediately got the message and was very satisfied. He paid for his beer, offered a smile to the transformed Claire and immediately went towards the farmhouse. Luck smiles upon the brave ones, but this time luck outdid itself! It suddenly presented them with an original solution that would free them. They would never exculpate themselves if they remained buried in that desert!

Canakis turned out to be a leading player in this effort to complete David's memories. This additional contribution of his could be, literally, a gift from heaven. He slammed the door as he came into the house.

"Guys, we're saved," he yelled with enthusiasm. After the explanation he gave, the atmosphere was more relaxed and they could smile again. Larry patiently waited for Canakis to end what he had to say.

"We also have some wonderful news for you, of equal importance!"

Canakis looked puzzled. "What kind of news could you have from in here? I don't understand you!"

Larry, excited, almost with tears in his eyes, said, "My old father, Jonathan Keith, managed to spot one of the doubles. You remember he'd bumped into them at Nassau's Sheraton?"

"Yes, I do remember!"

"Well, it seems that was the place where they produced the porno movie we saw at Brigitte's."

"The one on the Internet?"

"Yes, that one! My father had the presence of mind to ask for information and he found out that my double is a psychiatric patient in St. Petersburg, 122 Menomoni Street."

"That's impossible. It's a trap! Certainly the old man was deceived. I, myself, Larry, have lived so many things that I really don't believe in easy solutions when they appear."

David started laughing. "And the solution with the plastic surgeon? So, isn't that news? That, indeed, offers an easy solution! Could anyone imagine that the solution would come out of the blue, in a brewery?"

After they offered several toasts and had a good dinner from the Chinese restaurant, the morale was uplifted. It was time they acted!

"I would like to speak with surgeon René Fontaine, please," David asked on the phone.

"Speaking! Please, inform my secretary about anything you would . . . "

"Professor, you personally . . . "

"I am not a professor, sir," the doctor replied rather displeased.

"Doctor!"

"Now, you're doing better! Go on . . . "

"Doctor, what I have to say is in two parts".

"Well, let's start with part one, then . . . "

"I am David Mason!" There was silence on the other side. The doctor did not react immediately. He was shocked by this unexpected contact with one of the two most wanted persons in the world. He was aware of the hunt that had been organized for their arrest.

"The anthropologist, the paleontologist, the pederast?"

"Yes! So, you're aware."

"Yes, I am! But, believe me, I'm no little man, I'm not easily convinced. Deep inside I believe this whole impressive scenario has been built to discredit you. You're messing around with devils."

David was touched. He understood his future savior was also to become a friend, a faithful ally!

"I couldn't describe my enthusiasm, doctor! I think you're a very open-minded person and, I think I can trust you." Barbara, who was listening to the conversation, let some tears run down her cheeks.

"Absolutely! Where are you? How can I meet you?" the doctor asked anxiously. This time the telephone line was disconnected on David's initiative. Exactly then, the door had opened and the boy from the Chinese restaurant had come back, pretending he had not given the right change. The way he examined their faces showed he had returned to verify his assumptions. He wanted to be sure he had found the sadists, the wanted ones. Danger, once more, was immediate.

When the boy left, Barbara yelled, "Pack up immediately! We're out of here."

"Where are we going?" Natassa asked, completely lost.

"Find the doctor's address. We'll go straight there!" David wrote it down on a piece of paper, 151, Avenue des Alliés. He picked the phone up again. The doctor was there.

"We're coming immediately. I think you are our only hope."

"I'll be expecting you," the doctor said and hung up.

In a few minutes time, the five friends were in the doctor's waiting room. The first explanations concerning their incredible adventure made the doctor shiver

"I've called my summer house, at Knokke. It's ready for you. Meanwhile, everything is ready here for Larry and David to be transformed into men who look 20 years younger than they look now. Collagen does miracles, believe me! When you are in my summerhouse, the staff won't recognize you. They couldn't do so even if they were relatives of yours!"

Barbara immediately reacted. "Really, your rapid positive response leaves us speechless. You're literally saving us at the last moment."

"Let's not talk about this, we're losing time! We'll discuss it later! The doctor said, rather rudely. You and the other lady will be my assistants during the procedure. Come over here to wash your hands and wear sterile gloves, please!"

In the rudimentary operating room, one by one, first David and then Larry, were transformed, thanks to the plastic surgeon's golden hands, into two fresh-looking 30-year-olds. During the operation, the doctor told them his opinion about Roswell's crash and the Puerto Rico embryo about which the Americans, on purpose, had made no official statement.

"Doctor, we'd like you to tell us about your fees," Natassa said.

The doctor smiled. "The fee for what I've done, according to the law, is twenty years of forced labor for each one of you. But, due to my previous honest life, it will be reduced to only thirty years instead of forty. Lady, my fee is my contribution so that the whole world will know the truth!"

The doctor had also arranged things so that the two patients would not stay at the villa with Barbara, Natassa and Canakis.

"Now you are unrecognizable, he told them, but your environment could betray you. If Hitler had changed his face but went on hanging around with Goring and Goebels, no one would believe he wasn't Adolph!"

His decision was wise although the two women didn't like it that much. Natassa, annoyed, said to her friend, "I think René has his eyes on you and wants to corner you alone. But it is not your fault!"

"The fact that we have to deal with a horny doctor is obvious," Barbara said. "He undresses me with his eyes. Still, I don't think he's ignoring you, either."

The welcome committee surprised the ambulance that arrived at the doctor's villa. Two police cars waited patiently. In the back seat of one, a teenager, about 16, watched the ambulance's arrival with interest.

When he returned to the restaurant, the assistant said to his boss he had found the two wanted men. The boss lost no time and called the police. Because they found the farmhouse empty, the police immediately looked for and spotted the car outside Doctor René Fontaine's Medical Centre. The doctor was known for his extraterrestrial beliefs, and the Chief of Police very wisely thought the doctor would hide his friends in his villa and not in the wolf's nest.

The Chief's disappointment was big when the young boy said, "Officer, I saw them, it's not them!" When, after further search the police discovered the two women in a small pension, they told the Chief they had not seen Larry and David "for quite a while" and that, anyway, after the orgies, they did not wish to see them again.

The Chief was infuriated. "The wanted men escaped and there are no charges against the ladies. If there were any charges, one could certainly get precious information from them."

David and Larry's efforts to call their friend, Theodore, remained unsuccessful, because the grandfather had already taken his grandchildren and vanished among the wonderful Greek islands for the whole summer.

The seven-day convalescence period passed without complications. In order to test the results, Larry and David took a taxi and visited the pension, Renoir, where their friends were. Natassa and Barbara, silent, were on the terrace enjoying their filtered coffee and a piece of cake.

David and Larry sat near them and loudly ordered champagne.

"Please, a Veuve Joyeuse, with flute glasses," Larry said in French. Barbara, unable to hide her feelings, said in English, "They must be nouveaux riches . . . How in hell did they get the idea to sit near us?"

"Champagne at this hour?" Natassa added. "That's crazy! They certainly don't know how to spend their money!"

"To Niak's health, we wish him luck in launching his satellite-spacecraft!" Larry said loudly.

When the two women heard this statement they stood there, thunderstruck. Not even for a moment would they have thought those two elegant young men were their own friends. For safety reasons, they showed no enthusiasm. Only, during their conversation and without even looking at them, they praised Rene.

"René is a real genius! We couldn't recognize you! You look like college students! Not a single wrinkle is left! We're so jealous . . . Tomorrow we're leaving for Florida. Our tickets are at the American Airlines office for Brussels to Atlanta and Atlanta to St. Petersburg. We've got to help old Jonathan!"

"Where's Canakis?" David asked.

"He went to send a message to his newspaper. He's preparing things so they will receive us. How's it going with your headaches, David?"

"I had to record another tape. You'll hear it in the plane, it will keep you company."

# Space
# Ark

The two women had two copies of the tape with them on the plane. Comfortably seated in business class, they were listening to the extraordinary events that followed the final argument between the father-MANTA and the son-successor.

"Niak was travelling at incredible speed with his personal vessel, thanks to progressive gravity neutralization. He left KEROPS never to return. It was his life's most decisive moment. He was leaving chaos behind him, literally, an entire world that had no ruler and was on the brink of destruction. A solution had to be found. Yet, the only person that could reverse things was the one that had created them, MANTA's son, the successor that refused to rule. He was the adventurous, rebel son!

"When he arrived at the satellite, he immediately convened a General Assembly. His Angels, the greatest geniuses of their time, had moved close to him. They had put their trust in him. They believed in their new leader's visions.

"Life's dullness on planet KEROPS was the reason every

221

bright Angel was looking for something new. Niak's proposal, although it was irrational, seduced even the most intelligent Angels, because it gave them a higher goal! There were 381 Angels participating in the General Assembly. The other nine were trapped on KEROPS. They were going to miss the opportunity and lose their lives, when the MANTA woke up.

"In the center's spherical room, Niak was clear and brief. 'We're leaving immediately! In one day! Everything is ready. I'm arriving from the O.E.C.R, Orbit Extraction Control Room. If anybody has questions to ask, please submit them!'

"A tall, corpulent Angel stood up. 'The generosity you have, leader, of letting KEROPS live proves you're mature and that your decisions will be respected by all of us. We shall be with you, in grief and in glory.'

"On the other hand, a swarthy, short officer had a different opinion about KEROPS. 'Leader, your generosity may have negative side-effects, in the future. Perhaps the perception of betrayal that those you are saving now may have, will create problems for future generations.'

"Niak smiled. 'Soemgyp, thousands of years, thousands of centuries will pass before they could finally become a threat to our new society. By then, our descendants will be able to defend themselves. Let's leave it up to them. Do not forget, Soemgyp, that the need for action was the flame that will fire ANOL's launching towards a new Angels' adventure.'

"Before the Assembly was over, an ultimatum arrived, sent from the Peace Guardians Headquarters of planet KEROPS. It was the personal guard for each MANTA and its chief was, now, a clone-copy of Niak. He called himself 'Niak the Second'. In case the legitimate successor was lost, he would be proclaimed successor himself.

"The wording of the ultimatum was stern. 'MANTA dead. Successor murderer sentenced to death in absentia. I am new MANTA. Order you appear in 18 hours at floating MANTA Administration Hexagon. Signature: MANTA.'

"The developments were moving fast. Most likely, the Second had killed the MANTA, helped by the doctors, in order to become the successor. Only, the brainless, drunk with glory, had not realized that his and KEROPS Angels' salvation depended upon Niak exclusively, the very person that was sentenced to death.

"If he went there to defend himself and ANOL did not leave on time, then the killer-comet would turn KEROPS and ANOL into stardust.

"Niak, losing no time, in front of his 381 advisors, took the remote-control device and pressed a button that allowed communication with his dead father's office. He was sure the new MANTA of the Praetorian Pgs was already installed there.

"Sure enough, he had rapidly occupied the MANTA's office and, filled with pride, admired himself and the trappings of his power in the mirror. When he received the signal of an incoming urgent message, he took his time answering. 'I am giving the orders, the others wait . . . let them wait! Citizens are like meat. The more it is kept around, the better it gets. So they become more tender to their master.'

"He finally decided to take the call. He was furious that the traitor was calling him. 'How dare you?' he shouted. 'How dare you, after what you've done?'

"Niak replied calmly. 'Pay attention to what I tell you and don't be hysterical.'

'You have absolutely no right to give me orders. It's only curiosity that makes me listen to you begging me for your life. Isn't that it, the reason why you've called me?'

"Niak, as if he had not heard the hysterical reply, continued very calmly. He knew he had an important advantage that could stand no objection. 'If by the day after tomorrow, ANOL does not disappear, as you know, the magnetic forces shall pull comet ZX03 into collision with the planet. I was saying, thus, that ANOL has to be launched, at any cost, for you to be saved. If I obey your orders and come to defend myself, our chance of salvation shall vanish. You may consult your astronomy advisors if you wish. It is all up to me! Do you understand that? I'm waiting for an answer! Yes, or no? Not in 18 hours! I want an immediate reply!'

"There was a pause but no response. 'Your silence convinces me that I'm perfectly understood. Do you insist on my coming? I'm asking you for the last time! If you do insist, I shall come and the responsibility for total destruction shall be exclusively upon you.'

"No! Don't come here! The voice sounded gloomy, scared. Anyway, this crazy trajectory of yours on that satellite-ghost shall also be your sentence! It's just that you mislead the intellectual elite of our planet. I'm warning you. If you're ever saved and create the kind of society you've planned, we shall be against you. From now on, future generations shall be raised and indoctrinated to come and take revenge for your betrayal. They shall destroy your colony, even if it manages to prosper.

'Leva, I think that's the name the biologists gave you when they created you from one of my father's cells . . . You murdered my father.'

'I have? Who's accusing me? Have you no conscience at all? Shame on you!'

'Leva, take good care of the planet I'm generously offering you to protect by my departure. Prepare for the storm that shall follow our launching and ZX03's appearance.'

'So, you became our protector! Traitor! You have some nerve . . .'

'Of course! Because, if I delay and depart close to the comet's arrival, KEROPS will collide but I shall escape! If you don't wish me luck, I don't promise you I'll leave on time.'

"This was purely sadistic. He wanted to have the satisfaction that his father's murderer wished him a nice trip. There was no answer from KEROPS."

"I take your silence as a refusal. Then you shall be the reason why our tribe is sentenced to turn into stardust!" Still there was no response.

"Non-existence awaits you . . . You deserve the punishment. But your victims don't! Then . . . I shall delay my departure."

'Have a nice trip!' Communication was cut off for forever. Leva had capitulated. Those listening to the exchange laughed. They noticed the cowardliness and thoughtlessness of KEROPS' new leader.

"'It's time we left,' Niak ordered and went to his headquarters. There the cryobiology booth was expecting him. It was his temporary tomb. For him and 1,010,000 angels and slaves."

"One hundred thirty-two tunnels filled with Plasma-INH explosive material, a substance similar in characteristics to our nuclear energy, would have the task of tearing away the satellite from KEROPS's magnetic field. Immediately afterwards, 157 rockets, equipped with powerful reactors, would produce a spiraling move forward that would free them of the pull of the two suns. Thus, they would become totally unleashed from the elliptical planetary system.

"The biologists allocated the hibernation booths to the officers and they themselves reclined for the long sleep that could (there was a 73% chance of that) send them to non-existence.

"Niak, seated at the helm, pressed the lever labeled Cryonics with a determined hand, and 1,009,999 crystal coffins were automatically covered. The hollow noise that filled the room was the cooling system that had kicked in. For the last time, he was thinking about the scope of the project and that it might be plain utopia. He took a last look to check the trajectory they were to follow. After a journey of three centuries at a speed half the speed of light, there might be some hope of salvation. Their target was to reach a planetary system whose four out of twenty-one planets presented conditions that should allow them to make a new start, to create a new world based on the principles they had chosen.

"The 'Go' lever was in Niak's cryobiology booth. Pressing this lever would automatically freeze Niak's body and start the launch procedure. He lay in his coffin-cell and pressed the lever. He saw the transparent coffin's cover lowering irrevocably on top of him. 'For a new life!' he shouted and pressed the launch button. Before automatic firing, an anaesthetic gas was released to put everyone to sleep. Thus, they would spare themselves the pains caused by progressive physical freezing.

"The satellite's launch in space could only be compared with ANOL's 'departure', when he still was a mountaintop of KEROPS. One hundred thirty-two lightning flashes preceded one hundred thirty-two thunders. KEROPS's sky was bright, as if a piece of sun had approached their atmosphere. The satellite immediately became smaller. In a few minutes, a new roar was heard coming from the one hundred fifty-seven rockets. Now the travelling ANOL, the former God, the former rock, the former shelter for swarthy angels, departed for its big journey, its fateful adventure. It was a bet on fate, a bet on nature! It was a ray of hope for those who escaped the world of KEROPS."

"All systems functioned perfectly and, in less than one earth day, the satellite-spacecraft had already reached the desired speed of 75,000 miles a second. A meteorite rain began falling on the satellite's surface increasing, slowly but steadily, its volume and weight.

"Because Niak wanted to know what was going to happen on KEROPS, he had installed a complete televideo-recording system. When they found a friendly spaceport, he would be able to see the past he had not lived. Niak had made provisions to record not only all that had happened on KEROPS but, also, all the conversations MANTA-Leva had with his officers. He wanted to know how they would solve the problems they were to face.

"Creatures on KEROPS expected ANOL's departure to cause a reduction of atmospheric pressure with the immediate consequence of feeling much lighter. Of course, the darkness that came back would be solved by satellite-mirrors that would provide some light. A tidal wave rolled in but was easily handled, as preparations for the killer comet were more than adequate to meet with the side effects caused by departure of the satellite.

"The KEROPS inhabitants were literally shocked by the news of Niak's escape. They were unable to rationally explain that act. They all wondered, 'What more did he want? What ambition could surpass the glory of being the leader of the only civilization in the universe?'

"The only plausible explanation was that he obviously went crazy. Those who were accustomed to dealing with metaphysical issues, that is with religion, had a different opinion. As a soul may change its body, a portion of a tribe may suddenly change where it lives. They thought it was very natural that a part of the population should try to create a new entity. 'As in birth,' the famous metaphysician, Sanoy said, 'inside every organism a new one is created, full of life and will for progress.' Thus, in our society, an embryo was created, at ANOL, that demands to live wherever it wants and the way it wants. Let's hope it is not stillborn.'

"The astrophysicists announced—through the new MANTA—that the comet's passing would be followed by earthquakes and tidal waves. They predicted abysmal crevasses would be created and natural rains would stop. All this terrified the Angels.

"The passage of time brought the inescapable. The hour of the apocalypse had arrived for KEROPS. Suddenly, everything trembled. For a few minutes, gravity disappeared and everything was floating in the air. KOX's ring collapsed, as easily as one breaks a nut, under the conditions created by the comet approaching KEROPS. About eighty percent of the floating towns and grounds disappeared in just a few seconds. The sudden equalization in the level of the two oceans radically modified the planet's geophysical structure. No matter how the most advanced brains of the planet had tried to study the possible disasters, they had never been able to predict reality. Everything happened in such a short time that no corrective action could be undertaken. For the MANTA's headquarters and the erudite Angels, unsinkable submarine shelters had been constructed. They could resist terrible pressure.

"When the ring was shaken and collapsed, huge dust-clouds covered the suns' light. Darkness over the planet lasted for six earth days.

"After the quakes and flooding ended, life returned to normal, the calm mindful of a motionless body after a bullet has hit it. When the submarine shelters slowly resurfaced, the Angels had a breathtaking view over the new 'Creation.' They were terribly disappointed. Their planet was nothing more than a huge spherical sea. Here and there, the former mountaintops had turned into bald islands, shining under the light of the twin suns.

"There was no longer a need for satellite mirrors because KOX's ring no longer blocked the sun. KOX had been blown apart and transformed into a chain of islands of various sizes. The planet's axle had been displaced and its rotation was earthlike. There were nights and days, cold and heat. The 'good' and the 'evil' had survived the disaster. What had irrevocably died was hope.

"Very few survived, one in a thousand. An important percentage of the survivors had severe psychological problems and could not be part of the active population. It had to be recycled! Euthanasia was legally practiced in psychopathic cases.

"The new MANTA, seeing that an acute feeding problem would be faced, immediately ordered the DE.A.T.H. system to be applied without exception, even to Angels! Only, the pace of extermination of psychopaths had to be according to availability of food. Tragic! In case of urgent need, they would pick up food at the DE.A.T.H. systems of the slaves. 'Hunger has no religion and 'love' as well as all the other emotions on planet KEROPS, were controlled 'through stomach.'

"In his delusional announcement after the cataclysm, MANTA-Leva ordered that nothing be allowed to take place if it undermined survival of the Angels. Knowing that a leader, in order to calm his furious civilians, has to find an escape goat, he did not forget to strike with his mouth. 'Niak, my father's murderer, is responsible for this disaster! When everything comes back to normal, I shall explain to you how he betrayed his father and me and all of you! He is doomed! By force he imprisoned the planet's brightest brains and took them with him in a journey with no return and no destination! I give you my word that, if they survive and we ever learn where exactly they are, we shall annihilate them! One of our survival's purposes must be our future revenge! Death to the traitors!'

"While the paranoid leader was delivering verbal fireworks, his officers were working hard."

"The Old Testament's cataclysm looks like a summer spatter of rain in comparison," Barbara said.

Natassa was thinking of her David, fighting to win his "Goliath."

"After a careful study, conclusions on the nature of the population were disappointing. Only 1 in 1,000 had survived. If a selection were performed to find the ones who could live productively, only one in 50,000 would be chosen. Their species would disappear. That seemed the most probable end. They had to fight it. They had to work hard to heal the wounds of the planet and of their souls."

Here, the tape was over. The two women were really impressed. That description was the most interesting of all.

# The
# Detectives

Canakis, using the airport's fax, sent a message to his newspaper, the *Urbana Daily Mail*.

"I have disappeared for reasons that have nothing to do with the newspaper. I am sure that, when I inform you about the case I am working on, you will understand. I am forced to live as an outlaw. You will, very soon, have dreadful revelations on the so-called deceit by Mason and Keith that was published on the Internet. However, you can print that, according to very reliable sources, there are serious doubts about the veracity of the charges against David Mason and Larry Keith. Within the next three weeks I will be able to provide the detailed story. I know that it will be an extremely important story for us. Signature: Stray Canakis".

When Jonathan, Larry's father, informed them that he had spotted one of the doubles in St. Petersburg, Canakis was already in Atlanta with Barbara and Natassa, and they were planning to unmask the conspiracy that aimed at their defamation.

The surveillance measures over Canakis and the two women had slackened as Michael Donovan and Cardinal Patrick were assured they were getting closer and closer to the two targets and that, sooner or later, some "Judas" would send them to rot in Attica's jail.

Canakis's reunion with the two women was a gala occasion. Hugs and kisses, at the beginning; back to reality afterwards! The tireless Canakis had already bought tickets for Tampa, leaving at 4:30 p.m. with Delta.    Natassa did not share her friends' optimism. She was thinking about David's headaches and the difficulties of the mission they had to fulfill. Her distress forced the others to slow down listen to what she had to say.

"I'm saying, guys, before we board the plane, we should take a map and study the place where we are to work. Then we'll draw up our plan."

Canakis, who had visited the area, said, "Ladies, don't worry! I know the area pretty well. I know, from a reliable source, that the Franklin Cross Foundation is well known and respected. Famous scientists have worked there, like that Neurology Professor, Van Gehuhten. He's has been an associate there for many years."

Natassa interrupted him. "But, he's the surgeon that operated on David! Now, he's at Memorial Hospital, fortunately, far away. He knows me. If he ever recognized me . . . "

Canakis continued, "You're right! We've got to be very careful and discreet. Of course, first of all, we've got to meet Jonathan Keith. The old man has probably created the proper beachhead." Mario was not wrong. He knew that Larry's father, for safety reasons, had already rented an apartment in Northeast Tampa, close to South Florida University, at Busch Gardens. He told the two women about that. Meanwhile he found Jonathan's phone number and wrote it down on two pieces of paper and gave one to each of his friends. "It's 1, 272-133-2270. In case we're lost, we meet there!"

Barbara and Natassa made sure they had the right number. Barbara foresaw, despite her initial enthusiasm, that finding the doubles would not be such an easy operation. Certainly, the others must have taken their own measures, so the friends had no time to lose.

"And how are we going to the asylum?" she asked. A kidnapping isn't an easy thing to do."

"You won't mention the word asylum again, Barbara! "Everybody knows it as the Franklin Cross Neurology Foundation! As far as going there is concerned, there's no problem at all." Canakis unfolded a map and showed them the itinerary. He left unanswered the second part of Barbara's question.

"We'll leave from Busch Gardens with Jonathan. We'll pass Tampa's Zoo and enter Dunedin, where we see National Route 19. From there, headed south, we pass Clearwater and get into St. Petersburg. The Clinic is between Salvador Dali's Museum and the Sunshine Skyway. They say—'cause I've asked—it's a marvelous place!"

"Would they be crazy to go anywhere else?" Natassa said laughing. On the plane, the conversation became more optimistic. Landing was great and their morale was high. Even Barbara's pessimism was weaker. They took a taxi and, in ten minutes, they were at Jonathan Keith's address. The old man had the name "Johnson" written on the door of Apartment 22. Despite repeated ringing and pounding on the door, nobody answered. They finally went to the apartment next door. Still, no answer. They were ready to leave when a man, probably the gardener, came near them. "I see you're looking for Mr. Johnson in 22.

"Yes!" Canakis said.

"The police came two hours ago and took him in for interrogation, I think. I'm not sure." The gardener extended his open palm.

Canakis improved the gardener's memory with a fifty-dollar bill and learned that the order for Jonathan's removal came from a hospital. The three friends left as fast as possible, trying not to arouse the gardener's suspicions.

"Certainly, the old man escaped again from the institution.

He owes us $375. We're done again . . . Come on, girls! Let's go to the police. This time we'll get it from him"

"$375 . . . That much," he gardener said, going back to his job. They immediately went to Carlton Tower on 3rd Street South. They registered under false names. They then sat down for a while to recover and draw up a plan based on the new data.

"We've got to save the old man," Canakis said. "He's certainly in bad trouble! Probably imprisoned. Since we know what's going on, I think we can help him."

They left, resolved to succeed. Canakis called the Central Police Department. The trick he had in mind had to work, at any price.

"Hello . . . "

"Central St. Petersburg. Officer Louis Moreno, I'm listening."

"Just a moment! I'm connecting you with Secretary Donovan!"

"Listen, my son, Louis! Jonathan Keith is useless to us. We have just learned he is a storyteller. If you keep him there, scandal is assured! Moreover, he's a hero, Korean War."

"Mr. Secretary, thank you! Your call solves a very difficult problem for me."

Jonathan fell into their arms when he came out of the police station, as a fruit falls from the tree when it's time has come. Moreno had almost thrown him out! The trick had worked marvelously. In the rented car, Jonathan was trying to tell them what had happened.

"I did no harm! They came just like that, out of the blue! They picked me up and took me to jail! The officer asked me about Larry and for what reason I was at St. Petersburg! I told him that . . . my nerves . . . that I didn't feel too well and I had come to relax."

"That was really good, Jonathan! It's exactly what we've told them. They believed us!" Canakis then told the old man about the order from Secretary Donovan.

Jonathan continued. "David's double is mentally retarded

but he works in the kitchen. He used to be a patient in the clinic. He doesn't show up anywhere. He lives at the Clinic all the time."

"He has no family?" Natassa asked.

"Yes, and no. He has a foster mother that seems to be interested only in taking from her son whatever he manages to steal from the kitchen and, first of all, of course, his salary. The night before, I saw them exchanging big packets. Of course, I didn't show up but I know where and when this is going on."

"How can we find her address?"

Jonathan looked into his pockets and took a paper out. He gave it to them saying, "She lives far from the Clinic on purpose. So they don't suspect her."

That night they set up a trap. But it was the full moon. Four unfruitful days passed before the trap worked. Son and mother were arrested on the spot. Canakis shouted with all the authority he could muster.

"Inspector Louis Moreno! Follow me, please."

The woman, carrying the stolen goods, was in shock. Fortunately, the double had already gone and was not there to see his mother was in real trouble. The fake women detectives had recorded the scene on videotape.

"Give the evidence to the detectives and take us to your home, immediately," Canakis said.

"I live very far from here, in Northeast Tampa, at a niece's of mine. She doesn't know anything. Please, anything you want. Don't let her know," she said, scared to death. Of course, Canakis, Barbara and Natassa were recording every single word.

"No, lady! We know you live alone at 1016 54th Avenue. We'll search your house for additional evidence."

"Food's the only thing my poor Adam brings me," the woman whispered, shaking like a leaf.

Canakis, wanting to take advantage of her psychological state, said, "Food . . . and who took the thousands of dollars? Answer me, now. Either you tell us the truth, or I'm taking you in and it may mean at least ten years."

"Legally! My Adam said they gave him the money in a bank at St. Martin Island, in the Caribbean.

"He won all that in two days?"

"He didn't tell me he won. He said he may lose his job if he tells anyone, even me." In the meantime, they had arrived at her home. It was a real mess.

"I want all of Adam's photographs," Canakis ordered The poor lady came back with a faded picture-album.

"Not old ones . . . New ones," Canakis barked. The woman went away and, in a while, reappeared with a dozen photographs.

"Bingo!" Natassa exclaimed. On two of those pictures, Adam was with Larry's double. The resemblance was astonishing! Even the facial expression was the same. If those pictures were shown to friends, they would certainly be mistaken.

As if she was trying to apologize, the woman said, "He brought them back from the trip . . . He told me he got them secretly with a friend of his, because it was forbidden. They're weren't kidding."

"Who?" Canakis asked.

"I've no idea! Certainly those that gave them the money."

Canakis, putting the picture right in front of her, asked "And, who's the one with Adam?

"I have no idea."

Canakis pretended he pitied her. He was familiar with the interrogation technique, "the carrot and the stick."

"Listen, lady . . . "

"Whatever you want. But, the money, I've spent it. I had debts, you see."

"Who cares about the money! What I want is for you to ask your son who the other guy is. It's the other one we are looking. We want his address, his phone number, everything! He's wanted for armed robbery and murder."

The woman seemed relieved. "Since you don't want the money, everything can be arranged. Just let me go. I'll go and ask him now; it's certainly dangerous to do that on the phone. Anyway, he only speaks to me. He trusts nobody else!"

They made a terrible mistake. In their enthusiasm, they let the woman go. Jonathan, being more experienced, saw time passing without a word from the mother, and became more and more anxious. He suddenly rang the alert signal. "Guys, let's get out of here! Take the pictures, all of them and go. Also, take a picture of the house."

Indeed, they just had enough the time to leave before two police cars arrived and the house was surrounded. It all made sense. The mother knew the police officer and knew they were lying to her. But she was scared. They could be federal investigators who wanted to blackmail her.

When she left, the mother went directly to the police department and Louis Moreno. She told him what had happened. Meanwhile, he had learned the earlier phone call had not been made by Michael Donovan. He was furious.

The four had to act without any delays. They had no reason to stay in that place. They returned the car and rented a boat and sailed along St. Petersburg beach, north of the Gulf of Mexico. In two hours they reached Tarpon Springs. They left the boat but made sure that they were carrying the precious pictures. The pictures, the videotape and the recording of the conversation with the mother demonstrated without any doubt that the "official accusation" was nothing but a conspiracy. The enormous, really satanic plot was, at last, coming apart.

They made photocopies of the pictures and sent them to three different addresses. Jonathan took one more pack. An envelope containing the pictures and all the evidence was sent to the newspaper's managing editor in Champaign-Urbana. The second one was sent to Doctor René Fontaine and, the third to their friend in Paris, Brigitte Marcais.

Jonathan Keith, after thanking them for helping him get out of prison, wished them luck and went away. "I think I'm going to get some rest. At my age, it's no good competing with you youngsters. I'm sure you don't need my services any more. I hope I'll soon meet my son and take him into my arms. Until then, Barbara, you may replace me."

The old man's devotion and sense of self-sacrifice touched

them. Jonathan's contribution to the case had been essential and effective. He had the right to retire now. If he went on with the same intensity, his heart would certainly betray him.

Canakis, relieved because David and Larry would soon be exonerated, had a suggestion for the two women.

"I invite you to Chicago. I've already booked airline seats for tomorrow morning, 11:00 a.m., at my paper's expense, of course. You'll have the Westin Hotel's Royal Suite on the Executive Floor. Right on the Magnificent Mile, Michigan Avenue."

Natassa was less optimistic. She usually was circumspect and terribly suspicious. "All this is fine, guys! Everything here is settled! But, have you thought of David and Larry? How are they doing?"

They had agreed that, on the phone, they would use different names. David was "Daniel" and Larry was "Tom". Natassa took it upon herself to call them. After several efforts she got them on the phone.

"Daniel, my boy, how are you? Is everything fine?"

"Both Tom and I are doing perfectly well. We're thinking of coming as soon as he's got his business finished."

"Daniel, tell Tom that everything went all right! All four of us are doing fine!"

"Four?

"Yes, sure! Haven't you heard? Granddad is fine. He just got out of the Clinic! Tell Tom, he'll be glad! But, he was tired and went home."

"What about the twins?"

"It's too long to explain now. But it was a lot of fun!"

"I wouldn't think so!"

"We've got pictures of the twins! Their mother took them when they were in the Caribbean.

"You're serious?"

"Absolutely serious. Everything's great."

"Then, Natassa, I think that . . .

"You'll soon be in my arms, my love! Really, how's business doing? The headaches?"

"I had two crises but, fortunately, they're over!"

"With the same medicine?"

"The cocktail works well. Of course, with the same medicine, but I am going through a very strong phase."

"I see . . . I can't wait . . . I miss you! I'll be at the Westin Hotel on Michigan Avenue. If you need anything, communicate through the overnight courier."

"Today, in one hour, they'll be sent! Kisses . . . " The two beside her understood and felt relieved as nothing particular had happened to the aesthetically altered "mutants" of Doctor René Fontaine.

Natassa, at last, was not pale anymore. She walked on cloud nine now that David was fine!

"He has recorded two tapes and, as he said, they must correspond to very interesting parts of the MANTA history," she informed her friends.

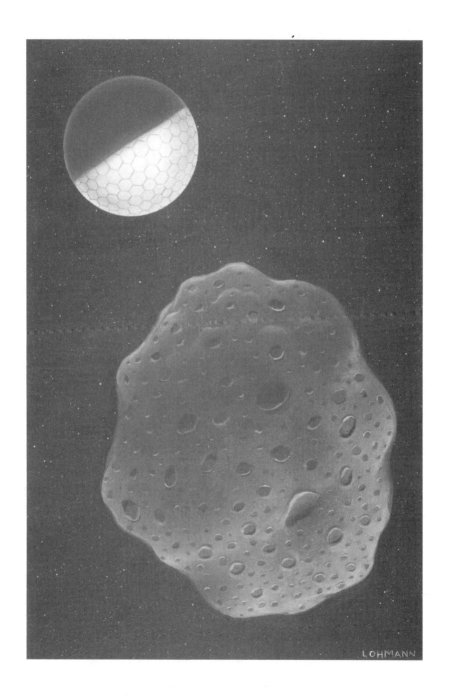

# Space Journey

"You mean to tell me that two months have passed already since David woke up?" Canakis asked, surprised, looking at his calendar.

"It seems to me like many years have passed, my friend," Natassa said. "You came in half-way. Do you realize what we've been through? At least double the trouble!"

Barbara confirmed. "When I think of the day I kidnapped my Larry out of the quarantine in Nairobi, in Kenya . . . Then, imagine, by helicopter . . . a blind flight over the jungle . . . Madness! Pure madness!"

"You must tell me what I don't know," Mario protested. "But, I don't have time now. I must organize a meeting of all those that will help us . . . I wish you a good rest. Bye!" He left, but his brain was working at full speed. Now that they had reached the final stretch, they should not be making any tactical errors.

Natassa opened the DHL parcel the roommate had just

240

brought in, while Barbara went on murmuring. With intense emotion she took the two tapes out of the envelope.

"Barbara, calm down! David's sent us tapes. I don't think I need your authorization to put them into the recorder, do I?" Barbara took her into her arms, kissed her and, seated side by side, in full view of beautiful Lake Michigan, they turned on the recorder.

"When everybody was hibernating, including Niak, P.A. the Hypercomputer was the real captain of the satellite-spacecraft. P.A. was the pride of their space technology. His memory was enriched with billions of data, and he was absolutely capable, with his 'electronic reasoning', to make decisions and implement them successfully. Everything had been predicted. Everything was to function according to the specific orders MANTA-Niak had introduced in P.A.'s memory. Everything was working perfectly, at the beginning, on the Space-Ark.

"MANTA Niak's aim was to reach a planetary system that belonged to Alpha of Centaur. That system consisted of one sun and 52 planets. Only four of them were inhabitable according to the fully reliable data collected by the astrophysicists. The research had been conducted under the personal co-ordination of Hax, assistant chief of this mission.

"According to the plan, when they were close to their target, and thanks to gravity laws, their satellite would acquire its own orbit, revolving around the same sun. Afterwards, they would try, at the proper moment, to migrate to one of the four inhabitable planets. Yet, the 'Angels' wishes are one thing, God's orders are another,' as the proverb goes.

"Indeed! The Hypercomputer functioned well for many months but at some point stopped controlling the journey's course for a whole earth year. The malfunction was caused by frost in one of the circuits that operated at 203 degrees Celsius! Despite intervention by the automatic corrective mechanisms, the problem was compounded. When it resumed working under very low temperatures, the computer's speed was temporarily affected.

"When, at last, P.A. woke up, he immediately went to work

after he first managed to repair himself. When he studied the new data, using his cold reasoning, he considered it was utopian to insist on the initial plan. Anyway, they had long ago passed by their initial target. The excellent data he had reminded him there was one more hypothesis to examine.

"In the remote past, a MANTA suffering from a persecution complex had ordered a detailed research about the universe, in order to discover possible alternative solutions in case of a severe threat. At that time, there was no danger; not even a prediction of disaster. The information coming from that useless research had, fortunately, been stored in P.A.'s memory. The chances for the initial plan to succeed did not exceed 27%. The chances for the alternative one fell to 3%! Plain suicide! 'I prefer suicide to execution!' This phrase appeared on P.A.'s screen when the dice were thrown and the kamikaze satellite changed direction. The target P.A. was aiming at was a star with the strange name of 'Alphomega.'

"Fortunately, during the journey's ungoverned period, speed had remained stable at 88,000 miles. If it had increased, the satellite would have turned into a comet and would, for eternity, be a vagabond spreading fear among planetary systems. Its new speed, imposed by P.A., was studied so that, if ANOL approached a star, like Alphomega, four times its mass, this planet's gravitational forces would diminish it even more. That would render ANOL a prisoner, a satellite. Certainly things were much worse now because, instead of four, only one planet of that system filled conditions for survival.

"Everything became more difficult. In order for ANOL to reach that planet it had to travel, without colliding, among other huge stars with strong gravitational forces. Furthermore, those stars were totally unfriendly. Their climate would not accommodate any form of life. So, they had to avoid being trapped, at any cost! Time was running out fast on the easy part of the journey.

"The critical moment arrived. P.A. cleverly avoided three planetary giants and, finally, managed to point at planet Alphomega. That planet, according to its volume, weight and density, had already fallen into a comfortable orbit around its sun. There was some unknown data. Did the planet's atmosphere have the gases needed for the comfort of the Angels? Of course, they could settle there in protected colonies yet, that would be a temporary solution, before their final extermination, unless the biologists . . . or Goddess Luck . . .

"In view of ANOL's forthcoming arrival at the planet, speed started to decrease. P.A. had literally risked their lives and, finally, had managed to bring them to a port. In three earth days, ANOL would become a satellite and, according to the plan, the big moment had arrived. It was the awakening. First of all, Niak was the one that would have the honor of seeing planet Alphomega.

"In some ways, this would not be an awakening, but a resurrection. An entire population—a complete survival system, organized to its last detail, would finally reach its aim. Or, more correctly, would approach it with more hope of success. Under P.A.'s orders, millions of coded messages would be sent to activate everything, as long as, of course, the Leader agreed. P.A.'s first message was to be received by Niak. The hibernation booth opened and light impulses in his body stimulated the leader to open his eyes, at last.

" 'I knew I would get here! Let's stay calm, this is where difficult things start.' Those were his first words.

"Complete recovery demanded injections into his body of various substances and foods, for forty-eight hours. Niak put his hand into the recovery recess and the countdown started for the procedure that would bring him to a normal level of activity. He was given a tranquilizer gas that would keep him calm during those endless 48 hours. When the monitors notified P.A. that body and brain functions were satisfactory, authorization for activity was given. The officers and the population would be awakened only after Niak's orders. Niak passed his hands over his eyes, moistened his dried lips, exercised his fingers and hands and sat up. 'It's time to go! We were lazy enough,' he thought, and stood up. The first thing he did was to take a look at the chronometer.

" 'Impossible!' he murmured. 'We exceeded scheduled time by 375 years . . . ' He tried to remain calm. He stepped out of his transparent coffin and immediately ran to the Control Room. In a glance he discovered the radical change of direction and panicked.

" 'What if we've become the satellite of the wrong planet? This would be our definite end!' "

"P.A. heard his monologue and replied, *'Alphomega is our target-planet and, in less than three hours, we shall be its satellite. The planet is inhabitable. After phasmatoscopic research, I have reached the conclusion one can live there under tolerable conditions. On screen ZKPS I am giving televisual images of the planet in order for you to acquire personal information on the given conditions.'*

"The huge screen was on with a light blue color surrounded by a white frame.

" 'P.A., What's all this?'

" 'Vapors. As we approach the planet, the denser they become.'

" 'I don't see anything! I want to see what exactly is going on, on the surface of this strange planet.'

" 'I would not advise you to do so.' Niak pressed a button. 'P.A., what's happening?' No reaction came from the Hyper-computer.

" 'Why don't you answer?'

" 'Under the clouds, Master . . . '

" 'What is it? What is happening?'

" 'It is Hell itself, Master! It's the only name I recall for the situation down there! We begin to experience side-effects.'

" 'What do you mean?'

" 'Something comparable to what happened to KEROPS when we left and had the visit by the comet. Only, here, things happen on a much larger scale!'

" 'Niak suddenly remembered something and ran to put on the screen of ZKPX (KEROPS's information system) where he had recorded on video everything that happened on the father-planet, beginning when they left their orbit. He was horrified, watching the collapse of KOX's ring and the destruction of thousands of floating towns and arable grounds.'

" 'P.A., was anybody saved on KEROPS?'

" 'I have received a message from the MANTA, your brother. One out of every thousand Angels was saved, but . . . '

" 'But, what?'

" 'Only one in ten thousand is not out of his senses . . . I think that is rather an optimistic statistic.'

" 'Niak covered his face with his hands. 'At least they're saved,' he whispered. 'Fortunately, we escaped. At least some were saved. Let's see what shall become of us . . . '

"He returned to the ZKPS screen that gave information on Alphomega planet. On that friendly place were four solid surfaces. While he was watching, these solid surfaces were torn apart, like a piece of paper tears into smaller pieces. One of the four ended up looking like a piece of lace.

"From the mountaintops, fire and melted metal were spewing out, powerfully ejected with a tremendous roar. At the beginning, Niak thought this phenomenon was threatening.

" 'P.A., are they shooting us?'

" 'No, Master! You should not worry about that. Our arrival caused very significant disturbance on the planet's crust. It cracked and flames are jumping out from his burning core.' Niak did not seem appeased by P.A.'s explanations. 'How are we going to live in such a hell?'

" 'Master, nature always finds its way to equilibrium, no matter what happens. Suddenly it intervenes and realizes the perfect solution. It shall certainly do so, now. Without minding about the losses.'

" 'Niak was not yet satisfied with the explanation. He needed some more details. 'P.A., where is this pandemonium leading?'

" ' . . . to dynamic equilibrium. In less than twenty-five KEROPS days, everything will be calm. Tranquillity that will radically modify the landscape will follow.'

" 'Yes, but the inhabitants shall be aware that our arrival is the cause of their disaster. They shall know we have brought them destruction. Have you thought of their reactions?'

" 'Master, I have to apologize! As we are talking about our own losses, I completely forgot to inform you. There are no superior forms of life on this planet. This means there is no organized enemy. You may consider as given the submission of the creatures whose intelligence does not exceed the animals. The intellectual level of the most developed creature does not exceed fifteen percent of the NOVO-OMOHS' level.'

" 'That low? But, how is it possible you have so much detailed information about this planet, P.A.? Who had been interested in all this before?'

" 'Master, first, my information about the animals is not complete. As far as the other data is concerned, it exists thanks to an ancestor of yours who risked losing his place because he was considered peculiar.'

"The MANTA reacted, 'Oh, I see! The one that had the nickname Tremulous?'

" 'Yes, Master, exactly! Deep inside, he had this premonition something was to happen. He had sent 850 missions to all directions, to study the universe, to find out where we could live without enemies, in case of emergency.'

" 'It seems he was a Prophet rather than a Tremulous. Really, P.A., we've forgotten the most important thing! What about the atmosphere? Are you sure we won't have any problem?'

" ' . . . Yes . . . well . . . '

" 'What do you mean? Niak asked anxiously. I see you're hesitating. Tell me immediately! Tell me the truth!'

" 'Well, Master, something strange happens here. We, excuse me, I mean you, the Angels, might have some difficulty breathing, while . . . '

" 'While . . . ?'

" 'While, Master, your OMOH slaves and, particularly, the NOVO-OMOHs shall be better adapted to the new atmosphere. I am terribly sorry!'

" 'If this isn't a surprise . . . " the MANTA said furiously.

'Well, it doesn't matter. We've got the better biologists with us. They'll certainly do something to help us. They might equip the new cloned generation with the slaves' breathing gene.'

"On the screen, P.A. showed close-up images of the planet. While the pandemonium continued with the same intensity, terrible earthquakes shook the ground! Deep fissures wrinkled the surface. Huge and strong plants cracked down like matches or were swallowed by the ground that abandoned their roots. From the mountaintops, rivers of melted metals were flowing down, burning anything alive on their way. Living creatures that had ruled over the planet for thousands of years thanks to their muscular power, now tried vainly to avoid the fatal end.

"Later, P.A. showed a group of monstrous creatures, huge in their volume and weight. They had fallen on the ground and were shaking, as if an invisible hand was pressing them and glued them to the ground

"P.A. made the long story short. 'The end of this world is here, now, Master!' Niak got up, walked a little and, turning his head, said, 'Is this the dawn of our own world? Or, are we to follow . . . '

" 'With no doubt,' the hypercomputer P.A. declared with technological self-confidence, 'it shall be the rise of a new home-planet!'

"P.A.'s answer satisfied Niak. He sat in front of the ZKPS screen and thought of enriching his knowledge to be ready for the forthcoming landing. Wasn't it his father who said 'Information is power?'

" 'P.A., why do the animals die right on the ground? There's not even one walking although they have very strong feet! What has changed?'

" 'Our arrival increased this planet's and our mass. At the same time, its orbit has been modified.'

" 'What do you mean?'

" 'Without us, Alphomega, according to law of gravity, had a defined orbit around its sun. This was predetermined, according to its mass. Now, we are part of it. The combined mass of the two of us is heavier, so, we are also in a new orbit, at another distance from the sun.'

" 'I see! Gravitation has changed! It increased!'

" 'Exactly! Every creature, every object is, at this moment, 60% heavier. If those animals' feet could lift up ten tons, they now have to lift 16 tons. They are sentenced to be immobilized.'

"Niak remained silent, thinking. 'They shall all starve to death! They cannot move their bodies, I am sorry.'

" 'Not all of them, Master! Certainly, nature also has provided for such a case. There certainly exist animals with auxiliary body power. Moreover . . . '

" 'What else?'

" 'The axle of revolution has been modified and the poles also changed location.'

" 'This means the climate will change, too?'

" 'Master, the new climate will be more favorable to us, sorry, to you.'

" 'P.A., I really hope you're right. In fact, what about my sleeping Angels? I would like to have some more details, before I wake them up.'

"There was no response.

" 'P.A., what's the matter, again? I think you're trying to avoid the bad news.'

" 'Master, it might be a disaster, but it is not a complete one . . . '

" 'What do you mean? What do you mean, a disaster?'

" 'I will show you the data on the ZKPS screen. You will allow me to interrupt communication in order to recharge myself.' The screen was turned off while the other one turned on. P.A.'s recorded analysis presented the following data: "73 percent dead, 25 percent in a non-reversible state. Awakening is not advised for them. 1.8 percent alive, yet impossible for them to be active members, shall be handicapped. All of the officers, saved. Rest of living, capable. They are 2,406. 1,188 are OMOHs in 594 couples."

"Niak shivered. If he had been made to have tears—like the NOVO-OMOHs, he would be weeping now.

" 'P.A., are you ready?'

" 'Yes, Master.'

" 'It's a real disaster! Only 1218 Angels have been saved! The DE.A.T.H. System must be applied to the total of the impotent. This shall help us maintain complete food autonomy. Thus, without haste, we shall organize our descent to the planet and our colony, there.'

" 'Yes, Master. Do you allow me? I have some good news. According to my calculations, eight spacecraft are in flight condition. Four others are in a reparable state.'

" 'But, we had hundreds of them.'

" 'They were completely shattered due to extreme temperature variability and to de-pressurization.'

" 'At least, the remaining ones are reliable?'

" 'Absolutely, Master! There are eight spacecraft. Already, the stone-breaking mechanical rats have reached the surface.'

" 'Are the exit tunnels ready?'

" 'Yes, Master! I have ordered their opening.'

" 'Tell me, P.A., how is it possible you have every detailed information concerning the planet? When did you have the time?'

" 'Master, when our course's deviation occurred, I had calculated the only solution was to direct ANOL towards Alphomega. While you were asleep, I had all the time and necessary equipment to study our target. Furthermore, I have drawn up a map of its surface. I know all the areas where you may find the necessary minerals or, other areas, that look like our floating fields with soils that we can cultivate. But they are not floating here.'

" 'Very well! Your contribution to the plan's success was extremely important. This is why I am to take you with me in one of those spacecraft.'

"The Master of the game isolated P.A. Niak had to concentrate. He suddenly was realizing that data had changed and new problems came up that were awaiting his solution. The plan was to colonize another planet, with different data, different prospects, other kinds of enemies. The plan did not predict such extensive losses in people and materials during the journey. That was a disaster beyond anticipation. The only positive thing, that was also his most effective weapon, was P.A. He functioned perfectly well.

"His closest collaborators, Hax, Salta, Soemgyp, and the technological elite, had managed to build up that extraordinary mechanical brain that was able to think, to judge, and even dared to take initiatives. The equivalent to KEROPS's planet system had been enriched with all of the knowledge and all the information coming from every imaginable area. It contained anything that had been written, said and created.

"All the data concerning every life's area, from fashion to astrophysics, were already in his memory. This vertiginous condensation of information was followed by a synthesis stage. Information was evaluated and put together into a dynamic equilibrium state that could be activated at any moment and result in what we call 'thinking.' This distillation of the knowledge and information, and of the synthesis that followed, became so necessary, that it could be compared to the gospel of a religion. Of course, this religion had no prejudices and no superstition.

"When the old MANTA had announced the hypercomputer's maturing, he had said:

" 'Thanks to my son's genius that invented it, the whole world shall, from now on, obey the Father-Computer that will belong to all of you. Through your Personal Computers you shall consult it and I would like you to execute, in every detail, its decisions and advice because it is error-free.'

"Niak, its inventor, had managed to install on ANOL an exact copy of the Father Computer. He named it P.A., after the initials of the two suns' names. The one was 'P' and, the other, 'A'. This was to imply that, as the two suns bring light, thus P.A. would enlighten them to find their way again.

"Their salvation depended precisely on that characteristic, that it was capable of decision and the execution of that decision without error. It was their own Savior-God. With P.A. as an ally, Niak had no need for advisors. Yet he needed good collaborators, Angels he could trust.

" 'I shall first awaken Hax, Salta and Soemgyp,' he thought out loud. 'We shall try together to evaluate the situation that is created and prioritize our action. When evaluation is completed, I shall wake up the 381 members of the general assembly.'

"He pressed the button that activated the communication system with P.A. He immediately asked, 'What about the 381 that are asleep in the central sphere?'

" 'Master, I am sorry! According to a later check, only 218 are alive and in good psychological shape, that is, capable of survival. They are part of the 2,406 capable ones I have calculated. The 1,188 OMOHs that are alive are in the central sphere. Do you want the awakening procedure to start?'

" 'No, P.A , it's too early! Wake up only my three assistants!'

"The ZKPS screen displayed the macabre statistical figures that showed his tribe's destruction and horror. The MANTA knew the only reason for this evil was his limitless ambition. Would he, at least, reach his target? Or would he simply be considered the greatest butcher of an entire world? Perhaps, he thought, the calamities that fell upon KEROPS, at the moment of his departure, and the cataclysm that followed the comet's passing, would leave wounds that could never heal. They might disappear as a species!

" 'If I fail, I shall be my generation's murderer! If I ever fail, I shall be the worst criminal of the whole universe,' he thought. He got up and went near a wall, so bright it perfectly reflected his image.

"He saw himself and said, 'No! I must not be disheartened! No! I'm close to the solution! Reproduction shall fill up the gaps. My biologists will certainly be able to create a new generation, not only through cloning. They will offer it new features that shall help it to adapt perfectly to our new home-planet's environment.'

"He gained encouragement from his own words and when

he fell asleep at the end of the day he enjoyed a few refreshing hours free of nightmares and cares. The next day, he put his agenda in order. He had many things to discuss with his three assistants. They already were in the final recovery stage. By night he sought to settle the matter of the distribution of the NOVO-OMOHs: 65% of the 'romantic-sensible-actors' would fall under his jurisdiction.

"After the three assistants completed their recovery procedure, they abandoned their cold graves and moved towards the administration center to meet their idol and savior.

"For the occasion, the MANTA wore all the colorful decorations corresponding to his status. As soon as they entered, he got up to welcome them. He was very touched by their presence.

"The giant Salta put his arms around Niak and told him. 'We are alive and this gives us hope for our future survival.' The other two, less emotional and more pragmatic, disregarded the formalities, and went straight to the heart of the matter.

" 'Hax and I, MANTA, are waiting for your orders. Certainly many urgent things have to be done so, let's not waste any time! P.A. informed us about the target's modification.'

"Niak briefly explained the tragic situation concerning the losses they suffered during the journey. Afterwards he took them into the tunnel-elevator that would lead them to ANOL's surface.

"First, according to P.A.'s instructions, they had to wear the equipment that would allow them to survive, as there was no trace of atmosphere. ANOL, anyway, had its weight and volume expanded because of its journey.

"The landscape they saw when they reached the surface was discouraging! The ground, full of scars, resembled a dead man's face. It reminded them of a bombed battlefield. In ANOL's case, the bombs were small or big meteorites that had blasted innumerable craters. Deadly silence reigned. The dominant color was gray, the color of death. They looked at the sky. It was an instinctive move because, seeing their unfriendly, spherical, gray homeland, they looked up to the sky for salvation. Indeed, at that moment, in the middle of the sky, there was the planet that, despite the great distance, sent them reflections in blue and gold.

" 'We shall be saved if we manage to colonize that wonderful celestial body,' Niak said. Salta, who always spoke the most, asked, 'MANTA, what does P.A. say? Are we going to succeed? Will we manage to go there?'

"Niak paused before answering. 'Yes, my friends! We will! Yet, reaching one's destination does not necessarily mean one may also prosper there.'

" 'Are there enemies, obstacles, dangers?' The giant assistant asked, biting his lips.

" 'No, Salta, there aren't and this encourages us to try our landing sooner than I thought.'

" 'Still, we have to choose the landing area,' said Hax, who had not spoken a word until then. Niak did not reply. He just gave the signal for them to return to headquarters. They got rid of their equipment and then their leader described his plan in detail.

" 'My friends, the answer to Hax's question is that, yes, we have to choose, not one, but three areas for landing on Alphomega.'

" 'Why three?' Soemgyp asked curiously. 'Wouldn't it be better if we were all together? Separately, we might make it easier for our hostile environment to harm us.'

"Niak smiled. 'Your argument is very reasonable but we are not supposed to face a directly hostile environment. Even the stronger animals have been exterminated. The reason is more serious than one could imagine. In P.A.'s geographical analysis, I have noticed there are three different areas on this planet that could be equally convenient for us to settle.'

" 'Divide our population into three groups? But, since we all have the same possibilities . . . '

"Niak nodded. 'My friends, we are the same, but we are not able to work. Whether we like it or not, we depend upon our labor force.'

" 'You mean the NOVO-OMOHs will determine our actions in the end?' Hax asked, amused.

"Instead of any other answer, Niak turned on P.A.'s screen and asked him to display the planet's geophysical map. In a few seconds, a first part was displayed, showing high mountaintops and a very uneven ground.

" 'Of course, Hax! Imagine we landed at precisely that point and didn't have the corresponding mineworkers, those Cut-Eyed NOVOs that dig tunnels in places where not even a machine could go. In my opinion, one of us, together with those workers, should land here.'

"The MANTA went on with the demonstration and reached an area of the planet where temperature was very high and everything was covered by tall trees.

" 'Here, we will land the dark Angels. Sun's radiation doesn't cause them any problem; thus, there will be no losses.'

"Soemgyp, who was fat and short, proposed, 'I would like to lead that mission.'

"The MANTA looked at him seriously. 'I have no objection, provided Hax agrees to control the mines. Anyway, you're swarthy, too.'

"The proposal of turning the mines over to HAX was tempting to him. Everybody was aware that, he who would have under his possession the mineral wealth would also be the most powerful."

" 'I accept with no reservations,' Hax said, managing to hide his enthusiasm.

" 'You, MANTA, where will you be? Where are you going with the unskilled and delicate actors of the NOVO-OMOH race?'

"The MANTA pressed the button again and displayed a piece of land surrounded by a small ocean filled with islands.

" 'As your leader, I shall have the administrative responsibility and my instructions shall be transmitted through the channels. My NOVO-OMOHs will, anyway, have to deal with occupations that have nothing to do with manual work. Of course, in order for us to survive, I shall take with me 200 un-skilled OMOHs, for agriculture.'

" 'We all have incorporated bio-tele-trans-receivers (BTTR) and we just have to activate them in order to communicate directly, even if everything is destroyed. From my headquarters, I shall display in your electronic bulletin your work-program, based on your information. For the time being—I am to judge how long this will be—I shall have absolute power and I warn you that, for our common aim's sake, for the sake of Survival, I might lead you to the limits!'

"Hax, Salta and Soemgyp exchanged glances. Afterwards, they came near the MANTA and, with a typical submission gesture, they showed they agreed and placed their lives at his disposal. Each one of them separately swore the same unconditional submission oath: 'EVERYTHING for the tribe's salvation! EVERYTHING in your hands!' "

# Showdown

**B**y the time he was ready to leave the Westin Hotel, Canakis had planned and organized a counterattack on every front. From Chicago's O'Hare Airport he took an American Eagle flight and, in no time, he was at his newspaper's office in Urbana. Choked with emotion, the Managing Editor himself, the one that had fired him before, held him in his arms and kissed him.

Canakis got straight to the point. "Sir, before I came here, I took an antidote for your kisses! You never know!" Without giving him time to respond, Canakis continued.

"Call everybody here. I want to speak to them! Things are developing with lightning speed, and we've got to catch up with them and take advantage of unexpected opportunities. We have to act in an organized fashion to be effective."

In a few minutes the office was filled with reporters, notebooks and tape-recorders in hand, ready to receive instructions. Canakis, like a general before the battle, started giving orders to his "officers."

"George!"

"Yes, sir!"

"You'll contact geologists Milio Kosta and Vladimir Lisenco. You'll also get in touch with Jonathan Keith and Dean Thomson, the astronaut's father. Tell them, George, to stay close by; we shall give them instructions very soon. Also, contact Brigitte Marcais, in Paris, and Theodore in Athens or Brussels!

"Pietro!"

"Yes."

"You'll immediately contact the Center for the Study of Extraterrestrial Intelligence (CSETI)!"

"You mean Steven Green, the one who had organized that famous convention last April?"

"Exactly! Congratulations, Pietro, I'd forgotten his name! Also find Edgar Michael, the former astronaut who walked on the Moon, in 1971. Also find Major Philip Corso!"

"The one who wrote the book, *The Day after Roswell*?"

"Precisely! Also, the four doctors at Walter Reed Hospital in Washington! They did the autopsy on the Roswell corpses. Also, find Richard Huot and Jacques Lavois, who photographed a UFO, in 1978, in Montreal. Let's not forget John Eckles, the medical philosopher, Nobel Prize in Medicine, who mapped out the human brain. I almost forgot! At any cost, find me Dr. Weissman and Martin, the ones who studied the Puerto-Rico embryo!"

"Yes, sir!" Pietro said and bolted out.

After Canakis gave some secondary instructions to the rest, he turned to his happy managing editor.

"Chief, I think that, especially in this affair, what interests me most isn't all that much the newspaper's success—that will certainly be astronomic. What interests me more is to help the truth shine for all to see! Gods and demons are after two persons whose only mistake was to mess around, without even wanting to, with a terribly revealing story about where we come from and who we are."

The editor replied, "My son, I don't think you can convince

me we're Angels. My conviction is we're doomed. Yes, we're Angels who came from Hell and, instead of creating a new paradise we fell back again into a horrible technological hell that is the creation of our own hands and twisted brains. Tell me, son, what are your plans?" the chief asked, smiling.

Canakis pounded his fist on the editor's office for emphasis and said, "I shall bring them all to the Westin Hotel, including David and Larry and their women. All nineteen of them shall be there! I'll call all the television stations and ask questions in front of the cameras."

"It will be a huge story," the editor said, drunk with satisfaction.

"It will take about four hours and I'll have over two hundred journalists and reporters torturing me!"

The managing editor patted his graying moustache. It was true that he had no reason at all to be displeased with what he had heard. His many years on the job signaled to him the beginning of a windfall that would benefit the newspaper. Trying not to show too much of what he was thinking, he simply said, "Four hours on every TV station is worth a lot of dollars, isn't it?"

"Finally, I shall invite Michael Donovan and Cardinal Patrick to a live television debate. They will be shaken. I'll ask them, 'Why this hunt? Why was David considered Public Enemy Number One?' "

The managing editor seemed to disagree with that last idea. "Ok . . . Ok! But let's not mess around with the federal government and the Catholics! Let's not make all our readers mad at the same time. First do those interviews and then wait for the reactions. Meanwhile, we'll see! We'll give it some thought?"

"OK, Chief! I guess you're right! You're more experienced and think more calmly than I do!" The editor's personal secretary came in without knocking.

"What's up, Tommy?" the chief asked. Tommy approached and gave him a fax. The editor glanced at it casually and handed it to Mario. "It's from Athens, from old Theodore. He must be thanking you for the invitation."

Canakis said nothing.

"Why don't you say something? Is he ill or what?"

Canakis still did not answer. He seemed hypnotized by the text in front of his eyes. "It's impossible! This is simply impossible!"

"What's impossible? Can't we find out?"

Canakis lifted his eyes. His face was pale. He looked as if he had seen God in person.

"Chief, in Greece, down in a valley there are some huge, egg-shaped stones on which priests have built monasteries . . . "

"Is this a geography lesson or what?" the editor teased. "I've visited Greece, as a tourist. On the way to Delphi, coming from the North, I've seen what you're talking about. They've got an easy name—the Meteora."

"Congratulations, Chief! Those Greeks have got the devil or . . . the Angels inside them! It's a prophetic name!"

"What's the prophecy in all of this, Mario?"

Canakis, shaking the paper, shouted, "There's been a terrible earthquake. The earthquake just toppled one of the stones. That meteoro was thoughtful enough to break into two pieces, like a watermelon. Fortunately, there was no monastery on it. In it, they've observed metallic construction. Like the one in Beni's cavern, the one David investigated!"

"How do you know exactly what it looks like?"

"Theodore Papadopoulos, who saw the first, now saw the new one, too. He's the only eye-witness of both events!"

"He's sure? What's he saying exactly?"

Mario unfolded the paper, sat beside the editor and read out loud. "I have visited the locale and, approximately at the center of the fossil, I observed a strange gap. It is like a huge hive-room with a stone cover."

The managing editor was feeling uneasy. He wanted to protect Canakis whose enthusiasm might lead him to reach conclusions too fast.

"I think . . . don't forget your friend has reached some respectable age. The quality of judgement and perception of an event is almost always directly related to age."

Canakis, left the office without a word, and went to the information Center of Illinois University, three blocks away from the newspaper building. At the Geography Department, he found Professor Alex de Greef and checked the Internet about information on the Meteora. He learned that the origin of Meteora is still unknown. The mineral structure has nothing to do with the rocks of the nearby mountain. Research showed the Meteora were not the product of erosion like Arizona's equivalent formations. There is no continuity; they have no "roots." It is as if something supernatural had positioned the huge rocks there like stone-guardians; it surpasses imagination. The results of an incomplete research project showed that the rocks are not compact. They are empty inside!

"Vehicles for transportation of personnel!" Canakis shouted in his enthusiasm and drew the professor's reaction.

"But, what are you talking about? Those are just stones! Nothing more!"

Mario smiled. He was certain the professor was surprised and it was only logical, as he was not yet informed about David's File.

"Professor de Greef, I don't have the time now, but I promise you that, very soon, through the media and the documents I'm going to send to you, you'll understand the deeper meaning of the phrase: 'The Meteora are camouflaged vehicles for staff transport!' "

As Canakis was departing, carrying the printout about the hollow Meteora, the professor crossed himself and murmured, "The poor guy is going crazy! Roswell's virus from space must have contaminated him. That's it for him, then!"

Canakis returned to the newspaper building and instructed his nineteen guests to be at the Westin Hotel in four days. He made sure rooms were available and told them to confirm the space two days before their arrival.

He went to bed. He was home for the first time after such a long time! That last stormy day had exhausted him physically and, even more so, psychologically. He slept for twelve hours without even changing sides. But a nightmare disturbed his sleep. On one side were tanks and aircraft, fully equipped, driven by priests and, on the other side, Angels with swords and thunder.

"What a strange instrument—the human brain," he said to himself when he woke up and realized with relief that, what he had dreamed of was a simple cocktail of the information that was on his mind. He took a shower, shaved and, while preparing himself a good cup of coffee, he pressed the button of the answering machine.

"I see you so rarely that I've almost reverted to being a virgin! Sorry! Now, I'm seeing Renato! Good luck!"

"At last, I got rid of her."

Yet, the second message did not come from a girlfriend. "I'm calling from the Department of State. Please notify everyone concerned. Following the latest developments, a World Convention will be held in Cancun, Mexico. Its purpose will be to study all the pertinent cases in the CSETI reports through unbiased interrogation of Roswell's eyewitnesses and fully detailed analysis of David Mason's narration.

"The convention will last seven days in order to provide adequate time in case we need to call any essential witnesses. All charges against David Mason and Larry Keith were dropped and we are instituting an investigation against those responsible for the defamation plot against the two. In order to confirm receipt of this message, you are kindly asked to respond personally, number . . . "

Canakis, sporting a smart-aleck smile, dialed the number on his mobile phone. Before he was able to say a word, he heard a voice.

"Secretary Michael Donovan."

"Mr. Secretary, this is Canakis!"

"My friend, Canakis! I'm very happy to meet you, at last! I'd prefer Michael to the pompous Mr. Secretary."

"OK, Michael! I've got your message and I'm very pleased you are finally taking David's File seriously.

"But, of course! Ever since the beginning of it all, I . . . Be certain that I shall exercise all of my influence so that this affair reaches its natural ending. The truth will come out."

This entire apologetic monologue was aimed at hiding the unsuccessful efforts of the state and the Church. An effort that had one purpose, that of muzzling David Mason. Canakis had every reason not to complicate the situation with accusations of his own. On the contrary, he had to show he was willing to forget for the sake of reaching a respectable solution.

"I've called you to confirm my participation at the convention. It's a marvelous initiative of yours! Congratulations!"

"Mr. Canakis . . . "

"Mario, to high government officials!"

"OK, Mario! Everything will go fine, with one small condition, as far as your friends are concerned."

"I'm listening, Michael!"

"Let's not have anything that has to do with religion become the direct subject of criticism. I promise you, this matter shall be discussed privately during another meeting."

"I'll do my best, Michael, and I hope I am successful. Of course, we need the agreement of those personally involved."

"Mario, please, if possible, send us a copy of every one of David's tapes so that we can study them."

"OK, Michael! When do you think this convention will take place?"

"It's rather difficult to say right now. In any case, I would not think that you would object as to the place . . . Mexico."

"No, I don't think there will be any objection but I think the narration is too incomplete for me to send you copies."

"Are you serious? David's still speaking? He might get addicted to that!"

"But, this is the complete theory of creation, Michael; it explains almost all the unanswered questions. Nobody knows, not even David, when exactly the narration is to end. Personally, I think that in twenty to thirty days it will be completed."

"Amazing! And here I thought . . . "

"No, Michael! This isn't done according to a schedule of

ours. It depends on the stimulation generated by the microchip in David's brain, that electronic device that was placed in his memory's center when he was injured."

"Extraordinary! I think we all had underestimated the importance of this matter. I'm looking forward to listening to the tapes. Write down my personal phone number, if anything important comes up. It's number. . . . "

"Michael, I'm a journalist and, starting tomorrow, I'm going to start publishing the first hot stories in the *Urbana Daily*. I invite you to read them. I'm about to tell everything!"

"In God's name! Just keep gods and religions out of it."

"OK! I swear to God, our own God . . . "

"Thanks, Mario. Bye."

Mario Canakis was jumping with joy, completely forgetting the coffee that he had prepared for himself a while ago. He had succeeded, all by himself, in freeing David and Larry. Furthermore, a convention was organized to clear up this entire messy affair. "I see myself, everyday, on all the superchannels, defending the New World theory . . . At the very least, a new kind of Star Trek series will come out of this story."

He was talking to himself. It was a glorious thought, a hymn to victory.

# Truth Over Lies

**D**avid Mason and Larry Keith learned the good news this time, without having to take any conspiratorial safety measures. Larry always cherished the opportunity to tease his friend.

"Fortunately, things are moving faster now, David, because I see the collagen on your face deteriorating; it has lost that impressive look! You know, you're full of wrinkles . . . You're ugly again! When Natassa sees you, she'll be disappointed!"

David could not leave a challenge unanswered. He touched Larry's jaw with his fist and remarked, "Larry, I'm ugly, now . . . OK! But you who, even after the surgery were a mess, imagine what an aesthetically discouraging stage you've reached by now!"

Emotionally, they were in a state similar to that of two convicts who have suddenly received reprieves from a death sentence. When they went out on the street to breathe freedom's air, they wanted to yell so that everybody could hear them. "We are the ones accused unjustly of being pederasts!".

"Larry, have you read the newspaper *LE SOIR?*"

"What? They've started the chase again?"

"No, calm down! Biologists in Germany have determined that the Neanderthal man wasn't an ancestor of Man, as they were saying up to now."

"Perhaps he was an ancestor of the Nazis," Larry said.

"Ha, ha! You're terrible! But that was very good!"

They were now carefree, no worries about personal safety, and were acting like children. They chatted and they joked. They were happy. They took the train and soon arrived at Brussels' Grand Place.

"Excuse me! Where can we have a really fine meal?" they asked a stranger.

But despite all the insider views of the stranger about dining in Brussels, they entered the first restaurant they saw, Chez Vincent. Everything was so tasty; they almost gorged themselves to the emergency room. They spent the afternoon trying to digest their huge meal in the comfortable armchairs of Café Metropole at Brokers' Place. David remained silent, not even answering his friend's irrelevant questions. But there is a limit to everything.

"David, have you noticed the lady that just passed by?"

"What's on your twisted mind again? Yes, I saw her! What's bothering you?"

"Nothing, but I think she comes from St. Martin's Island, in the Caribbean."

"And based on what criteria have you reached this amazing anthropological conclusion, Doctor?"

"If you had visited the island, you would have noticed that all of the women, with no exception other than the Dutch, have terribly prominent behinds."

David propped himself up a little, exhaled heavily to indicate this displeasure, and said, "You are the famous professor? You are the one who's madly in love with Barbara, the one upon whom the scientific world depends for interrogating me? Aren't you ashamed? If I know you, if it were within your absolute jurisdiction, the next generation would have its DNA enriched with the 'prominent-behinds' gene of this lady."

Larry changed the subject conveniently. "OK, David, sorry! For a long time I have wanted to ask you about the DNA of monkeys and humans."

David jumped out of his seat. His face was lit up and the smile of victory bloomed on his lips. It frightened Larry. "He is going to have one of those headaches, again! We must find some private place," he thought.

"Eureka!" David shouted, totally indifferent to the people around them. The customers of Café Métropole looked around uncomfortably. Larry tried to calm his friend.

"Do you have a headache?" he asked, as David was returning to his seat.

David smiled and turned his armchair around so he could look his friend straight in the eyes. "I've thought of something that may actually connect the Roswell and the Puerto-Rico incidents with KEROPS's history!"

Larry shook his head in disappointment. "Two dissimilar events that are separated, perhaps, by millions of years! It's impossible that they are related! Extraterrestrial corpses, on one hand, Angels on the other . . . but . . . just a moment . . . Yes! The corpses had two humps! They could be inactive roots of wings! Tell me! Help me understand!"

David was listening with satisfaction. Then, seeing Larry had reached a dead end, he said, "Let me help you, Larry. Listen and tell me if my thinking is unreasonable. If we study and compare the DNA from Roswell's corpses to that of the Neanderthal man, or even to today's human beings, we might discover something really important."

Larry scratched his head. He was impressed by David's unexpected suggestion.

"David, you're a genius! You're incredible! I think that if this comparative study is done it will produce some surprising conclusions!"

"Even if no relationship with us is concluded—which is

most probable—we shall probably reproduce the dead space travelers in a human uterus, through cloning,."

"Who knows? Perhaps memory is hereditary in those creatures and then . . . "

"Then, no other 'David' shall ever again be abused in order to narrate the history of their civilization."

David got up and was followed into the Metropole by an astounded Larry. They asked to book a room.

"Do you have a headache?" Larry asked anxiously.

"No, my friend, I'm in a hurry. I want to transmit my idea to our coordinator, the amazing Mario Canakis!

At the Hotel, in Chicago, the champagne was flowing in celebration of their victory. Just half an hour earlier, Barbara and Natassa had heard the wonderful news and they tried, in vain, to locate David and Larry. At last, David called and they told him about the other great news concerning the convention their opponents were finally obliged to organize.

"So, even a convention will be organized on our behalf," David said obviously moved. Mario, your news is really extraordinary! But, we also have some news of equal significance!"

"What do you mean?"

David explained his thoughts about reproducing the aliens through cloning. "One condition for us to accept the invitation to the convention Donovan is organizing is to receive an official promise that this cloning will be performed," David said.

A surprised Mario was unable to utter a single word. Finally, he managed to speak. "David, I must admit your brain gives birth to great ideas! Anyway, your humility and modesty are almost disguised behind a mask of vanity! Take good care of your image," he advised jokingly. "I think this demand of yours will be too much, but it costs us nothing to try."

"Thanks for keeping my feet on the ground, Mario; you understand the effects of drinking from the cup of glory!"

The more Mario Canakis thought of David's idea, the more ingenious he found it. "How is it," he thought, "nobody up to now ever thought of reproducing the dead aliens? Law prohibits such action on humans but there is no law stopping David from implementing his idea about 'non-human beings.'

"There will be serious problems that will have to be resolved. We cannot estimate their consequences right now. What would happen if we could replace the nucleus of a monkey's ovary with that of an alien? If we could not, we would have to find the proper receiver for the alien root. Imagine if that receiver were a human being!"

Mario found his conclusions extreme but revolutionary. "That's what enthusiasm does . . . Enthusiasm is the brother of fanaticism, and the mother of both is superficiality . . . But enthusiasm is also the motor that drives progress."

Natassa, who sat beside him, respected his daydreaming. But, when he expressed his philosophy out loud, she could no longer take it. "Who is the superficial person that inspired this phrase in you—a philosopher? I want to learn, too, so that some day I may be able to reach your level!"

Mario reached out and grabbed her nose with his two fingers. "I'm the superficial one, I'm the philosopher."

But beautiful Natassa would not give up so easily. "After this declaration I must know if superficiality is a condition for becoming a philosopher."

The telephone rang. It was Mario's managing editor calling from Urbana. "Mario, I've been talking to a Cardinal"

"Bless you! Did you get any advance relief medication?"

"He absolutely wants to meet you. Anywhere."

"Never! I refuse!"

"Why?"

"Because I don't see the point. Because I don't see what could be gained from such a conversation; what would be the subject of discussion."

"David's File."

"Chief, there are new developments, even though the storm has not even settled around David's File. But, we have some incredible news! By the way, tell those we invited not to come to Chicago. It's better we postpone that. The news has forced a change in my immediate plans."

"What news?"

"The news is David's proposal for cloning."

"Is he going crazy, Mario? He wants a copy of himself? He knows it is strictly forbidden. And, anyway, what would be the use of such a cloning?"

"You don't get it! You won't even let me speak! That's the problem with being a managing editor. They never let anyone complete a sentence."

His boss interrupted him again. "Mario, the chairman of the Board of Directors proposed that you should become talkative like me."

"You mean, I'll also prevent others from completing their sentences?"

"Congratulations! You've been named director of our new television station, based in Chicago and underwritten by the newspaper. We're waiting for you to baptize it." A long silence followed.

"Are you there? Have a drink to revive yourself."

" . . . Thanks! Thanks! Thanks!"

"So, tell me about David's cloning."

Mario explained that it was about the cloning of aliens, not David's own cloning. But the boss was predictably and irrevocably against further complications of the situation. Everything seemed headed towards a reasonable resolution which would mean both a near future and a long-term financial success.

"Chief, I think you're right! I'll see to it that our demand is postponed for a much later date."

The discussion ended, but the door of opportunity was just opening up for Mario. The David Mason case could feed the new station with endless and original material for at least two more years. "Really, what am I going to name it?" he wondered. He ran to announce the news to the two women in the other room.

"For over two hours we have been drinking to one toast after another . . . Guys, I've got solid evidence that I'm really drunk," Barbara said, pretending to be stuttering.

"You think I'm in a better state?" Natassa added, gulping in one attempt the glass of champagne Mario had just pushed into her hand.

"Mario, if you continue with your rapid success up the company ladder, you'll soon be carried to the hospital in a hepatic coma," she blurted out.

The very next day, David and Larry were on American Airlines' non-stop flight from Brussels to Chicago. On board, several passengers who recognized them showered them with questions and wished them well. Fortunately, David did not seem to be facing any of his usual headache crises.

"David, when somebody's after you, you seem to be inspired more frequently. Do you think the transmission is interrupted, now that you're calm?"

David shook his head. "I wish I hadn't been injured even if that would mean I wouldn't have the honor of becoming the curiosity item of the scientific world. Larry, I feel that not only my mental Odyssey isn't over yet, but, on the contrary, it is in its most interesting phase. I don't know what's to follow but, certainly, there will be one surprise after another."

The landing at O'Hare, at 1:30 p.m., was a turning point in their lives. They were returning to their home country not only without handcuffs but riding on a wave of glory. Even before they had a chance to meet their girlfriends, a lawyer representing the federal government shook their hands, wished them well and reminded them of the legal venues available in order to rehabilitate their name and wounded dignity.

A little later they were hugging their friends.

"Incredible! It seems incredible to me how fast things have been moving," Larry said to Barbara.

"If old Jonathan, your father, hadn't discovered your double, I don't even want to think where you might be now," she muttered. "Your father is the only unrecognized hero." Larry's eyes misted with tears. He pulled back from Barbara and dialed his father's number on his mobile phone.

Canakis followed the conversation from a distance but was touched at the thought of old Jonathan's heroic efforts. He approached Larry because he also wanted to express his gratitude to the old man who had literally been the hero in his own rescue.

"Jonathan Keith, please . . . This is his son." A momentary silence followed. "Hello, I wish to speak to . . . "

"Just ten minutes ago, your father was watching on TV that everything had worked out for you . . . and he left this world. I am the doctor that examined him and signed the death certificate. I am so sorry! My sincere condolences . . . but . . . also . . . my congratulations to you."

Mario saw Larry's face turn pale and realized right away that something had happened to the old warrior.

"Have we lost our hero?"

"Yes, Mario . . . he completed the rescue operation and, after he'd learned the results, he quietly fell at the bastion where he had always lived. I wanted to hold his hand, Mario. I wanted to thank him once more as I should have. He was my father, my hero. He never asked for anything. He never begged for recognition. He was a really proud man. He loved deeply yet he never showed it. He only demonstrated it with his actions. Farewell, proud father! Farewell, my immortal hero!"

Larry's last words were drowned in tears. He collapsed on the sofa. Barbara and Natassa watched speechless. Mario shattered the silence.

"In a few days, Larry, I'll inaugurate a TV station, here, in Chicago. I predict its future will be comparable only to that of the success of CNN. Everything's ready, except for the name. I am now announcing that the call letters of the new station will be *JKS* for *Jonathan Keith System*. I think it's an expression of gratitude he deserves."

Larry and David ran to Mario and embraced him. The three cried silently as the women watched and shed their own tears.

The room was charged with their unspoken gratitude and the memory of old Jonathan.

That night, Larry, Barbara and Mario left by plane to attend Jonathan's funeral that was scheduled for the day after. Natassa and David remained in Chicago. The moment David was approaching the gate at O'Hare, he felt the usual symptoms, headaches and vomiting. He was taken immediately back to the Westin, over the objections of the airport doctor who accompanied him from the gate to the street curb where David and Natassa took a cab. The doctor, of course, had no idea about the peculiarity of David's condition.

# The
# Beachhead

"**N**ormally, the rescued Angels would have needed fifteen earth months, utilizing their super-modern technological equipment, working all day long, to prepare their last attack and achieve their landing on planet Alphomega.

"Of course, earlier, the MANTA and his officers would make one or more reconnaissance trips, to gain personal experience on the conditions prevailing at the three areas they had selected.

"When P.A. woke the OMOHs up, everything went smoothly. Yet, when the NOVO-OMOHs, who were much more demonstrative, woke up, there was chaos! Those that had been perfected according to Niak's orders felt the loss of some of their comrades and cried, yelled, and wept, lying on the floor like babies. Furious about their behavior, the Niak almost ordered their execution. P.A. advised him against it.

" 'Master, you own a limited number of slaves-workers. You will be able to eliminate them eventually, only after the biotechnologists create a sufficient number of common hermaphroditic ones, and only after they adapt to the new environment. Unless . . . unless . . . their own evolution would allow them to replace the Angels themselves in jobs that are boring and not so responsible.'

"The worker teams toiled ceaselessly, according to Project Thunder. A solid state, condensed gas was the energy used and it moved the colossal machines that cleared the obstructed tunnels and picked up the corpses. Utilizing automated procedures, the corpses were transformed into dehydrated, protein, pyramidal pieces. Thus they were conserved until their final consumption as basic food. Other machines, resembling gargantuan rats, continued to open corridors so that the starcraft that had survived would reach ANOL's surface. Work was so intense that the entire satellite-ark was shaking as if hit by an earthquake, a constant earthquake that had reached three degrees on the Richter scale!

"MANTA's officers were at their assigned posts, seeing that Project Thunder was implemented to its minutest detail.

"Two months before launching the twelve starcraft to conquer Alphomega, the MANTA and his officers had decided to proceed with the first reconnaissance flight. Using a digitally processed oscillatory Doppler, P.A. studied the area where the supreme leader was to visit. This mission had been named 'Blue Vision.'

"The MANTA's personal spacecraft and its navigating system were technological wonders. The steering system was fully ergonomic and its propulsion was exclusively laser powered. At the spacecraft's tail was a powerful laser source. The photons emitted by laser are matter, just like the photons of any other light beam. Yet, when the laser is activated, it emits photons in an absolutely straight line, like a stick dotted with infinitely minute spaces.

"If a substance existed that not only could reflect but also stop the photons, then instead of the forward movement of the photons, the body carrying that laser device would be moving. The Angels had already discovered that substance. And, of course, if the body carrying that laser device is a spacecraft, then, theoretically it travels at the speed of light, that is, 300,000 kilometers a second! To reach lower speeds, they emitted not continuous, but intermittent photon bursts.

"This propulsion technique was the MANTA's own invention and he kept it strictly for his personal use. Everything was ready for operation Blue Vision. Niak took his position in that extraordinary and completely silent starcraft. His comrades, sixteen of his most trusted officers, took positions around him. Of course, Niak would do nothing unless he was in constant communication with P.A.

" 'Are we ready, P.A.?'

" 'Yes, Master, we are ready. The trajectory of the starcraft during operation Blue Vision is predetermined, according to your precise instructions.'

"Niak's comrades, who ignored the meaning of the word vision, thought it was a strange name. Niak understood what they were thinking but provided no explanations. He recalled the old MANTA saying: 'Followers give explanations. Leaders simply demand them!'

"He did not have to use the laser reactors because the distance could easily be covered with the power of the compressed gas turbines.

"A thick layer of vapor covered planet Alphomega. At first, his fellow travelers were disappointed, because they had no idea what was hiding underneath that layer.

"Flying vertically for a few minutes, the starcraft passed through that layer and, to the amazement of the officers, before their very eyes, a fantastic world appeared like a painting. The myriad colors of the landscapes and the transparent blue color of the oceans would enchant Ulysses himself. The scenery was magic with the splendor of the rainbow. That was the picture from afar.

"In a few minutes, the starcraft gently touched the ground covered by a green carpet, unlike anything they had seen on KEROPS. All seventeen passengers deplaned, wearing their helmets, spherical plexi-glass helmets filled with a gas mixture that assured their breathing.

"P.A. performed some very rapid calculations and transmitted the good news: 'You may take your helmets off; density of oxygen is ideal. Gravity changes have resulted in modification of density.'

"They jumped with joy. The team now could spread out in order to cover as much of the surface as possible. They had landed in a beautiful valley, but it was filled with hundreds of huge skeletons. The flesh had mostly disappeared and the sun had left some dried up scraps on the giants' skeletons. At the horizon, the mountaintops emitted smoke calmly. As P.A. had predicted, nature had reached its dynamic equilibrium. Niak pointed to a proud-looking, high mountaintop that no longer gave up smoke, where a halo of white snow was forming, reflecting the unique sun as it was setting.

" 'My dear colleagues, I will set up my general headquarters on that mountain, in that region. All the orders shall be communicated from this place.' No one spoke. They considered it wiser to just nod their heads as a sign of obedience and total submission.

"The ground tour lasted several hours. They collected plant and ground samples and when they finished they decided to return to the starcraft because the dark night had arrived.

"Suddenly, something moved at Niak's feet. Surprised as he was, he jumped up and everybody's lights went on almost immediately turning the night into day. Something like a thick rope was moving round their feet as if it were trying to strangle itself. One of Niak's comrades approached the thing and lifted it with his three fingers. The others approached, curious to examine the strange rope. As if powered by lightning, the "thing" twisted its body and bit the officer's hand. In pain, he screamed and threw the thing to the ground.

"Niak took a pair of tongs from the starcraft and picked the thing up again. By the time they returned from their first exploration, one of them was already dead! He was the first victim of adaptation. The planet had exacted revenge because they had violated it. It was all Niak's mistake. Before the officer had picked up the 'rope' he should have asked P.A..

"Niak informed the supercomputer about the incident and placed the strange, long, deadly animal in a small booth for biological analysis. P.A. conducted a detailed analysis and the results were quickly available.

" 'Master, unfortunately, I do not have any information on the remaining animals. Yet, in ten days, I shall know everything. Our biotechnicians will process the information I shall give them. Thus, anything that moves on the ground, anything that swims in the oceans and anything that flies shall be studied in order to avoid surprises.'

"Of course, the Angels did not face death as humans do. Simply, biologists took two cells from the body, for cloning. One 'copy' was destined to serve as a bank for parts and the other took the place and fortune of the departed. Still, the important losses the Angels had suffered did not allow them to casually risk the life of those that had survived. Each one's role was already defined and, for that reason, each was considered irreplaceable.

"Time passed and the work reached its end. The twelve giant starcraft had been installed and the time for the staff selection had arrived. Selection was based on strict criteria, such as aptitude and biological adaptation to work environment. Every officer would have three starcraft, one of which would carry the protein supply that was needed to feed the Angels until their first harvest.

"MANTA would take one personnel transport starcraft, another filled with supplies and, a third one to transport the biotechnology and biotherapy team and their labs in full readiness. The cunning Soemgyp had managed to extract the promise of a full cloning unit, which he received.

"MANTA's orders were the immediate increase in the pace of reproduction in order to replace the heavy losses of the journey. Of course, in his personal starcraft, powered by the SCL (Star-Chip-Laser) propulsion system, the first and main guest would be a unique creature. The landing area he had shown to his officers was a beautiful part of a region where mountains alternated with flat surfaces ideal for cultivation of crops.

"Salta, as MANTA had promised, would be in charge of immense fields that could feed many hundreds of millions of Angels. The future was assured and, certainly, the laws governing the number of dependents and heirs would be adjusted accordingly.

"Indeed, Salta made the first suggestion. 'Great MANTA, our Leader, there are so few of us in this chaos of fertile fields . . . we'll get lost!'

"MANTA answered in a very diplomatic way, 'My dear Salta, you know we all have an implanted communication device, how are we going to get lost? If, as I predict, the experiments that have started here in our new homeland are successful, then, we shall be able to communicate with our minds, our thoughts. Let's say I am thinking of you. You shall immediately feel it and be expecting a message. I shall be thinking of it and you shall answer me the same way. Isn't this fantastic?'

" 'Great MANTA, I've heard of this but I cannot recall the name of this system.'

" 'Bio-tele-connection, or BTC. It is the application of the transfer of thought. Some Angels used to have this aptitude, during the Albinos era. As far as your basic question is concerned, which I did not address, I tell you that, if everything goes well for three centuries, the population increase shall be out of control and, more importantly, the way of life shall change radically.'

"Salta thanked the MANTA and left because he saw swarthy Soemgyp approaching. He instinctively did not like him.

"When MANTA saw Soemgyp, he asked him to come closer. 'My friend, you shall probably have the more difficult part.'

" 'My life is in your hands, great MANTA.' Did he actually believe what he said, like the other two? The iron discipline imposed by the leader was a basic factor of Project Thunder's success.

" 'Soemgyp, you will land on a huge, very hot and solid surface. There is dense vegetation and lots of unknown animals
that may be extremely dangerous. You must establish strong
foundations there, with the help of the swarthy and tall
NOVO-OMOHs. Of course, you shall be in permanent contact with me to receive the necessary instructions.'

" 'Great MANTA, yesterday, when I was resting, I had a
nightmare. It was so realistic, it shocked me.'

"The MANTA smiled. 'I am listening, although I should not
. . . I don't have time for fairy tales.'

" 'I dreamed that even though I had settled perfectly well,
suddenly communication was interrupted with you and Hax
and Salta. I felt falling into the emptiness without a balloon
uniform. I was shaking like a leaf, like a young child that had
been abandoned. I shouted: I am dying! Save me, great
leader!' "

" 'Ha, ha, ha! My dear friend, you are still young and feel
rather insecure . . . We all do, some of us more, others less.
The guarantee that the nightmare shall never be repeated is
my inseparable friend and constant collaborator, P.A..' "

"The supercomputer's receiver was on, so P.A. heard the
conversation. Flattered by his master's praise, he reacted properly.

" 'May I, Master?' P.A. asked. 'Each of the three mission
chiefs shall be allotted two exact copies of my telecommunica-
tion system. Even if you lack a single ergion, the smallest unit
of energy, you shall have enough energy to communicate with
me by using muscular power equal to only three OMOHs. If
both the copies are destroyed, you will have a device that re-
sembles your beam-gun. If you press a button, the gun shall
emit waves covering the entire planet and will reveal the coordinates of your position.'

"The short Soemgyp, listening to all of this, was very happy.
'I feel ridiculous, great MANTA. But, the way I see it, we all
have to trust you with every single thought of ours.'

" 'Congratulations, my friend. Your words are wise.'

" 'May I ask one more question, Master?' he asked with servility.

" 'I am listening. Speak freely.'

" 'Instead of landing in dense vegetation, why couldn't I land more north where things seem clearer, at least, from here?'

" 'This is a very good question, my son! But, where you are assigned to land, you shall be able to immediately respond to your food needs. Those plants are full of fruit. Thus, without a food supply problem, you shall have all the time you need to think of the proper ways of conquering the regions you have mentioned.'

" 'Yes, and specifically the point where the huge river flows into the little ocean.'

" 'But, a place where nothing grows,' the MANTA added. 'The audience is over. I see you have imagination and this is a positive trait for the work you are in charge of. Do not forget that you are the only one to whom I have granted several NOVO-OMOHs and a complete biotechnology team. You are one of the three seeds, perhaps the best one. If you fail, it shall mean the end of our ancient people. Their fate is in your creative hands. Never forget that!'

"With these solemn words, the audience came to its end and the MANTA retired."

Natassa, taking advantage of the interruption, and according to Canakis's instructions, assisted David to stand up and prepare for departure. They had to leave the Westin Hotel.

They had hardly settled in a nearby Holiday Inn when David reacted. "Natassa, I don't feel well. Changing hotels exhausted me." David put his head in his hands and lay down.

Natassa sprang from her chair and ran to the adjacent room. In less than 30 seconds she was back with a glass of water in which she had poured the content of two ampoules.

"Darling, drink this! It's some Calmo Bionevryl."

"But, I've never taken that before . . . "

"You'll take it now." Natassa would not accept any objections. David stood up and drank the preparation with the vile taste. Natassa kissed him.

"You'll sleep for 24 hours, my love. My diagnosis is you are overly stressed—you have Brain Fatigue." Instead of an answer, she heard him snore.

# The Hour
# of Decision

It was natural that M. Donovan, "Michael" to his friends and Cardinal Patrick, would coordinate their actions, in view of the convention they were organizing in Cancun.

They were convinced they were going to be assaulted not only by David Mason and Larry Keith, but also by the mass media and, particularly, the foxy Mario Canakis and his brand new JKS TV, whose large audience was a source of concern.

The Secretary and the Vatican owned a complete list of sympathizers and of those pretending to have had an encounter with a UFO. Their plan dealing with them needed to be carefully prepared. Donovan had already been indirectly in contact with most of those that Mario and his *Daily Mail* had invited for an informative meeting. The plan was that, before seeing David and Larry, they all should meet with the Secretary and the Cardinal.

The unsuspecting group accepted Donovan's kind gesture to receive them and "brief them on serious matters preoccupying the public." But they had made it clear that they would not discuss anything that had to do with David's File. Donovan did not show any disappointment. He had other methods at his disposal to impose his will.

Mario Canakis heard about the meeting at the last moment. It was impossible for him to prevent it from taking place. He knew that what Donovan was doing without informing him first was improper. So, he called up the Secretary.

"My friend, Michael, this is Mario."

"Oh, I've heard about your TV station . . . JKS, I believe."

"If you weren't the first to know, who else would? The CIA?"

"Ha, ha, ha! Mario, now that I have you on the phone you're saving me a call to inform you about the Mexico convention."

"I accept the invitation, Michael. I've heard all of *my* friends are to be *your* guests over there . . . Don't you think it's a rather interesting coincidence?"

"Mario, there will be 600 guests! It will take place in Cancun, on Mexico's Yucatan peninsula."

". . . . 600 guests in Cancun! This means anyone that has data about aliens and UFOs may speak? This means there will be more than the VIPs?"

"If you wish to add some more, I could send you another 300 invitations for your guests. Of course, the agenda will also cover issues beyond those of David's File."

"What, exactly, is the agenda? I've heard something but it wasn't that clear."

"Mario, everybody has his job to do. I represent the administration. The public, the establishment, the Governors, Senators, the financiers, intellectuals, the Church, everybody who should be informed directly, by responsible persons, where exactly we do stand . . . as a State. We've got to give some direction, advice, to avoid losing control. Whatever we consider a major problem, it must be solved during this convention. Of course, David's File is part of that problem. I guarantee you we will be neutral, both the Church representatives and I, as long as none of you talks about the subject of religion. "

284 / The Last Dynasty of the Angels

Canakis felt lost. Up to that point, everything was fine. Suddenly he was barraged with a message of friendship and cooperation. The Secretary continued.

"Mario, I am now preparing the agenda, and afterwards I want to see you."

"About what?"

"Since you are starting this new TV station, I think I'm in the position to offer you some assistance that will help you in your initial steps. Of course, I'm asking nothing in exchange. Truly . . . "

Canakis' telephone rang again, soon after his chat with Donovan.

"Mario!"

"Oh . . . Theodore!"

"I'm in the hospital with a fracture . . . old age, you see! I've got so many things to tell you! Donovan called me in person! And you know what I told him?

"Dear Mr. Secretary, in my home-country they say, 'To make grimaces in front of an old monkey makes one look ridiculous!' "

"Ha, ha . . . That's real good."

"I gave him a piece of advice—to organize the convention but to talk about everything else but *the* issue. I've warned him that there are matters he is totally unaware of and that if he puts too much pressure on us, he'll be the one to lose."

"What did he answer?"

"Like an ancient oracle—nothing clear."

"That is?"

"He said, 'Mister Theodore Papadopoulos, I had no intention of doing a thing like that. In a few days, when the agenda is printed, you will see. I make reference only to security and terrorism measures and other matters we consider timely, such as David's File. Mario, we Greeks are gamblers, although I have never played cards in my life. I smell a trap in his game. Be careful, son . . . However, I'm sure about your final victory."

"He wants to scare me?"

"It's obvious, my friend! Yet, things won't go his way. As you say, he uses the carrot and the stick method, the perfect method to convince someone. Mario, I think you're dealing with a professional tamer."

When he hung up the phone, Mario felt overcome by the warmth of a feeling of optimism. He said to himself, "The experiences of a long life, cold logic and intelligence coexist in this man, Theodore. I thank God I have had the luck to meet him. It's a pity, though, he won't be able to be present, on our side, at the convention."

Old Jonathan's loss was recent. Twenty-four hours ago he had been buried—where else?—at Arlington Cemetery, because he was among those whose life had the one and only aim, to defend their country. Of course, this is perhaps the only country that is not unthankful towards its defenders. Larry, his son, was really inconsolable for his loss. When he received the folded American flag and his father's decorations he almost fainted in front of all the high brass that came to honor his father. Fortunately, Barbara comforted him and he slowly regained his composure.

When they returned to Chicago, to the Holiday Inn on Ohio Street, David, Natassa and Mario were waiting for them.

Canakis wasted no time and began the briefing.

"Guys, I just talked to Michael Donovan."

"He probably keeps a low profile and wishes a truce, " Larry said.

"No, my friend! On the contrary . . . he has begun the guerrilla warfare . . . and a campaign of bribery. He hands out dollars everywhere. The four of us, we've got to organize our defense and—why not?—our counter-attack!"

"You said four," Larry repeated, "because, unfortunately, we're not going to see the fifth one again . . . "

Mario put his arm around Larry's shoulder. He felt his friend's pain and wanted to share it with him.

"Be brave! Do what the 'fifth' would expect you to. I'm sure that he'll help us, wherever he may be now. As I was saying, before we reject anything, before we move forward, before we suggest anything, we'd better think seriously.

"I'll be precise. We can't afford to mess up with the government. The state does its job; it wants the country to be calm, not bothered by any questions that would interfere with everyday life. When the Church realizes that somebody is promoting a point-of-view that's accompanied by real proof, it automatically considers him a heretic, an enemy, a danger. I don't blame it. They do their job.

"For the moment, David, your story's not over. We don't even know if it concerns them. Now, why is the Church so worried? This is something that makes me suspicious. Perhaps, the Church knows much more than we do. Perhaps what the Church knows is far more extraordinary than what we do know."

Larry interrupted him. "Mario, why wouldn't we adopt a rather naïve policy of non-aggression—no criticism, no empathizing, no fanaticism. We mustn't lose our temper!"

Barbara apologized for interrupting them. "Gentlemen, here is something to consider. We do not add or subtract anything. We do not pretend that all this has anything to do with our own planet. Anyway, we ourselves are not certain about all this. We cannot make you believe us, even as far as David's File is concerned. We let the specialists judge. However, since 'KEROPS's Story' belongs to us, we all simply exploit it on television, in literature and in movies, without adding or removing anything. Whatever you see or hear, shall be accurate. Goodbye . . . "

Her statement was followed by heartfelt applause. It was the most intelligent plan of action. But David had some objections.

"Guys, I think we don't have the right to conceal our opinion. Nor have we the right to pretend to be deaf as we face those who have evidence. At Roswell, the aliens—according to Brigitte Marcais' information—had wings, just like our own Angels. I may be formulating assumptions, but maybe the origin of the Roswell's aliens is planet KEROPS. Maybe it's a vendetta story . . . Maybe they were commandos that came to punish the runaways — Leva's curse."

Mario interrupted him. "First of all, at our station, JKS, all of you will have the opportunity to present and defend your opinion. I think that, instead of a frontal attack — as I thought at the beginning — a step-by-step attack, by doses, so to speak, would be more effective. We've got many more chances to succeed, this way."

Natassa added, "Thus, simple people will solve the problem through what they hear. We all know that, next to the power of nuclear weapons, what governments fear most of all is the increase of an audience on issues opposing them."

"I agree with the queen of your heart, Larry," David said.

# Cherche
# la Femme

It was the first time David woke up after a 24-hour coma-like sleep. In another hour, Larry and Barbara would arrive at the Hotel, returning from Jonathan Keith's burial.

The CBN cocktail Natassa had given David was effective as usual but there was a side effect; vomiting and headaches began as soon as he woke up.

Natassa and Larry, with Barbara, were worried. They were ready to take him to Memorial Hospital when, unexpectedly, they heard him trying to calm them down.

"Natassa, my love, and you, my friends . . . I see you're worried and I thank you for your interest. What's happening to me, this absence of a resting period between two headaches/transmissions is due to something really exceptional and not to a simple worsening of my condition."

Larry, who was already beside David, massaging his wrists, asked, "David, how do you know? How can you be sure? You were in deep sleep!"

David smiled, looked at them ironically and said, "Cherchez la femme!"

Natassa did not take this remark very well. "You mean you were cheating on me, in your sleep, with some pin-up girl and you woke up tired? Is this what you mean?"

"No, darling . . . but, for the first time, in my sleep, this electronic devil that's in my brain managed to intervene in my dream world. Not only with words but also with images."

"What do you mean?" they all asked, as if in a chorus.

"I mean a totally weird creature appeared in front of me. As if it was made of foam, it looked like a human embryo and was just about four feet tall. It had very big eyes with no eyelids, no eyebrows, and no hair. Its body was covered with very thin pink feathers and a pair of colorful, atrophied wings sprang out of his shoulders."

"Was it alone?" Larry asked.

"Yes! All alone! It was as if we were together in a huge pink egg-shell."

"Was it standing up? Dressed?"

"No. He was sitting on some kind of a throne made out of stone, like that of Minos's one can see at Knossos Palace, in Crete. He was covered only up to his genitals. Around his neck was a chain with opal spheres and in front of them hung its symbol of power.

"What was it like?" Larry asked again. "Anything extravagant? Something precious, perhaps?"

"Not at all. It was a circle with two lines crossing vertically."

"Like a wheel with four spokes, if I've got it correctly!" his friend said again to help him forget.

"Exactly as you say. It had no teeth. Instead, it had an uninterrupted, sharp piece, just like the sheep."

"You mean you couldn't distinguish its teeth? It was like an uninterrupted denture? That's a terrible presence! It was Niak!"

"You've guessed right . . . he came into my sleep because, as he declared, he didn't know up to what point of the Angels' history the chip had taken us or how long he could wait before it was completed. He wanted, before he would continue with the story of the landing on Alphomega, to mention something that had been forgotten. Listen to me, now that everything's still on my mind, before I forget the details!"

They quickly installed the recorders and David started.

" 'Stranger, right now, I do not know whether the story of the inhabitants of KEROPS continues. Anyway, if there is more, you shall have it; otherwise, what you are about to hear will seem to be completely irrelevant to colonizing. Yet, all this is essentially important to the motives that made me revolt and get uprooted along with my family.

" 'Yes, it is true I wanted a new society, new laws that would be more reasonable, according, of course, to my own judgement. This is true, and I have decided to trust you with the other aspect of the truth, my second motive. I do not know if it was stronger than the one concerning social justice.

"I think you already know that most of the Angels were controlled, except for the MANTA's dominant generation. Among a MANTA couple's descendants, through biological intervention, there were two males and one female. The first one was the successor. In my case, I was the successor, Niak. Leva was my brother or, to be more correct, the vice successor. The MANTA-Father's spouse was, let's say, the Queen of the planet. It was up to her spouse to decide whether or not he would offer her power or education.

"MANTA-Father had a weakness for his wife—our mother. A whole floating hexagon belonged exclusively to her. It was a real palace, built by the more experienced engineers and decorated by the finest artists. It was her paradise. Her education had reached such a level that father, himself, consulted her. Many of the informational transmissions were her work. She was Ave. When father would die, I was to marry our sister, to reactivate the dynasty. I was an adolescent when, for the first time, I was allowed to visit Ave. This visit had taken place, as I learned later, on her initiative. Not even the MANTA was informed about it. When I had reached the audience room, she told me with her velvet voice, 'Many times have I admired you for your scientific deeds and COFA's perfection.' "

" 'And,' she continued, 'I wanted to touch you. Something inside me, a very strong impulse, compelled me to invite you. I cannot sleep at night because my thoughts are close to you. And, even in my sleep, you are always in front of me, so beautiful, with your sparkling eyes!'

"I was really surprised when I first saw her. She was a wonderful Angel with long wings that were nothing like my atrophied wings. They were huge and colorful, with all the colors of the rainbow. On her head there was a waterfall of golden hair that reached her waist. She was naked when she received me, not wearing anything, not even a jewel or a decoration.

"For a moment, I thought I was dreaming. I had never seen such a beauty in my whole life. I felt as if my whole body was but my eyes and my sex. Suddenly, she opened her wings wide and unveiled two desirous breasts! When she closed her wings, she embraced me tightly; she had really trapped me close to her. This female creature was the sweetest trap any male could imagine. For three days I was in that luxurious paradise. Three unforgettable days! No! I did not leave after those three days. I stayed for another one. During that last day, that Angel of Paradise proved to be a monster of intelligence and an endless treasure of knowledge.

"The creature I had in front of me stopped talking for a while. He was very moved. Then, he continued, 'Stranger, mouthpiece for my orders! Unknown stranger, future Messenger! I want to trust you with all of my thoughts and the deeper reasons of the decisions that radically changed my life and that of a whole planet.'

"After the fourth day, at the moment I was ready to abandon her forever, according to custom, she told me, 'You are different from the others. Whatever you decide to do, I shall help you. Yet, you have to promise me that you shall take me with you wherever you go.'

"Her prophetic words were probably the motive for me to find a way of going somewhere else with her. I wanted her exclusively. When we parted, with no hope of ever meeting again under normal circumstances, I began seeing my father as a rival and my sister, and future wife, as an enemy. I forgot to tell you that, as I was leaving her, she gave me an object with the inscription, 'precious surprise' . . . "

David stopped the narration. "Natassa, darling, give me something to drink. I feel the headache is decreasing but not disappearing."

Natassa went to bring him something, as Larry asked, "David, imagine! I was saying to myself, an entire history with no trace of female influence."

Barbara, as if it were her responsibility to reply, thought out loud. "It all depends on the woman, but once she's made up her mind, it's impossible not to achieve what she wants. That's why, Larry, and you David, you should be careful! Every woman's mind is an abyss. As you see, all Niak had achieved, he achieved it thanks to a woman! 'Woman is the brave man's muse.' "

Larry could no longer stand it. He got up and said, "Yes, of course! But, don't forget, Barbara, the millions of corpses on two planets, and the satellite that this Queen's intervention has created. You could say, yes, they may be dead but that caused the flourishing of the pyramidal protein food industry . . . The expansion of DE.A.T.H. Super-markets! That's the final result of that lady's acts. It's true I could never imagine that the beauty of a woman could trouble a brain like Niak's. Oedipus in Space!"

David was embarrassed listening to that argument. "Natassa, do something before I continue . . . the headache is here again."

David continued as if nothing had interrupted his narration.

" 'My sister, the woman that she is, felt something was not going well and complained to our father. But he absolved me of any responsibility when I pretended that because of work I did not have the time to respond to her extraordinary sexual demands. Fortunately, they did not know anything about my visit, because the 'Empress of My Heart' had organized it at a moment when my father, brother and sister had gone for an inauguration ceremony to the other side of the planet.

" 'The idea of creating the NOVO-OMOH race was hers. She gave me her own genetic material. That was the "precious surprise." With that, my biotechnicians managed to create new female OMOHs. With hermaphroditic semen and after removing some specific genetic material, they have created the male NOVO-OMOHs. The sensitivities they inherited, such as laughter, singing or dancing, are Ave's features. It is strange that up to now, nobody had suspected the strange resemblance.

" 'Now that I am dictating to you, I am very tense and, perhaps I have left many questions unanswered. I hope that if everything goes as it should during our landing on Alphomega, I will finish it up. At this moment, what is most important is the success of Project Thunder.

" 'My officers await me at the launch pad of the first mission. The first to go is Salta, with three starcraft, who will descend to the boundless valleys, the place of the rising sun. Of course, he and his officers, in addition to P.A.'s transmitters, had the implanted BTC for direct communication with their master.

" 'The second is Hax and his slaves-assistants, a few NOVOs.

Most of the NOVOs shall be part of my own mission. Few others will follow Soemgyp. Indeed, I allowed him to do the selection. His are short, with squinting eyes to protect them from dust when they work in the mines.

" 'Then, it shall be the swarthy and bright Soemgyp's turn, who is already asking for more space. His appetite is in reverse proportion to his dimensions. I shall be the last to leave, together with the queen of my heart that is already carrying planet Alphomega successor. Yes, that unique encounter of ours had not been fruitful. Yet, fortunately, before the Great Escape we had already decided we would create the conditions to acquire a successor, as soon as possible. Thus, even if I had died in an accident, my people would not remain ungoverned. My landing area is neither rich, nor hot, but it has an important advantage. The queen of my heart likes it. It is the brightest place of the planet.'"

David breathed deeply. "I feel relieved at last! For a moment, I thought my head would shatter into pieces because of the pain. Now, I'm fine! If anything has happened to the MANTA and the others, including the queen, then these are certainly the last you have heard of them."

Larry, who was still furious with Ave, seemed not to have heard David's last words.

"Have you heard? She's even chosen the place they would live! She's certainly telling him when to go to the toilet. I've lost all respect for Niak. Such a surrender . . . to a female . . ."

Barbara, not one to give in easily, now found the occasion to defend her own sex and declared to Larry, "Behind every famous man, there is a woman, my dear."

"Imagine how much more famous he would be if there were no woman," Larry replied.

"You are mean," Barbara said, seeking a different kind of surrender. "If you don't kiss me right now, I'll never talk to you again."

They embraced and immediately stopped talking because their lips discovered much more interesting things to do. When the conversation started again, Natassa said, "You mean, this lady behaved exactly like a queen bee."

David seemed surprised. "Darling, I really don't see how you came up with that comparison . . . I just don't see it."

"You don't see? Then what's the reproductive mechanism in a hive? The queen gives birth to genetic material that is distributed and, at the end, what comes out of it is what she dictates—some drones, a few strong 'stallions,' workers, that is, NOVO-OMOHs. Whenever she wants to, with a drone or without him through cloning, she creates a new queen.

"That's what she did, the winged, bright queen of the stupid drone-like Niak-MANTA. He didn't realize he became her toy, the puppet whose strings she's pulling. Thus, her desires are fulfilled. Of course, she also pretends to be the victim. She certainly complains about having left a whole floating palace for him. This entire colossal operation, this titanic effort, all those hecatombs, had but one aim, the changing of the guard in the New World, on planet Alphomega."

"A matriarchy," David stated simply. "What do you expect when a woman dominates every man's heart? If you generalize it, you come to exactly the same conclusion as my Natassa." Then, with his arms wide open he said to her, "Come, queen of my heart, let's change the world."

Larry remarked, "Guys, very much to the point, I remember a funny story."

"We're all ears," someone said. "It's time we relax a bit after all the tension caused by Niak's confession."

"Ok . . . hear this. The final hour, the destruction of the world, is here. Everybody died except for two. The male who survived, a young, white man, was walking in a deserted area. Suddenly, he sees an Indian girl approaching him. The young man was a refined individual, from a good family and status, but the situation begged for practical solutions. So, he tried and found the right approach. When the girl was close enough, he said, 'Excuse me for the proposal I am about to make, but . . . would you like to come with me and create a . . . pink world?' "

They laughed; the tension had evaporated. The rest of the day was uneventful. At night, they went to an Italian restaurant, Capri Delicious, to partake of its delicate tastes and selected wine. Then, in a stupor, they went to sleep.

Suddenly, David's screams made everybody jump out of their beds. When Larry and Barbara opened the door separating the rooms of the suite they found themselves in front of a freakish sight. David, like a sleepwalker, his eyes bloodshot, foaming at the mouth, was crawling on his hands and knees. He was screaming and tearing at his pajamas, vainly trying to shed them.

Natassa, no longer a stranger to her lover's odd behavior, knew exactly what to do. With steady, calm hands she readied an injection, and confidently planted into David's behind a mixture of tranquilizers and fortifiers. The first were for the brain, the other for the body. David sighed deeply and spread himself on the carpet within a few seconds. They took him to bed and Larry and Barbara walked towards their bedroom door, ready to return to bed.

"He must have had a nightmare . . . It's over now, Natassa . . . Anyway, we admired your calm."

Natassa smiled. "I hope to turn out to be a liar, but I think all this was a warning . . . "

Larry hesitated and held Barbara back before entering their bedroom. Natassa's statement puzzled him.

"What you've seen is a symptom of intracranial pressure. Now he's calm but this doesn't mean the pressure is not continuing."

"What do you suggest, Natassa?" Barbara asked, and hugged her. "Tell us, how can we help you?"

"Get the recorders ready! I've got to wake him up so he can unload what's on his brain. No doubt, that god damned awful microchip has started sending its unrelenting new orders. It's the second time he has had such intense symptoms. We're to hear something very important, I'm sure. The safest way to wake him up is to give him the Synegotamine serum."

They placed David's anaesthetized body in a half-seated position and Natassa immediately injected the serum's needle into a vein. They patiently waited to witness the Synegotamine work. Indeed, David slowly regained his color. His blinked his eyes and began the narration.

# Treason

"Fourteen months of preparations had already passed. Everybody was at his post where he had worked very methodically to complete his task. Niak, accompanied by Salta, Hax and Soemgyp, went up to the surface of ANOL, the satellite turned spacecraft. He boarded his personal starcraft with his officers and began reviewing the three launch bases, following the first phase of Project Thunder.

"At the base that was under Salta's control, the preparatory work was almost completed. Niak landed there in order to congratulate the staff for their excellent behavior. Salta was to take Skyship No2; that would be his temporary headquarters and the officers' quarters until they had built permanent installations on Alphomega. Salta had proposed calling the MANTA 'Master,' as P.A. called him. His heart's queen was to be called 'Queen O'. Salta informed the master about the latest events.

" 'Master, P.A. received an RCH-location broadcast. It certainly comes from KEROPS. I suspect your brother is looking for us. P.A. assured me he has not located us. We are on the other side of the hemisphere that received the RCH transmission.'

" 'Thank you, Salta . . . but why wasn't I informed by P.A.?' "

" 'He did not want to wake you up, as he did not consider the event that urgent.'

"Niak thought for a while. Then, as if he had found a solution, he put his arm around Salta's shoulder and told him, 'We must not leave a single trace of our presence on that place. As we leave, we must heal every wound, erase all our fingerprints. Every construction, done by Angels or OMOHs must disappear forever. Leva will certainly do everything he can to locate us and get his revenge.'

"Salta was carefully listening to the instructions and, without wasting time, gave the first orders to the computer that planned their moves.

"The other two officers reported to him that in ten days, they were to abandon the satellite in order to land on Alphomega."

"A touching farewell ceremony was to take place before they abandoned ANOL. In the main hall—one would say 'the throne room'—the master was dressed for the occasion with the MANTA's imposing uniform and the simple yet precious decorations of his rank. The elegant, beautiful Ave, perhaps so that jewels would not interfere with her beauty, was dressed in a simple transparent veil that allowed a lot of room for the imagination. Her only jewels were three rings, on her left hand's three fingers. Very thin chains kept the rings together.

" 'EVERYTHING for the salvation tribe, EVERYTHING is in your hands,' they all repeated individually, kneeling on the floor, head down, thus indicating submission to the Master and Ave.

"Gesturing ceremonially, Niak offered his three officers the decorations suited to their new authority, decorations which were just copies of his own decorations, but in smaller dimensions.

"Short and swarthy Soemgyp, who saw that beautiful and colorful Angel, the queen, for the first time, appeared dumbstruck. He could not move, nor could he speak. His big, almond-shaped eyes seemed hypnotized. The Master noticed and, as the others also did, approached him and tapped him, as he would do to a small child.

"This is not appropriate for a small child . . . "

"Those words wounded Soemgyp's touchy pride. Soemgyp who was hiding under a hypocritical veil of submission and slavish behavior. He did not reply to Niak's comment. He approached Ave, took her hand and kissed the rings with a passion. All the while, with the speed of a magician, before he let her hand go, he placed a stone into her palm. The eternal woman managed to hide her first surprise and the first gift she received from a stranger.

"Salta's departure from the satellite on Skyship No2, and his landing on Alphomega presented no problems. Hax's departure, with the cut-eyed slaves, was excellent. And when Soemgyp, the Master's favorite, reached the determined area, in addition to the official message of safe landing, sent a second one, just a little before Niak's and Ave's starcraft left ANOL.

"At the moment they received the message, they were in the P-Gass, their personal starcraft. The text read, 'I am in a real paradise. I invite you to come as soon as possible. I assure you, your stay here will remain unforgettable! Your eternal slave, Soemgyp, Equatorial Administrator.'

" 'I've told you, Ave, he's just like a child! I just hope he's not as thoughtless. I'll see to it that he is helped whenever something's wrong.'

"Ave had something rare, for a female. She was a person of

few words. And, whenever she spoke, she was so laconic one could say she was Pythia in person. People had to analyze her phrases to realize the depth of her statements. Niak regarded her silence as a plus, although, when on duty, he was afraid and avoided those that spoke too little. When P-Gass, with the SCL propulsion system, reached its destination, at the queen's request they flew over a huge area."

" 'My love, a real master has to live higher than the people he rules over,' she said. Then, showing him a beautiful mountain whose tops looked like bright diamonds, she spoke again.

" 'If I were God and had to live on this planet, I would certainly choose the top of that proud mountain. From now on I shall call it 'Gods' Residence.' "

Barbara, like everybody else, was surprised. She said, "But, then . . . there's no doubt! Olympus is the mountain where, according to mythology, gods lived!"

"Yes, Barbara! After this revelation there's nothing to hesitate about. Yes, the Angels did land here and on no other planet!"

Natassa said, "Let's not be in too much of a hurry. Perhaps it is a diabolical coincidence."

David was silent. He did not confirm anything they said. He did not contradict, either. He waited for them to stop talking, to continue.

"Before they even had time to land, an urgent message arrived at P-Gass. "Master, please . . . Come immediately! Very serious problems threaten the whole mission! I am waiting for you! Signature: Soemgyp." This time, Niak was furious. He called P.A..

" 'At your command!' "

" 'What is happening with Project Thunder—Equatorial sector?' "

" 'Everything is going as planned, except for the Equatorial sector, Soemgyp's landing area. While everything was going fine, both my copy and transmitters were destroyed, due to a short circuit. Information says that animals like the one that killed the Angel during the first mission, entered the machine and caused this terrible damage.' "

" 'Can it be repaired?' Niak asked nervously.

" 'Perhaps in two years!'

" 'Two years without any help. That's tragic!'

" ' No, master! Do not forget IN.CO, the Individual Computer through which communication may be restored. But there shall be no visual communication.' "

" 'What does this mean?' Niak said angrily. 'The ZKPS screen is not functional?'

" 'Of course it is! But, not in Soemgyp's area. The ZKP screen functions for ANOL, but now it is useless to us.'

" 'What would you advise me to do, P.A.?' Silence greeted both remarks.

" 'I need a responsible reply!'

"At that moment, a tiny light went on. It was the indication that what P.A. was to say, was extremely confidential. Niak understood and brought the receiver to his ear."

" 'Soemgyp's activity, for the past several days, is very strange. So strange I would consider it suspicious, unless he is mentally deranged. I cannot give you any advice because I have no access to the landing area. Even a secret system that existed is strangely inapt.' "

" 'What would you do, if you were me?' "

" 'Immediate destruction of the Equatorial Mission. Cause the self-destruction of the supplies. Do not forget that, through remote control, you may activate the partial or total destruction of every mission. Soemgyp ignores that fact.' "

"Niak interrupted the communication. Of course he was the absolute master. He had the right of life or death over everyone. He had the right and the power to enforce it."

" 'Queen of my heart,' he said to Ave, who seemed not to pay any attention to what was happening, 'I think we will visit the restless child sooner than planned and take a look. In two hours, we shall be there. I am sure that, after some hours of staying there, everything shall be settled. If you think this is too tiring for you . . . '

"With no reservation, she answered, 'My place is by you. I will follow you.' An enigmatic smile lit her face.

"During the journey Niak was in her tight and warm arms. When they approached, from 30,000 feet high, Niak saw fire and flames coming from explosions near the landing area. In many spots, the forest was still burning.

" 'I shall fix him . . . I shall replace him. I shall not allow him to create problems again . . . he even had demands, that incapable dwarf,' Niak shouted furiously.

"Ave, on the contrary, was strangely neutral. One might say she kept an attitude of equal distance. Landing was smooth. Niak went down by himself and noticed that only some low-rank officers had come to receive him.

" 'Where is your Chief?' he asked.

" 'He is expecting you," the officer said, his face turned to the ground.

"In ten minutes they had arrived at Soemgyp's starcraft/temporary residence. Everything was quiet there. No noise, no fumes, no fires. Nothing, nowhere. As if, what Niak had seen from above, was but fake scenery. He waited for ten minutes but Soemgyp did not show up. He took the IN.CO. from his belt, and called the P-Gass. No response! Complete silence!

" 'I fell into a trap,' Niak screamed suddenly. He took his gun, the one he had used to immobilize his father, and moved threateningly towards the starcraft that had brought him there. Those on his way avoided him, as if he was cursed. They all tried to avoid him, at any cost!

" 'Back to P-Gass! I have to leave immediately! Before this satanic Angel traps me,' Niak said to himself. 'Why haven't I followed P.A.'s advice? I was in a hurry . . . '

"He jumped into the staff transportation vehicle with ease and, in three minutes, he arrived at P-GASS. 'Fortunately, everything is quiet here,' he thought. 'Imagine if I was late! That criminal might have hurt me at the end'. He passed through an entry nobody else knew, which led him directly to the emergency flight control room. Even if the starcraft had been occupied by enemies, from here he could make it take off and lead them where an exemplary punishment awaited.

"He stuck his three fingers in a box and took a metallic piece that seemed to be there by accident. The octagonal door opened slightly. He had some difficulty passing. He saw something at the pilot's seat. He could not be certain because a strange, orange-colored fog was filling the room. A voice, that seemed to come from very far away, made Niak freeze!

" 'No one could say you're late to your rendezvous, Master! I've been expecting you. I was sure I'd find you here, in your secret shelter. But nothing remains secret to me.'

"Soemgyp, in his formal dress and carrying a gun like Niak's, was there. He did not have that submissive dreamer look, or the humble Angel's airs. Now, he was proud, he was sarcastic, he was ready to destroy anyone that was an obstacle to him.

" 'I believe the laser lights you watched from above have fulfilled their mission. Anyway, what am I saying? I have the confirmation right in front of me, Master! Master . . . Wasn't it your name? Well, Master, I'd like to inform you first, that the queen of your heart has changed heart.

" 'Second, there's no hope for you to escape from here because everything is planned and neutralized. I've already informed Salta and Hax that P-Gass exploded and there was nothing left. You are certainly considering P.A.. But it is nothing but a computer, a cold machine. I've already sent him P-Gass's destruction report, with images and proofs. We've blown up a false starcraft, so the view was lively and convincing. Anyone who asks P.A. about you shall receive an appropriate reply.'

"Soemgyp pressed a button that connected him with P.A.. Immediately, the lights were turned on. 'Master Soemgyp, I am listening!'

" 'I would like a description of this moment's situation!'

" 'Following your predecessor's death, Master, everything is now under your jurisdiction. Information says the other two leaders elected you to take the MANTA's position. You are the new master, MANTA-Soemgyp.' The criminal interrupted the circuit and started laughing.

"Meanwhile, Niak had fallen on a chair without uttering a word. There was a deadly silence. After a few endless minutes, the trapped MANTA asked his executioner, 'Why don't you kill me? Since you had the courage or, better, since you had the audacity to take revenge upon the one that made you what you are, since ingratitude is your religion, why are you so late in neutralizing me and throwing me away? You've stolen a planet from me . . . You've stolen my beloved one, Ave . . . Why don't you steal my life, too? What are you waiting for?'

"Surprised, the trapped MANTA noticed that, for the first time in his life, drops had begun flowing his eyes! He was crying! He was crying like a common NOVO-OMOH!

"Soemgyp did not reply. He secured the exits and left the once powerful master of the world, alone and miserable. The cunning traitor had everything planned. He had managed to incorporate certain texts into P.A., before the master could check all the texts and before he could check information accuracy."

"In the room where the imprisoned master was now waiting his fate, was the starcraft's automatic recording system, the opal sphere, that also included the archives of the tribe of KEROPS."

"Just as we have the black box that records flight, in our planes?" Larry asked.

"Yes, Larry, exactly! Only the opal sphere's aptitudes are millions of times superior. All the conversations and reports were recorded and listed by subject. For example, my microchip contains information about the species' evolution and its history. The master, even though profoundly desperate and disappointed, never forgot to inform the opal memory spheres. Ninety-two per cent of those spheres aim at informing future generations about their history. Such is my little devil . . . And he will soon leave me alone."

"Of course, following the master's death, you might get rid of . . . "

David reacted, "Don't be so sure about that . . . Never laugh before the story's over!"

"The master had all the time he needed to narrate all of the events to be recorded in the opal sphere. For ten days, the secret flight control room was his prison. The guards only gave him something to eat and drink and they never answered any of his questions. It was forbidden to give him any information. One night, as he was examining one computer, he noticed that if he connected it to the automatic pilot, he could hear anything that was said in the central room. He did not remember when he had installed that system but he had certainly done that to spy on the others."

"Watergate!" Larry said.

David did not react. "Carefully and keeping noise at a low level, he pricked up his ears and opened his eyes. On the screen, he could see ten Angels having a conversation in low tones. Judas-Soemgyp was not there. The imprisoned MANTA could not see the faces very clearly. He used a device to stop interference and gain a clearer sound. At last, he could hear."

'Eight more died, today . . . biogenetic engineers say . . . a new species will save us . . . ' An Angel that seemed very wise said. 'No NOVO is dead . . . we are the fragile ones . . . in danger of extermination . . . '

"Thirty more days passed and, fortunately, this channel's discovery had saved Niak's mind! If he had not found this little window in his isolation, he would have had a break down by now. During the entire period in there, in the room, the only topic of conversation was dealing with survival problems. 'They are having some difficult moments out there,' Niak thought. 'It's a pity they have left me inactive, here . . . I could be of some help.'

"One day before the thirtieth, Niak saw something on the screen. Something he thought was the product of irrationality!

" 'It's impossible! It can't be true!' He turned the receiver off and covered his face with his hands. 'I'm certainly losing my mind . . . This is certainly our end!' "

One need not emphasize the reverence with which Larry, Barbara and Natassa listened to David's description of Niak's Waterloo.

David shook his head. "Alas! What happened after Niak's imprisonment did not even happen in ancient Rome, during Nero's reign. Events followed one another in rapid succession, as if propelled by a typhoon that dictated them. One after the other, the officers disappeared from P-Gass's meeting-room; this is why the Master noticed in the monitor that more new faces surrounded the planet's rebel. Almost none of Niak's favorites were close to Soemgyp.

" 'I just hope he doesn't kill them,' Niak screamed. 'There are so few of us . . . and I'm through!' he thought. 'Of course, it's unpleasant but, what's more important is the tribe's survival. If this criminal brain has it in mind to annihilate anyone, for almost no reason, this shall be the Angels' end.'

"He had some difficulty in understanding what was going on in the last scene he had watched. Seventeen Angels were seated. Soemgyp was among them and, beside him, alas, a NOVO!"

"OMOH? A spineless one?" Larry asked.

"Yes, guys! It was a NOVO-OMOH!"

"Present, participating at the superior administration board? How do you explain this, David?"

"Yes! Not only that NOVO-OMOH was present but they also listened very carefully to what he had to say! It was like a conference! Almost as if he was the Chair!"

"He spoke? But . . . I thought that, mentally . . . " Natassa said.

"Yes, Natassa! They had feelings but mentally the biogenetics engineers blocked them so they had no initiative or demands. They could not and would not defend themselves if they needed to. Anyway, having feelings does not necessarily mean you're intelligent. Sometimes it's even considered a disadvantage."

# JKS TV

Urbana's *Daily Mail* had already allocated a respectable sum of money for the inauguration of its new Chicago TV-Station. Extensive advertising brought the message to every home and business—this new channel was going to be something totally different. It was the subject of daily conversations in Chicagoland, during evening cocktails and in meetings.

"Have you heard about JKS?"

"Yes! Everybody knows it starts broadcasting soon and they say it will be original, outrageous, and unbeatable . . . "

JKS had announced that, for six months, there would be discussions on subjects championed by and with genuine personalities or witnesses and decision-makers, and the public's participation would be free. Each show had two official guests, and two participants chosen by lot from the audience. Mario Canakis's aim was to make the State's and Church's representatives participate actively on the hot discussion whose central theme was: "Where do we come from? Where do aliens come from? And why are we hiding the truth?"

"D" day approached and Canakis was hiding numerous secret allies and real winning cards up his sleeve. Nobody knew of their existence except him. Everything had to function perfectly. Opinion polls showed that, even under the most pessimistic calculations, audience share would reach 64%. Given the competition with giant networks and programs of infinite variety, this figure seemed highly inflated. If it was true, this would automatically mean substantially increased sales for the *Daily Mail*. That, in turn, would mean resources to lead the newspaper to the top.

Mario was like a general giving orders. All day long, among his computers and his assistants, he led preparations for the assault. The new wars were also for conquest but they aimed differently. In this war, Mario aimed at conquering, from the very first moment, the public's confidence. He was determined that anything that would pass his lips would be right, true, impressive and unbeatable. "Respect for the Public's Intelligence," was his motto.

Autumn was already in the air, and the "Windy City," Chicago, was starting its annual rehearsal with the northern wind of the early morning. Mario was strolling on Michigan Avenue, around 7.30 p.m., when his mobile phone rang. Mario sought shelter in the entrance of a building.

"Hello . . . "

"We've landed," a woman's voice informed him. Mario heard, yet he did not understand.

"Hello!"

"Mario, it's Barbara . . . Can you hear me?"

"Yes, Barbara, I hear you. I'm on the road, would you like to . . . "

"I want to announce the big news to you. You're still not familiar with the rest of the story but, David said some things that prove the Angels had come down to Earth."

"Triumph!" Mario shouted. "I'm coming to the Holiday Inn. I'm very close to Ohio Street."

People on the street looked strangely at the man who, every three to four steps, jumped up. It was as if he walked and danced at the same. It was logical. There were some indications that Niak had lead his Angels to earth, but there was no clear confirmation of it. Now, fortunately, exactly before the Station's inauguration, Mario would be much more convincing having this extraordinary information.

"No . . . I first have to go to the station. The situation's changed. There must be some modifications to the program. Perhaps we should postpone the inauguration ceremony . . . "

The phone rang again. It was Natassa.

"Mario, what followed the landing was extraordinary. Come as soon as you can . . . I tell you, what follows is totally unpredictable!"

Mario ended his conversation and direction. He went straight to his office. His enthusiasm had no limits. Entering the building, he shouted, "They're here! They've landed! Anyone who says we're no Angel faces, bring him here! In front of me!"

His new secretary, Lillian—a very elegant and beautiful woman with red hair and green eyes—was really worried.

"Mr. Canakis, what's wrong?" Mario grabbed her waist and started dancing with her in the office.

"Some creatures like you, Lillian, are atavistic creatures! I have unbeatable evidence we're Angels' descendants! If not all of us, certainly you are!"

Lillian started laughing but came up with an answer. "Some creatures like you, Mister Mario, show we've got devilish origins. Not all of us but, certainly you do!"

His screams upset everybody. They ran to his office to learn the reason for this sudden explosion. The Director, indeed, was very anxious. "Let's hope Mario's not going nuts! Otherwise, we're lost!"

He was the first one to run. Before he had the time to ask anything, he received a big kiss on his forehead. Then Mario embraced him and whispered into his ear. "Bingo! It's great! Just as I'd predicted, the Angels landed on Earth. David Mason, during his last transmission, assured earth was the planet that received them. Isn't that extraordinary?"

"This means the story's over, so we'll have the complete scenario before the inauguration."

Mario agreed. He gave instructions to all the departments' chiefs about the program and the modifications that had to be done at the last moment. Then, he immediately called the Holiday Inn.

"What's up? Is everything over? David's torture's finished? He must be happy now that he's got rid of the MANTA's deadly embrace."

It was Barbara that answered the phone. She seemed worried.

"Mario, I've got to go because not only is David not through with it but, at this moment, he's saying incredible things! I am hanging up . . . if you want, come over. I'm telling you, it appears that the end surpasses the wildest imagination."

The line went dead. Mario was really surprised. He did not expect David's narration to continue after landing. "I hope he's not losing it! I hope he's not going crazy narrating stories of his own now! If something like that happened, it would really have negative effects upon the new TV-Station. One could very easily jump to the conclusion, then, that not only the end is false but the whole story is." With those depressing thoughts, he asked for help:

"Lillian, please, I want you to find me the most famous psychiatrist in our city. It's urgent."

Lillian was surprised. "Do you think success will cost him his mental health?" she thought.

"Lillian, I see you are not concentrating. I want you to find him immediately."

Lillian pulled herself together and turned to her personal computer. She finally discovered there were many good psychiatrists but, also, for different kinds of problems.

"Mario! What psychiatric specialty?"

"Mythomania! Paranoia, or something like that!"

She finally found the perfect one. "Pritikin!" Lillian shouted.

"Lillian, are you nuts? I haven't asked you for a lawyer! I was asking for a medical doctor!"

"Pritikin, Jeremy; La Salle Avenue, telephone . . . ." If that was not a coincidence! Some Pritikin had helped to get rid of his ex-wife through a very successful divorce.

Mario smiled. "If that Pritikin does his job as well as the lawyer, then everything will go fine."

"Lillian, let me speak with . . . Hello . . . "

'Hello! Doctor Pritikin's office. You're speaking with his secretary."

"It is very urgent. Would it be possible for me to speak to the doctor?"

"No, because he's at a meeting in St. Petersburg."

"At Franklin-Cross?"

" I am surprised you've guessed!"

"Yes, it's a little farther than Salvador Dali's Museum and near the Sunshine Skyway . . . I even have the phone number."

"Have you been a patient there?"

"Thank heaven, no! I am Mario Canakis, the journalist!"

"Oh, you're the one that owns JKS TV-Station? I am sorry, I thought you were . . . "

"ABC nuts? Ha, ha, ha! I'll call the doctor later. Meanwhile, inform him I'm perfectly well. It's about a possible patient."

Half an hour later, the specialist assured Canakis he would meet David the next morning. He had agreed with the doctor to conduct a discreet examination so that David would not misunderstand this act. Anyway, it was important that those who were to take part in a TV or radio show and that were to announce information of general interest were in good mental health.

"Lillian, I think your opinion on a case you're about to hear will be very important to me. I, personally, am already influenced and perhaps my judgement isn't that reliable. I'm inviting you to come to the hotel with me. Things are getting very serious. As you know—you've heard about David Mason's tapes—it's about a history that's our to gain public opinion."

"Yes, I'm fully aware of that!"

"I suddenly am informed that, while KEROPS's Angels have landed, David goes on telling stories that could, this time, come out of his own imagination . . . understand? We've got to stop him, otherwise . . . "

"Otherwise, the whole story would seem false while we're trying to demystify the sayings. Mario hid his face in his hands. He had acquired a tic from repeatedly seeing David doing it, in moments of despair.

Lillian came close to him and put her hand on his shoulder. Mario opened his eyes to see two beautiful green eyes that approached him slowly. In a moment, their lips were so close they finally kissed. It was not a simple friendship kiss.

"I admire you," she said.

"It's logical," he replied, taking her into his arms.

"Mario, what about modesty?" she ironically asked.

"The same as about . . . humility! Really, what would you say if we called the fiancé?"

A small tap was the punishment Lillian imposed on him for his indiscretion.

# Clones to
# the Rescue

eanwhile, at the Holiday
Inn, there was panic
everywhere! David was talking and nothing could stop him.
The flow of information rushed from his brain to his vocal
cords. The pyramidal, opal microchip had almost melted. It
had less than 1/40 of its initial power. Yet, it seemed that the
negligible quantity left contained a fantastic conclusion to the
story, so interesting it thrilled even the narrator himself.

The unexpected developments with Niak's imprisonment,
P.A.'s falsification and the progressive disappearance of the
mission's officers, was an unexplainable mystery.

At the hotel, Lillian and Mario joined Larry and Barbara,
who were already there.

Lillian had taken things very seriously. She brought with
her everything she needed to take notes. Of course, as she listened to the incredible things David narrated, she was so absorbed that she wanted to do nothing but find out what happened at the end.

David continued the story from the point where a NOVO-OMOH appeared at the meeting and sat beside Soemgyp.

"Niak could not believe his eyes. 'Is it possible? Is it possible for a slave, a nothing creature, to be speaking? It's crazy! They are listening to him, although it's known that genetically his brain is unable to acquire knowledge and exercise judgement. It's probably an error the genetic engineers have made . . . it's probably atavism', he thought.

" 'Atavism . . . Yes!' Now Niak remembered that often the OMOHs were born with wings, although it was theoretically impossible after the alteration of their DNA and the removal of the corresponding genes. 'I may understand atavism concerning wings, but the brain! Why had this NOVO-OMOH not shown his mental aptitudes earlier? Millions of questions flooded his mind. This event really downgraded his generation. Reason and animal instincts were placed here, side by side, in a deadly degradation. If there was revenge on their minds, it could lead to a tragic end.

"Suddenly, while Niak was asking questions of himself and trying to repair the damaged voice transmitter, he heard a noise coming from the octagonal exit. The noise became increasingly louder until the familiar sound of the metal door, filled his heart with joy. So, there was still was some hope, hope that somebody had thought of him. Even if death awaited him, he would prefer that to rotting away in isolation.

"He saw the most puzzling picture in the octagonal frame of the door. Soemgyp, muzzled, with his hands tied behind his back, was in the middle. Beside him stood four NOVO-OMOHs, with the smile of triumph on their faces. Behind them, there were Angels that had literally been beaten, not because of violence but because of myriad color marks one could see on their skin. They were bent and an unusual cough shook their bodies after every few breaths they took.

"Before Niak had a chance to speak, one of the NOVOs crossed the opening and came close to him. Articulating perfectly, in a precise language, he said, 'We do not forget you are our Father. We do not forget you lifted our generation. Of course, your motives were rather wrong, but what is important to us is the outcome.'

" 'But, how?' Niak whispered, shocked by this unexpected visit and the NOVO's explanation. 'How is it possible you are so different and, furthermore, in such a short time?'

" 'The death of the animals on ALPHOMEGA caused the development of microbes, in other words, microscopic animals that fester on dead bodies.'

" 'They are very small?'

" 'They are not visible unless one uses special instruments. On KEROPS there were no comparable organisms.'

" 'P.A. discovered that. We asked him to analyze a piece of flesh we took from a dead animal, one of those huge reptiles that died because of increases in the atmospheric pressure. He reached the conclusion I just revealed. Yet, microbes do not only eat dead tissues. They also attack the tissue in the Angel's body.'

" 'What do you mean?' a terrified Niak asked."

" 'Well, they entered the bodies of most of you and some are already dead. We are immunized. P.A. said so. It means the microbes do not like us . . . ' "

" 'You mean, they don't get inside you?'

"The NOVO-OMOH ordered everybody to sit and sent Soemgyp away with his guard."

" 'They enter our bodies, but they only go to our brain. There, in our brain, instead of killing us, they finally die. Their corpses produce a substance that dilates the blood vessels and awakens our brain. Instead of harming us, they are beneficial . . . '

" 'What brain of yours?' Niak asked naively. He never knew they had a brain.

"The NOVO-OMOH laughed. 'The cerebral substance existed, former-Master, but was blocked by your genetic engineers. All the centers existed but there were no activated connections. That substance recreated contact areas in the brain. The result was this awakening. All those infected are awakened now. We are trying to infect the others, too.'

" 'What happened to my Angels?' "

"The NOVO stood up and pointed to the ones he had with him. No one was in the mood to speak, yet, one tried.

" 'Master, your curse for Soemgyp's barbarian behavior to you has certainly become our sentence. We don't have any strength, not even for walking. Only about half of us are left. I don't think we shall ever get over this. I feel my body weighing five times more than normal.' "

"Niak felt sorry for him. He got up and walked towards him. But the NOVO stopped him."

"'If you touch him, the same thing shall happen to you. The microbes are transmitted through physical contact. P.A. said even we, the NOVO-OMOHs, might escape for a while, yet, he cannot guarantee our future.' "

"During the incident when that snake killed one of his officers, Niak had seen the huge dinosaur carcasses rotting away, but he never suspected the danger that was threatening his Angels. Nor did P.A.. It was the dinosaurs' revenge."

"'But . . . if neither of you are capable of . . . then . . . ' "

"The NOVO-OMOH looked at him sadly before answering him. 'Master, you must understand that both you and us, we are the last dynasty . . . '

"This phrase fell on them like a time bomb. The last dynasty! An entire race would disappear in such an inglorious way, vanquished by an army of microscopic enemies? One of the Angels, who wore the genetic engineer's tattoo on his forehead, moved a little forward. He looked sick.

"'As a specialist, I inform you that, for the first time I cannot answer with certainty. Probably, yes. Probably, not. I have an idea in mind, a solution.' "

"'You mean there is some hope? Do you think some may survive?' "

"'Not for the Angels, or for the NOVO-OMOHs, but, maybe . . . ' "

"Niak was sweating with anxiety. He felt dizzy with all the tragic news, all these maybes."

"'How can you say maybe? If we are not to survive, nor the NOVOs, then who? And how? Answer me!'"

"The Angel took a diskette out, inserted it into the computer and looked at his own image on the screen. He saw himself talking. 'In case the situation becomes extremely urgent we will have to implement project "Genetic Seed," that consists of the following:

" 'As soon as possible, using cloning techniques, we will transplant in the uterus of every female NOVO-OMOH many varieties of creatures so that, in the future, at least one of them is able to overcome the deadly barrier of Alphomega's morbidity. A variety of creatures will be created, but our goal is not to choose according to their intelligence. We aim to pick the one most fitting for survival. The evolutionary power of the species will take over and do the rest.

'I am saying all of this to make it clear that quite possibly, the creature that survives will be our descendant but will differ from us intellectually. Perhaps, through evolution, it will achieve our own perfection some day.'

"The geneticist then provided further scientific analysis on how to apply the plan and the screen went blank, even as Niak was still trying to fully comprehend the dimension of the disaster the beautiful but unfriendly planet had in store for them.

" 'I wonder what is going on with my people. Perhaps they were not affected by the infection, as you called it.'

"The NOVO-OMOH, his head bowing in despair, informed him that the other two missions had exactly the same problems and that the 'Genetic Seed' was being applied urgently.

" 'If the female NOVOs survive for nine months, then the plan shall come to fruition,' the engineer added.

"Niak was literally lost. 'Soemgyp?' he asked with simple curiosity.

" 'Ingratitude, my former master, is appropriately punished in only one way—exhausting work in a field he despises. This is his punishment!'

" 'What do you mean?'

" 'He shall be the one that will take care of you. He will be your faithful slave!'

"Suddenly, Niak was worried. 'And Ave?' he asked and jumped up. He had forgotten the queen of his heart.

"'She has proven to be the most sensitive of all, your Queen. She was the first one to die. Her last phrase was to ask forgiveness for her ingratitude.'

" 'Where is she?' he asked, and tears came to his eyes and ran down his cheeks.

" 'She was cremated . . . it was P.A.'s order, so her body would not infect anybody else.'

"Niak collapsed on the floor. Soon they transferred him to a sterile booth in the main part of the starcraft. He was to stay there until his death.

"The NOVOs may have been inferior creatures, but they had feelings. For two days, Niak was between life and death. The shocks he had suffered had literally undermined his physical and mental health.

"When the same NOVO visited him, Niak asked, 'You seem very advanced . . . intellectually speaking. What is your name?'

" 'SAPIENS!'

" 'Which means . . . wise!'

" 'It is well known that admirers always exaggerate. I am simply the head of the Generation Rescue Team.

'At what stage now is the plan Genetic Seed?'

"Sapiens did not answer immediately. He took a small computer out of his pocket and consulted the data. He finally said, 'Officially, it has been named Genesis-Creation. The genetic engineers have already operated on all HOMO females with no exception.'

" 'HOMO? You're wrong! You mean OMOH, Niak said.'

" 'As everything was turned upside down, all the key-words you have brought from KEROPS have been inverted . . . we did that . . . so, OMOH became HOMO.'

"'You mean I am ANTAM?' Niak asked puzzled.'

" 'Yes! In Alphomega's history it shall be written that the first intelligent creature that arrived here was ADAM.'

" 'ADAM and EVE. . . . '

" 'You had asked me, Adam, about our activities. I assure you we are very methodical. All HOMO females are already pregnant. We have used every possible variety, modifying DNA so that the races produced resisting the virus. We have even used intergene intervention.'

" 'The races?' Adam was horrified. 'You mean you are going to create polymorphism among the descendants?'

"Sapiens smiled. 'Of course! It is our only possibility to guarantee survival. Theoretically we will have 16 different genetic prototypes that fight against Alphomega's viruses. Even if one of these prototypes survives, it will be a real triumph!'

"Adam was impressed. 'Did my genetic engineers have the time to inform you about the cloning techniques and all the rest?'

" 'Unfortunately, no, Adam! We had very little information because of their egotistic perception of the subject. Most of them preferred to die rather than betray their principles and beliefs about purity of race.'

" 'Very selfish. I would say it is really criminal.'

" 'I agree. Moreover, this behavior of theirs may be the reason why we might not have the best results possible. Particularly as far as intellectual capacity is concerned . . . '

" 'The ones that will be created, what will they be?' Adam asked.

"Sapiens closed his eyes and said, underlining each word, 'What I have told you recently is not true. Neither you, nor we are to be the last dynasty of the Angels.' "

"Nine months passed. Only Adam and seven others were left from all the original angels. Pygmeos or Pygmy, which was the new name of Soemgyp, committed suicide because he could not accept life as a servant of Adam. Each female HOMO group gave birth to different creatures.

"The newborn of one group had a long and narrow skull, long arms and legs and blond hair. Another group brought to the world angelic creatures, very thin, with a long tail and no wings. Once born, the latter immediately climbed up the trees!

"The three groups worth being studied by those responsible for the project were the ones whose features roughly resembled an intermediate kind, something between the swarthy and the Albino angels. They had no wings and, instead of feathers, on their skin they had thin fibers, like our own hair. The expression in their eyes gave hope that reason did not seem to be absent. The bony formation between their upper and lower jaws was completely differentiated. Now, the new creatures had teeth!

"What surprised everybody was the delayed childbirth by a female HOMO. The whole cloning procedure for her had been under the charge of an Angel researcher who was the genetic lab's director. This Angel was furious with the way life turned out. He was unable to accept that he had to obey inferior former slaves. Revenge was in his blood. The night his cloned female was to give birth, there was panic!

"The belly of that HOMO was unusually swollen and extended and, touching it, one could feel the abnormal mobility of its content. When delivery time arrived, those present witnessed the strangest event. Small creatures, black, long and narrow burst out with great speed, bumping into each other. They counted one hundred and twenty such black embryos, each tightly wrapped in a membrane. Just as persons in the delivery room managed to get over the shock, another event brought fear in their hearts. One by one, the strange creatures unfolded their bodies. The membrane was nothing but transparent wings which they flapped forcefully and with ear piercing sounds they disappeared in the night."

"Bats!" The one who could not stand the suspense this time was Mario.

"Yes, Mario! Those creatures were miniatures of

KEROPS's inhabitants. Only the relation between wings and body was different. They were disproportionate, as were many secondary features—their ears and legs, for example.

"The researcher had taken his revenge. When they ran to arrest and punish him, he was dead. Literally dismembered. A Sapiens was standing by him, with a gun in his hand. He had already done justice.

"Let's forget the mini-Draculas and the vampires and let's follow the fate of the angelic substitutes," David said. "I consider it absolutely imperative, my friends, before I continue with the final section of the glorious history of planet KEROPS, to make an important announcement.

"Most of the names I have mentioned are phonetically accurate. That includes the two suns, P and A , KEROPS and KOX.

The officers' names were also accurate but if reversed, Salta, becomes ATLAS, Hax becomes XAH and Soumgyp, becomes PYGMEOS. Of course, MANTA is Adam."

"Pygmies was the name of very small people somewhere in Congo," Mario observed.

"Maybe. Who knows, for unexplainable reasons they may have kept the name of their ancestor. As for me, I gave them those names in a loose rendering of what has been transmitted to me in order to be easier understood. Let's, however, return to our subject.

"The newborn babies of those three groups were the proof that 'Genetic Seed' was a success. That new generation owed, in a way, its creation and existence to the intellectually superior Sapiens and his colleagues. The microbes had played their part: 'One's death is somebody else's life.' Sapiens took it upon himself to oblige the genetic engineers to get to work and perform to the best of their knowledge, until most of them died of septicemia. It is to honor him that Adam proposed the new creatures be called . . . "

"HOMO SAPIENS! Larry shouted, catching up with David.

From the moment David began talking about the development of the genetic project, everybody was standing with their hands crossed as if they were in a church. They felt what they were listening to was the answer to the eternal and unanswered question, "Who are we and where do we come from?"

With religious fervor they heard that the first human beings were the descendants—with science's help—of creatures endowed with higher intelligence. The vanity of their leader, Adam, and the influence of Eva, or Eve, literally moved "Sky and Earth," so that nature could reach its aim, the creation of the human being on earth.

"Adam and Sapiens soon noticed there were differences among the children of the three groups, including their color. Some were white, others black and some yellow.

"Sapiens proposed—and it was accepted—that the black babies be kept by those who lived in the jungle. The whites were to be sent on to the West, the others to the East. Thus, the "Distribution Plan" had already been activated, following the Genetic Seed project, on the entire planet Alphomega.

"The years passed and no one bothered to learn to care for the complex machines which were no longer of much use. Rust conquered the mechanical and electronic equipment of the abandoned space vehicles.

"Unfortunately, Adam lived much longer than anyone else. I say unfortunately because he was the witness of the worst curse that could possibly happen.

"The descendants of HOMO SAPIENS were anything but wise. As time passed, their life differed little from that of the other animals in the jungle. The only difference was that he was able to destroy himself and other creatures. Adam lived in hiding to escape the killer instincts of his tribes."

David suddenly bounced off his seat, and his face became red.

"I feel something is going to happen," he said with terror in his voice. " . . . Now.

"ATTENTION—ATTENTION! Announcement! Attention! The last announcement . . . Attention!" It was our ancestor's, Adam's, voice.

For 30 seconds there was complete silence. They all had literally stopped breathing.

" 'I am under siege by savages! I just had enough time to run into the "P-Gass, the starcraft that brought me to this damned planet. There is very little food. My drive to live is worn out. The only solution is suicide. Perhaps the story shall never be transmitted. Perhaps those savage creatures, those heartless cannibals, shall manage to come in here and cut me to pieces.

" 'Perhaps the other groups I distributed with Sapiens's help may have a better development, take another direction. Perhaps, one day, they will come to visit my grave. And, if they are intellectually developed, they shall certainly understand what I have done.

" 'Oh, you . . . unknown stranger . . . whoever you are narrating the story of the glorious KEROPS's inhabitants, I have promised you a gift for your supreme service to my people The hour has come for your reward.

" 'On your satellite that is on our ANOL there is a magnetic hyper-core that, if activated, can turn out to be your greatest benefit. It may allow you to win over earth's gravity forces! If all this had not taken place, in order to survive on Alphomega, we planned to activate the hyper-magnetic core and we would forever eliminate the need for other energy sources.

" 'The opal sphere of knowledge, in front of which I now stand, shall be enriched with the most important and precious secret I could ever transmit. I hope this giant and endless source of energy is utilized in the right way. I hope it doesn't become a source of disaster. To activate this colossal magnetic field you first have to do some research at satellite's co-ordinates LDE-72-GBP, 37 feet deep. There is a complete file that will help you build the devices you need and inform you about their activation."

Adam suddenly interrupts his transmission with a scream. "The savages . . . they broken down the door . . . Blood! Blood on my hands and in my eyes! I am dying! The savages are killing me. This is the end!"

David collapsed on the floor. His snoring showed he was literally exhausted. He was a real wreck. Nobody moved. They looked at each other. Deadly silence. One by one, they left the room, biting their lips, trying to hold their own fears back.

In a few hours, David was in complete control of himself. At last, his nightmare was over. He was alone with Larry.

"The Master kept his word but he couldn't complete his story," David whispered with sorrow.

" Too bad . . . " Larry said.

"Unfortunately . . . he wanted to turn our world into a paradise! Can you figure it, Larry? No motors! Aviation tragedies would be impossible! We would all live without problems on a clean planet!"

"Free energy! Food for everybody and work for none."

"It would have been heaven on earth, Larry! How different would today's reality be if we could exploit his gift! But, I' m almost going crazy! One might say that what I've just now narrated was the story of the Creation."

"What do you mean, my friend?"

"Adam, thanks to Eve, would have brought us into paradise . . . Until now we knew that, because of Eve, Adam was thrown out of paradise . . . taking us with him . . . "

"You're right, David! Anyway, what humankind has to take out of all this is the fact that, in order to be rewarded our paradise we must live the way that would make us worthy of it."

David stood up and walked to the other room with Natassa behind him. "We'll talk a little later," he said.

"Yes, David. It is time for you to pay back your guardian angel, Natassa!"

Larry was deep in his thoughts when the telephone rang.

"Hello!"

"It's Manuel."

'Where are you, my friend? Why haven't you called? You know, our friend, David, has completed the story!"

"So how did it end?"

Larry briefed Manuel Calango and mentioned that the Angels had landed in Central Africa. But he never expected to hear what Calango said.

"Buana Larry! I absolutely want you to come here because there is something extraordinary. I am almost going crazy! I am waiting for you in Kishangani."

Despite pressure from Larry, Manuel refused to go into details. "What is he afraid of?"

Larry, as he had promised Manuel, did not say anything to anyone about the call. "I've got to go! I've got to see with my own eyes," he stated with determination.

# Are We the Last Dynasty?

David Mason's torment might have ended, but recognition of the authenticity of the data had not even started. Only the convention was offering such a possibility and the prestige to confirm or to reject the story. Larry, Mario and David noticed that their supporters, those who had knowledge about UFOs and information on aliens, had begun to avoid them, using various excuses.

In fact, the authorities and the Church slowly but steadily managed to leave them almost no allies. This undermining of their authority had been very carefully organized and seemed to be very effective.

That night, Larry and the others were feeling rather disheartened. They had learned about more desertions from their camp.

"Something's got to be done," Mario said. By the opening of the convention, we'll be all alone. Already half of our previous supporters are now neutral!

Larry's mobile phone rang. He answered it without hiding his boredom.

"Hello . . . "

"Oh, Manuel . . . is that you?" It was their faithful Calango.

"Buana, I am not coming to the convention." This was another stab in their back.

"But, your presence is necessary. You're an eye-witness."

"I think you should come here. Don't wait for me to ask you again. It's extremely urgent!"

"Are you crazy? Just a few days before Cancun?"

"Yes! I'm telling you it's urgent! Somebody's got to come and help."

"What's happening?" David asked out of curiosity but with also some secret hope.

"I can't tell you, David. Anyway it's not worthwhile. It's just excuses for not coming, don't you know?

Larry grabbed the phone. He could hardly hear Manuel Perhaps the phone's battery was low. "Repeat, please . . . "

" . . . . . . . . . . . "

"Are you sure? Absolutely certain? Or are you just guessing?

" . . . . . . . . . . . . "

"Where did it happen?"

" . . . . . . . . . . "

"I'm sorry, but I don't believe you . . . I can't even hear you."

"COME IMMEDIATELY!" Manuel's words began to convince Larry.

"If I decide so, where can I find you?" Larry took a piece of paper and a pencil. He jutted down, "Kishangani—Congo Palace—telephone number 033251-3233210."

David shook his head in disbelief. "Not even Manuel is coming; my faithful Manuel has abandoned me. He can't come because something unexpected happened. Obviously an excuse."

When the call was over, Larry pretended he had something important to do and left. He did not go very far. He went to buy himself a ticket to the Republic of Congo.

"I would like the first available seat on the next flight. It is urgent," he told said the girl at the travel office.

"You shall be very comfortable on this flight, sir. Two thirds of the plane are empty. I am required to tell you that visiting Central Africa is dangerous, the government has issued a travel advisory."

The next communication between Larry and David took place while Larry was on the plane. "David, I'm on my way to Kishangani!"

It's a miracle David did not pass out. "Are you nuts? What are you going to do there?"

"First of all, I will bring Manuel to the convention. Then, I will take a last look. Perhaps some new or forgotten data can be discovered."

"Larry, you won't miss the convention . . . right? I need you with me, at least the last critical 48 hours."

"Ok, David! Don't you lose hope; the end is not here yet.

The team that organized the defense of David's File was already in Cancun. Mario's newspaper in Urbana had arranged for them, 18 people, to stay at Fiesta Americana Hotel. It was built in Punta Cancun, the most central place of the city and very close to the imposing Convention Center, where the main part of the discussions was scheduled to take place. This was the place where they would hold the concluding meetings and reach final conclusions.

The inauguration of operations at JKS TV was a big success. And the big story was David's File, where the station had many exclusives. Of course, the cunning general manager knew how to handle the story. There was never a mention or inference about religion or the religious beliefs of the Angels.

The convention had use of the fully-equipped main hall, Coral Island. Two days before the weeklong battle, the different factions were already sharpening their knives.

David Mason, now refreshed and without the burden of physical exhaustion from the transmissions, was the principal speaker of the meeting.

The mood of the convention participants was somber. They knew that an unusual game was being played out, a rather strange duel that would conclude with acceptance or rejection of David's long narration as a true story. These meetings would decide whether David's File was to be classified under "Mythology" or "Anthropology". If efforts failed to prove that the events in David's accounts were factual, the most he could hope was the title of best scenario in science fiction. But such thoughts did not occupy their minds for long. Defamation was not an option.

It was eight o'clock in the morning when David stepped up to the podium. After thanking the organizers of the convention—mostly to show that control of the proceedings rested in the hands of someone else—the customary greetings, acknowledgements, and introductions, he came to the main point.

"Ladies and gentlemen, do not forget that at this conference we shall try to promote the idea of a 'Modern Testament' that replaces, though that is not its intention, the 'Old Testament.'

"Ladies and Gentlemen, for thousands of years, no one has been able to seriously question the scriptures, and that is important. Our role in this meeting is not to question the reliability of the scriptures.

"We simply present the message we received. Our only role is to make public the narrative of the account of an alien people's historic events, the description of the various stages in their journey through time up to the moment of their landing on our earth.

"We are not here to draw conclusions. We are not here to defend world theories, or to become the enemies of any religion or dogma. We leave all that to the judgement of specialists. We are here to submit data and expect others to evaluate them. As far as our probable winged ancestors' religion is concerned, we've left that out of the discussion.

"Our opinion is that there is no reason to make the problem

more complicated than it already is. If the fundamental problem, the basic question is answered, then there is no reason for us to insist upon religious beliefs.

"The basic issues we are submitting to this body are simple. First, after you are informed about the complete text of David's File, without getting entangled in religious matters, we would like you to express your opinion on whether those creatures had any relationship with the origin of human beings and what that relationship was.

"Second, the resemblance of Roswell's corpses with the aliens in the file could lead to the following argument: Did the alien flying objects come from planet KEROPS and are they trying to destroy mankind to take revenge for Niak's escape? Third, if the answer to the second question is 'yes,' then what are the defense measures that should be taken to avoid a massive attack from our enemies? How can we survive a space vendetta?"

David's presentation was received with vigorous applause.

Mario Canakis was the next speaker.

"Ladies and Gentlemen, as you know, Larry Keith has decided to make a hopeless, I think, effort to collect information in the region where Niak's starcraft was discovered and destroyed, that is at Beni. We have had no news from him in 10 days. David's faithful friend called only once.

"Ladies and Gentlemen, speeches shall not help us advance our cause. I thus suggest we all study for a last time the "History of KEROPS and Its Angels." If anyone finds confusing or contradictory points, he should immediately report them to us.

"We must practice prevention. We must systematically study the text, so the critics and those who doubt have clear and reasonable responses to each and every question. Anyway, you all know that, of the 103 persons that offered to help us, only 18 are left. But the one who speaks the truth is the one who wins at the end. This is what reason says to us; this is why I am optimistic."

The convention participants studied, according to schedule, for six hours, and took a small break for brunch. They rested in their luxurious suites from about 2 p.m. to 4 p.m., and then on to the beach to enjoy the crystal water of Coral Beach's natural bay.

The next day, the program began with an excursion to an exotic spot with Mayan ruins, underground rivers and enchanting tropical lakes. The program included a visit to Cozumel. To get there, they took the boat at Playa Carmen and, in just half an hour, they were at the rendezvous spot of all Caribbean cruises.

No matter how many things David saw, he could not forget the important fight ahead. Moreover, he had to enter that fight without Larry's presence. The fight would last seven days!

"How on earth did Larry get the idea of leaving? What was so important to lead him to desertion? Oh, no! Not desertion. I am not thinking straight."

That night they went to La Joya, the hotel's nightclub. The excellent orchestra and their Mexican guitars offered them one of the most beautiful experiences of their lives. The joyful ambience, the excellent wine, the romantic music, it all made them forget the big moment that was approaching and allowed them to go to bed happy.

As David, Mario and their friends were touring, their adversaries, the official guests and representatives of the government and the Church organized their own assembly at the Ritz Carlton Hotel.

Michael Donovan's camp had methodically prepared the answer to every theoretically strong position in David's File. They acted like real professionals.

At first, by falsifying the minerals from the Moon, the geologists would confess their failure and would apologize for the early conclusions they had announced at the Martinique conference at Diamond Hotel. The enamel had simply been replaced by . . . porcelain!

Those who had dealt with the Roswell matter had no interest in losing the government's favor for something that was considered of little long-term value.

"Yes, they had wings. So, what? Do I have to lose my job for the sake of some freakish creatures? In God's name!"

It was the kind of reasoning that would be acceptable to David's camp, even by those who supported the truth. That was also the reason that the mood at the Ritz-Carlton meeting was festive.

Michael Donovan, resting on a lounge chair at the beach, enjoyed the hot sun and the soothing breeze. At arm's length was a transformed coconut shell that contained cool juice and plenty of rum. He propped himself up a little, put some lotion on his shoulders and dialed a number on his mobile phone.

"Mr. President, it's Michael! I'm calling from the Ritz-Carlton in Cancun." The other side remained silent, waiting for more.

"The only thing that is not worrying me at all is the convention. The final announcement is ready. I've written it myself. It will deliver the final punch. There's absolutely no reliable evidence that we haven't neutralized. Please be assured. Theirs is a very nice fairy tale, the kind that is 'in' these days, a soap opera of the past. Don't be worried at all.

" . . . . . . . ."

"I am sincerely grateful! I shall never forget your promise. Duty! Above all, our duty!"

" . . . . . . . . ."

"My best wishes to the First Lady."

Michael Donovan had all the reasons in the world to be satisfied. His agents had literally undermined every element that supported the theory contained in David's File.

The cunning Michael, to be assured of success, had sent a direct message to the adverse camp. They were to receive it the following day. He knew that reading it would completely destroy their morale.

The text had been studied by a psychologist, and said, "Dear Friends, Although it is still the rainy season, we are lucky that Cancun is offering us all the best a tourist could wish. Take advantage of all this, just as we are about to do. The issues before us are more or less familiar to all. We will, of course, have the opportunity to go into academic discussions and stage a dignified performance along the lines of our scenario. I am, of course, referring to the subject that is of immediate interest to you.

"The main reason for this message is to inform you that a few days ago, I received confirmation from an important Cinema studio that it is interested in making a movie. Regardless of the final box office success of the film, I am able to guarantee you even now royalties of at least 2 million dollars.

"I think my presence at every single meeting is not necessary, so if you wish to get in touch with me, just leave a message at my hotel. I shall very much enjoy the company of persons as highly esteemed as you are. Michael Donovan, Secretary of State."

When the message was read the following day, during the plenary session of their group, there was pessimism and panic!

David, folding the paper, said, "Ladies and Gentlemen! My friends! Instead of outlawing the murderers they are asking us to commit . . . suicide. No, Ladies and Gentlemen! I am convinced we have to fight this unequal battle.

"In a fair fight, the winner is not the only one who wins a prize. Everyone who participates is awarded. The struggle for truth is a duty for all of us. Who knows? Maybe a David shall appear to save us from Michael-Goliath . . . Do not forget my name is David! This could be a sign." They applauded warmly.

Yet, every day that passed meant a new retreat for them, a new defeat. David had nothing to put in his sling. Witnesses, who claimed to be certain of the facts, were unclear, contradictory and even clearly negative.

"There were no corpses at Roswell. They were plastic dolls!"

"Did they have wings?"

"Dolls with wings? Where did you get that idea?" (Laughter in the audience).

"How many dolls did you count?"

"Two that weren't inflated and three filled with cotton."

Donovan and his assistants had turned the witness interrogation into a comedy. More and more people arrived daily. They wanted to have fun and enjoy the strange stories of David's team.

David, Natassa and the others gave the appearance of moving shadows. Poor David and Mario Canakis tried for hours to convince the biased crowd of questionable intellectual level. Time was passing . . .

On the last day of the convention, at 9 p.m., final conclusions and recommendations were to be drawn and announced during a ceremony. After giving it a lot of thought, David decided not to participate. He would pretend he was ill. He wanted to avoid humiliation.

"No! It's a perfectly engineered farce," he said. I feel like a clown in a circus. I shall not be present there at the moment they'll demolish my dignity."

Mario agreed. He felt so bitter he was in the mood for nothing at all. Most of the time, he was found lying at "Pok Ta Pok", the Golf Club's terrace, letting his eyes scan the horizon aimlessly.

Very early in the morning, David visited a travel office at the Kukulcan Commercial Center where was he had to confirm his departure the next day. He looked at his watch, got into his rented car and went to Cancun's international airport.

He was absent-minded. He had tried hard and, finally, succeeded in disassociating his brain from reality. At the airport, there was chaos! Three 747 Beings had landed at the same time. One American Airlines plane from the U.S., one Air Mexico from Atlanta and one Delta from Congo, Africa.

Hotel hawkers, carrying signs with potential guest names pushed each other like flies over a carcass.

David was ready to get back into his car and return to his hotel when, suddenly, his mind returned to the events at the convention. He replayed everything. Then the question: Why should he return? Unfortunately, there was nothing left but further defeat.

He opened the door of his Fiat and was halfway in when he thought he had heard, "Buana! Buana!"

"Now I am suffering from delusions," he thought. "Can you figure this? I'm hearing voices, just like the Africans called me at Beni, when I was there digging my . . . future grave!" He recalled his faithful servant and collaborator, Manuel Calango. He also recalled Larry, who had not given a single sign of life. He turned the motor on. Again, through the roaring sound of the motor, he thought he heard the same voice calling "Buana!"

He reached the hotel. At the reception, he could sense the pity of those around him. "Poor man! But he seems to be a nice guy, after all."

"My key, please." He took it and went upstairs to his suite. Natassa welcomed him with a kiss and suggested they sit on the veranda. They remained silent for a while. It was almost 7 p.m.

"There will be a storm, tonight, David . . . "

"After the 7-day storm, darling, another one won't scare me." David's metaphorical reply showed his deep disappointment.

"I think the phone's ringing," Natassa said, and David got up to answer:

"David, is that you?"

"Yes, Larry, it's me, though I wish it wasn't. You've certainly learned about what's going on. Really . . . why didn't you come? Where are you calling from?"

"David, I'm calling from the Convention Center."

" . . . . . . . . ."

"Do you hear me? I'm in Cancun and I'm calling from the meeting room. Just a moment! There's a good friend of yours that wishes to talk to you."

"Buana . . . Buana David . . . "

"Manuel? You . . . here?"

Larry took the receiver. "David, it is late. It's eight o'clock and we're expecting you . . . Come quickly!"

"Why don't you come here?"

"But, David, we're not the only ones waiting for you . . . Everybody is waiting."

"Everybody? Are you kidding me? Don't you think this is not the appropriate time for jokes? Have pity on me. I didn't think you would . . . "

"David, just a moment . . . The Secretary of State wants to speak to you."

"The Secretary . . . ?" David thought he heard wrong.

"Mr. David Mason, I ask you to come as quickly as you possibly can. We cannot continue our meeting if you are not here."

"But, I don't think . . . " Over the phone David managed to hear parts of the conversation.

"Haven't you told him anything? Isn't he aware of the latest developments? That's a big mistake. You should have called him earlier. The world's upside down!"

"Larry . . . "

"David, come immediately because there have been some astonishing developments."

"But, what in the world is going on? It sounds like another farce."

"Come quickly . . . Everybody's waiting for you . . . I've got to hang up. Every moment is precious!"

The time it took the glass elevator to come down to the first floor seemed like a century to him. What did Larry mean? What was Manuel doing with him? How is it that Donovan was begging him to return to the meeting? So many questions demanded the one definitive response.

Almost 500 people were waiting for David by the main entrance when he arrived. They stood in silence. Suddenly, Larry started, and they all began to applaud. He looked stunned but they continued applauding . . . for at least two minutes. In the crowd, David saw the tall figure of Manuel Calango who was holding something in his hands. In the dim light, David could not see if it was an animal or an object, but Manuel moved forward, towards him. People stepped aside to let him pass.

"Buana . . . " Manuel was now close to David. "Buana . . . We have brought this with Buana Larry, from Africa. It's for you, it's a gift."

And with that, he deposited into David's arms a beautiful, naked, swarthy baby. Instinctively, David embraced it tightly, even though something was piercing against his arm. Puzzled he lifted the baby so he could see, and there it was!

"But it's impossible . . . ! It has a set of wings. It has a set of white wings growing out of his shoulders. It is an angel? Obviously, a sign of atavism."

"Yes, David . . . Finally, justice and truth triumph," Larry murmured with tears in his eyes.

Next, it was Donovan who came to congratulate him and to whisper his apologies. He added out loud, "On behalf of the government, I am appealing to you so that we may work together on the colossal issue facing us."

Natassa ran into David's arms. Spontaneously, he said to her, "My love, we've got a child . . . " And, showing her the baby, "He's our winged Eros. The love that fights on the side of truth!"

Dozens of newsmen milled around them. It was Mario, from JKS TV who asked the first question.

"Tell us about your feelings this moment, David . . . a billion people are watching us!"

David, tears running down his cheeks, lifted the baby up,

holding it under the arms so that everyone could see its white wings.

"I feel completely justified! I have proven I am a descendant of the last dynasty of the Angels. I have proven that we all are!"

"What is your wish for mankind?" a CNN correspondent asked.

"I wish the man of the future would really be an Angel, even if he has no wings on his back!"

*The End*